Christmas

Taste of Home BOOKS

RDA ENTHUSIAST BRANDS, LLC
MILWAUKEE, WI

Contents

Taste *of* Home.

© 2018 RDA Enthusiast Brands, LLC.
1610 N. 2nd St., Suite 102, Milwaukee WI 53212-3906

All rights reserved. Taste of Home is a registered trademark of
RDA Enthusiast Brands, LLC.
International Standard Book Number: 978-1-61765-802-0
International Standard Serial Number: 1948-8386
Component Number: 119600040H

Cover Photographer: Jim Wieland
Set Stylist: Melissa Franco
Food Stylist: Shannon Roum

Pictured on front cover: Herb-Brined Cornish Game Hens, p. 58

Pictured on back cover: Slow Cooker Burgundy Beef, p. 167
Chocolate Balloon Bowls, p. 98

Holly Illustration: Shutterstock/Leigh Prather

Printed in U.S.A.
1 3 5 7 9 10 8 6 4 2

Share the joys of the season with Taste of Home Christmas

1. JINGLE & MINGLE
What better way to kick off your seasonal celebrations than a sophisticated, grown-up cocktail party? These delicious small-plate appetizers and festive beverages are just the thing to get your friends in the holiday spirit!

2. MAKE-AHEAD BREAKFAST
Whether you're planning a special Christmas breakfast for family or a sit-down brunch for friends, these recipes will let you get a head start on your eye-opening menu.

3. HOLIDAY FEASTS
Create one of three beautifully planned, full-menu feasts—prime rib, crown roast or seafood—or choose any of the a la carte options to design your own meal.

4. FESTIVE SIDES & BREADS
Your stunning main course deserves to be surrounded with dishes that are every bit as special. Here are 20 incredible sides, rolls and breads to round out your holiday menu in style.

5. NAUGHTY BUT NICE
Yes, you can indulge yourself at the holidays without overdoing it! Each of these delicious appetizers, sides, breads, salads and desserts is light on calories and fat but full of flavor.

6. COMPLETELY CHOCOLATE
Serve up an amazing feast with chocolate in every course, from appetizers to roasts to salads! And then—of course—finish it off with a rich and decadent chocolate dessert.

7. 5-INGREDIENT ENTERTAINING
Sometimes the most fabulous dishes require only a few ingredients. All the recipes in this chapter come together with no more than five ingredients (not counting water, salt, pepper or oil).

8. SEASONAL GET-TOGETHERS
Fun and festive food for a kids party, delicious and comforting recipes for an informal buffet, or elegant dishes for a formal sit-down New Year's celebration—whatever your plans, you'll find a complete menu here.

9. WINTER SALADS
Whether as the centerpiece of a holiday lunch or a side for a family feast, these 19 seasonal salads are cool and refreshing alternatives to the marathon of hearty holiday meals.

10. SLOW-COOKED CHRISTMAS
Make your holidays a little less stressful by putting your slow cooker to work. With this selection of recipes for main courses, soups, sides and desserts, you can spend less time in the kitchen and more time with your family.

11. MINI DESSERTS
These single-serving sweets satisfy everyone's craving for dessert. Present each guest with their own beautifully prepared plate, or let them sample a selection of these 15 miniature pies, cakes and trifles.

12. GRANDMA'S FAVORITE COOKIES
Classic Christmas cookies are the ones you looked for on Grandma's cookie plate every year. The 21 recipes in this chapter are the tested and perfected versions of those much-loved recipes.

13. SPIRITED SWEETS
Why not offer your guests an after-dinner drink in the form of dessert? Each of these tempting treats is infused with wine, liquor or liqueur for a grown-up take on sweets.

14. GIFTS IN A JAR
Homemade is the way to go for gifts for co-workers, teachers, neighbors and friends. These jams, salsas, candies and mixes are delicious and heartfelt creations from your kitchen that will bring joy year-round.

JINGLE & MINGLE

*'Tis the season to gather together—and a party with a
selection of cocktails and delicious small-plate appetizers
is just the thing to get friends in the holiday spirit!*

SPICY CRAB SALAD TAPAS

I served these delicious morsels at a party and everyone went wild! They have a crispy, flaky outside filled with creamy sweet crab that has a little kick. I used scalloped-edge cookie cutters to cut my pastry, but you can use a small biscuit cutter. If you don't have a small cutter for the center hole, a shot glass works, too.
—Vanessa Mason, Summerdale, AL

PREP: 35 MIN. + CHILLING
BAKE: 20 MIN. + COOLING
MAKES: ABOUT 2 DOZEN

- 1 can (16 oz.) lump crabmeat, drained
- ¼ cup finely chopped sweet red pepper
- ¼ cup finely chopped sweet yellow pepper
- ¼ cup finely chopped green onions
- 1 jalapeno pepper, seeded and finely chopped
- 1 Tbsp. minced fresh cilantro
- 1 Tbsp. lemon juice
- 2 garlic cloves, minced
- 1 tsp. ground mustard
- ½ cup mayonnaise
- ½ tsp. salt
- ¼ tsp. pepper
- 1 pkg. (17.30 oz.) frozen puff pastry, thawed
- 1 large egg
- 1 Tbsp. water
  Minced fresh parsley and seafood seasoning, optional

1. Preheat oven to 375°. Combine the first 12 ingredients. Refrigerate, covered, at least 1 hour.
2. Meanwhile, on a lightly floured surface, unfold puff pastry. Roll each pastry into a 10-in. square; cut into twenty-five 2-in. squares, or fifty altogether. Using a round 1½-in. cookie cutter, cut out the centers of half of the puff pastry squares. Whisk egg and water; brush over pastry. Place cutout squares on top of solid squares; transfer to parchment paper-lined baking sheets.
3. Bake until golden brown, about 18 minutes. Cool to room temperature. Spoon 1 heaping Tbsp. of crab salad into center of each cooled pastry. If desired, top with minced parsley and seasoning. Serve immediately.

SPICED WHITE SANGRIA

I've been making this recipe for more than 20 years. My husband and I are in the wine and spirit business and we served it at one of our first dinner parties after we were married. It's a refreshing change from traditional red sangria, and an easy make-ahead option for gatherings.
—Ellen Folkman, Crystal Beach, FL

TAKES : 15 MIN. + CHILLING
MAKES: 10 SERVINGS

- 2 medium oranges, seeded and sliced
- 1 medium lemon, seeded and sliced
- 1 medium lime, seeded and sliced
- ⅔ cup brandy
- ½ cup sugar
- 2 cinnamon sticks (3 in.)
- 2 bottles (750 ml each) white wine
- 1 bottle (1 qt.) club soda, chilled

Combine the first seven ingredients in a large pitcher. Refrigerate, covered, stirring occasionally, about 4 hours. Discard cinnamon sticks. Refrigerate, covered, 2 hours longer. Just before serving, stir in chilled club soda. Serve over ice with fruit slices in each glass.

Holiday Helper
If red wine is more to your taste, go ahead and swap it in. This is a great make-ahead option for parties since you can mix up a couple of batches and have them waiting in the fridge for when your guests arrive.

FESTIVE TURKEY MEATBALLS

PICTURED AT LEFT, TOP

Turkey gives a twist to these slightly sweet and spicy meatballs. For the holidays, I serve them on a tray lined with parsley and garnished with red pepper or pimientos.
—Audrey Thibodeau, Gilbert, AZ

PREP: 25 MIN. • **BAKE:** 30 MIN.
MAKES: ABOUT 3½ DOZEN

- 1 large egg, beaten
- ½ cup dry bread crumbs
- ¼ cup finely chopped onion
- ½ tsp. curry powder
- ¼ tsp. ground ginger
- ¼ tsp. ground cinnamon
- ¼ tsp. salt
- ¼ tsp. pepper
- 1 lb. ground turkey

SAUCE

- 1 cup honey
- ¼ cup Dijon mustard
- ½ tsp. curry powder
- ½ tsp. ground ginger

OPTIONAL ADDITIONS

- Fresh basil leaves
- Fresh cilantro leaves
- Fresh mint leaves
- Lime wedges

1. Preheat oven to 350°. Combine the first eight ingredients. Add turkey; mix well. Shape into 1-in. balls. Place meatballs on a greased rack in a 15x10-in. baking pan. Bake, uncovered, until cooked through and juices run clear, 20-25 minutes.

2. Meanwhile, combine sauce ingredients in a small saucepan; whisk over medium heat until heated through. Brush the meatballs with ¼ cup sauce; return to the oven for 10 minutes. Serve meatballs with the remaining sauce for dipping and, if desired, fresh herbs and lime wedges.

HOW MUCH FOOD? HOW MANY DRINKS?

Planning how much food to serve at a party doesn't have to be daunting! Here's a quick guide to how many drinks and how much food to stock.

APPETIZERS

On average, each guest will have about six appetizers at a dinner party; this number should double if it's a cocktail party. Stock up on bulk items like nuts, pretzels and olives that guests can munch on when they arrive and that can fill in any shortfall without attracting attention.

DRINKS

Several factors govern how many beverages you'll need, including the type of party, its duration, where it will be held, and your guests' preferences. These guidelines are for parties that are two hours long.

- Ice: 1 pound per person.
- Nonalcoholic beverages: One drink per person if alcohol is provided, three per person if alcohol isn't.
- Wine: One bottle of wine for every two adult guests.
- Champagne: 1.5 glasses per person for a premeal cocktail, three glasses per person at dinner.
- Spirits: Three drinks per person. You'll get about 17 drinks per bottle.

HAM BALLS WITH BROWN SUGAR GLAZE

PICTURED OPPOSITE PAGE, BOTTOM

These smoky-sweet meatballs are a Pennsylvania Dutch specialty. I like setting them out when folks come to visit.
—Janet Zeger, Middletown, PA

PREP: 30 MIN. • **BAKE:** 30 MIN.
MAKES: ABOUT 6 DOZEN

- 1 lb. fully cooked ham, cubed
- 1 lb. ground pork
- 1 cup whole milk
- 1 cup crushed cornflakes
- 1 large egg, lightly beaten
- ¼ cup packed brown sugar
- 1 Tbsp. ground mustard
- ½ tsp. salt

GLAZE
- 1 cup packed brown sugar
- ¼ cup vinegar
- 1 Tbsp. ground mustard

1. Preheat oven to 350°. Pulse ham in batches in a food processor until finely ground. Combine with the next seven ingredients just until mixed. Shape into 1-in. balls; place in a single layer on greased 15x10-in. rimmed baking pans.
2. For glaze, cook and stir all ingredients in a small saucepan over medium heat until sugar is dissolved. Spoon over ham balls. Bake until ham balls are just beginning to brown, 30-35 minutes, rotating pans and carefully stirring halfway through. Gently toss in glaze. Serve warm.

TURKEY BOLOGNESE POLENTA NESTS

Here's a delicious appetizer that combines two of my favorite foods, polenta and bolognese meat sauce, in one incredibly tasty bite!
—Lidia Haddadian, Pasadena, CA

PREP: 40 MIN. • **COOK:** 25 MIN. + COOLING
MAKES: 2 DOZEN

- 3½ cups chicken stock, divided
- 1 cup yellow cornmeal
- ¾ cup grated Parmigiano-Reggiano cheese, divided
- ½ cup heavy whipping cream
- ¼ tsp. salt
- ¼ tsp. pepper
- 1 Tbsp. olive oil
- 1 cup chopped onion
- 3 garlic cloves, minced
- ½ lb. ground turkey
- ⅓ cup tomato paste
- 1½ tsp. Italian seasoning

1. Preheat oven to 350°. Coat 24 mini muffin cups with cooking spray. Set aside.
2. In a large heavy saucepan, bring 3 cups chicken stock to a boil. Reduce heat to a gentle boil; slowly whisk in cornmeal. Cook and stir with a wooden spoon until polenta is thickened and pulls away cleanly from sides of pan, 15-20 minutes (mixture will be very thick). Stir in ½ cup cheese, cream, salt and pepper. Spoon 2 Tbsp. of the polenta mixture into each mini muffin cup. As the polenta cools, press an indentation in the center of each with the end of the wooden spoon handle to create a nest shape. Set aside. Wipe out pan.
3. In the same saucepan, heat oil over medium-high heat. Add onion; saute until translucent, 2-3 minutes. Add garlic; cook 1 minute longer. Add turkey; saute until no longer pink. Stir in tomato paste, Italian seasoning and the remaining chicken stock. Cook, stirring occasionally, until thickened, about 5 minutes.
4. Fill the indentation in each polenta nest with about 2 tsp. turkey mixture. Sprinkle with remaining cheese; bake until edges are golden, 25-30 minutes. Remove from oven; cool for at least 10 minutes before removing from muffin cups. May be refrigerated or frozen for later use.

APPLE AMARETTO SOURS

An amaretto sour has always been one of my favorite cocktails. This version has a special touch that makes it perfect for enjoying throughout the holiday season.
—Amber Forbes, Roper, NC

TAKES: 5 MIN. • **MAKES:** 6 SERVINGS

- ¾ cup amaretto
- 4 cups apple cider, chilled
- ¼ cup lemon juice
- 4 lemon slices
- 4 cinnamon sticks (3 in.)

Fill six highball glasses with ice. Pour 2 Tbsp. amaretto into each. Stir together apple cider and lemon juice until well mixed. Divide evenly among glasses. Serve each with a lemon slice and cinnamon stick.

CRANBERRY SPARKLER

The flavors of this refreshing cran-raspberry cocktail are great any time of year. In winter, the cranberry makes it a good fit for holiday parties, and the raspberries give it a warm-weather feel in summertime. It's a favorite beverage for our girls' night!
—Susan Stetzel, Gainesville, NY

TAKES: 5 MIN. • **MAKES:** 3 SERVINGS

- ¾ cup raspberry rum
- ½ cup cranberry juice
- ¼ cup lime juice
  Ice cubes
- ¾ cup ginger ale or lemon-lime soda, chilled
  Fresh raspberries and cranberries, optional

Combine rum and juices. Fill three rocks or old-fashioned glasses with ice. Divide rum mixture evenly among glasses; top each with 2 oz. ginger ale. If desired, serve with fresh raspberries and cranberries

ROASTED CHICKEN & BRIE HOLLY MINI BITES

I got the idea for these appetizers from my favorite sandwich at a local restaurant. I re-created the delectable combination of fig, apple and Brie in a quick appetizer with bright red cranberries and green spinach to give it a holiday twist. They're the perfect party appetizer!
—Terri Gilson, Calgary, AB

PREP: 20 MIN. • **BROIL:** 5 MIN. + COOLING
MAKES: 2 DOZEN

- 1 French bread baguette (10½ oz.)
- ¼ cup mayonnaise
- 1½ tsp. garlic paste
- 12 slices deli chicken, halved
- ¼ cup apple jelly
- ¼ cup fig preserves
- 24 fresh baby spinach leaves
- 4 oz. mini Brie cheese wheel
- ⅓ cup sweetened dried cranberries

1. Preheat broiler. Cut baguette into 24 slices; place on foil-lined baking sheets. Combine mayonnaise and garlic; spread evenly over baguette slices. Add a half slice of chicken to each. Combine apple jelly and fig preserves; spread evenly over the chicken.

2. Add one leaf of baby spinach to each slice. Standing the Brie wheel on end, cut crosswise into six narrow slices. Lay slices flat; cut each into four wedges. Add one cheese wedge to each baguette. Top each with 3 cranberries. Broil 3-4 in. from heat until cheese is melted, 1-2 minutes. Cool 5 minutes before serving.

Holiday Helper
To help with party planning, make these appetizers a few days in advance, then warm them in the microwave for 20-30 seconds before serving. You can also give this elegant appetizer a peppery kick by using arugula instead of spinach.

PORTOBELLO MUSHROOM & CREAM CHEESE TAQUITOS

This party appetizer was inspired by a dish I saw on an episode of Top Chef. *I simplified it a little and tweaked the flavors a bit. These can be made ahead and reheated in a 250° oven for 10 minutes.*
—Lily Julow, Lawrenceville, GA

PREP: 30 MIN. • **COOK:** 10 MIN.
MAKES: 10 SERVINGS

- 2 Tbsp. extra virgin olive oil
- 8 oz. large portobello mushrooms, gills discarded, finely chopped
- 1 tsp. dried oregano
- 1 tsp. dried thyme
- ½ tsp. crushed red pepper flakes
- ¼ tsp. salt
- 8 oz. cream cheese, softened
- 4 oz. whole-milk ricotta cheese
- 10 flour tortillas (8 in.)
   Oil for deep-fat frying
   Major Grey's chutney

1. In an electric skillet, heat olive oil to over 350°. Add mushrooms; saute 4 minutes. Add oregano, thyme, pepper flakes and salt; saute until the mushrooms are browned, 4-6 minutes. Cool. Remove mushrooms and wipe out the skillet.

2. In a large bowl, combine the cheeses; fold in mushrooms, mixing well. Spread 3 Tbsp. of mushroom mixture on the bottom-center of each tortilla. Roll up tightly, making sure filling isn't seeping out the ends. Secure rolls with toothpicks.

3. In same skillet, heat oil to 375°. Fry taquitos, a few at a time, until golden brown, 2-4 minutes. Drain on paper towels. When taquitos are cool enough to handle, discard toothpicks. Serve with chutney.

CRANBERRY APPETIZER MEATBALLS

Everyone needs a go-to party snack, and we like tangy meatballs flavored with cranberry and chili sauces. Make plenty—they vanish!
—Jim Ulberg, Elk Rapids, MI

PREP: 25 MIN. • **BAKE:** 15 MIN.
MAKES: ABOUT 7 DOZEN

- 2 large eggs, lightly beaten
- 1 cup dry bread crumbs
- ⅓ cup minced fresh parsley
- ⅓ cup ketchup
- 2 Tbsp. finely chopped onion
- 2 Tbsp. soy sauce
- 2 garlic cloves, minced
- ½ tsp. salt
- ¼ tsp. pepper
- 2 lbs. ground beef

CRANBERRY SAUCE
- 1 can (14 oz.) whole-berry cranberry sauce
- 1 bottle (12 oz.) chili sauce
- 1 Tbsp. brown sugar
- 1 Tbsp. prepared mustard
- 1 Tbsp. lemon juice
- 2 garlic cloves, minced

1. Preheat oven to 400°. Combine the first nine ingredients. Crumble beef over mixture and mix well. Shape into 1-in. balls.
2. Place meatballs on a rack in a shallow baking pan. Bake until no longer pink, about 15 minutes. Transfer to a 3-qt. slow cooker or chafing dish.
3. Meanwhile, in a large saucepan, combine all sauce ingredients; simmer 10 minutes, stirring occasionally. Pour over meatballs. Serve warm.

MARINATED CHEESE

This special appetizer always makes it to our neighborhood parties and is the first to disappear at the buffet table. It's attractive, delicious—and so easy!
—Laurie Casper, Coraopolis, PA

TAKES: 30 MIN. + MARINATING
MAKES: ABOUT 2 LBS.

- 2 blocks (8 oz. each) white cheddar cheese
- 2 pkg. (8 oz. each) cream cheese, softened
- ¾ cup chopped roasted sweet red peppers
- ½ cup olive oil
- ¼ cup white wine vinegar
- ¼ cup balsamic vinegar
- 3 Tbsp. chopped green onions
- 3 Tbsp. minced fresh parsley
- 2 Tbsp. minced fresh basil
- 1 Tbsp. sugar
- 3 garlic cloves, minced
- ½ tsp. salt
- ½ tsp. pepper
  Assorted crackers or toasted French bread slices

1. Slice each block of cheddar cheese into twenty ¼-in. slices. Cut each block of cream cheese into 18 slices; sandwich between cheddar slices, using a knife to spread evenly. Create four 6-in.-long blocks of cheese; place in a 13x9-in. dish.
2. In a small bowl, combine the roasted peppers, oil, vinegars, onions, herbs, sugar, garlic, salt and pepper; pour over the cheese.
3. Cover and refrigerate overnight, turning once. Drain excess marinade. Serve cheese with crackers or bread.

RUBIES ON ICE

Ginger and pomegranate are made for each other and the color of this beverage is tantalizing.
—*Tara Deshpande, New York, NY*

TAKES: 15 MIN. + FREEZING
MAKES: 4 SERVINGS

6	Tbsp. pomegranate seeds
½	cup vodka
4	Tbsp. pomegranate molasses
3	Tbsp. sweetened ginger syrup
2	Tbsp. lime juice
1	cinnamon stick (3 in.)
	Club soda, chilled
4	each lime slice, optional
1	to 4 tsp. pomegranate seeds, optional

1. Scatter pomegranate seeds over an ice cube tray, about 1 tsp. per cube; fill with water and freeze.
2. Combine vodka, molasses, ginger syrup, lime juice and a cinnamon stick. Let steep for 15 minutes. Strain; discard the cinnamon stick.
3. Place four pomegranate ice cubes in each of four tall glasses. Pour molasses mixture evenly into glasses; top off with chilled club soda. Stir well. Garnish with additional pomegranate seeds and lime, if desired.

 Holiday Helper
For a drink that really sparkles, use the ripest, brightest pomegranate seeds possible. If you want a nonalcoholic option, you can easily leave out the vodka; it's still a delicious and festive drink!

BAKED BLUE CHEESE BITES

A friend of mine brought this appetizer to a party at our home and it was such a success that I now make it all the time...and not just for parties, either! These freeze well, but be sure to serve them warm.
—Charlotte Warren, Blackstock, SC

TAKES: 30 MIN. • **MAKES:** 2 DOZEN

½   cup crumbled blue cheese
¼   cup butter, softened
½   cup all-purpose flour
¾   cup chopped pecans

Preheat oven to 325°. Beat cheese and butter until blended. Add flour and pecans; mix until a dough forms. Shape into 24 balls. Place on an ungreased baking sheet. Bake until bottoms are lightly browned, 14-16 minutes. Serve warm.

SHRIMP & PINEAPPLE PARTY PIZZA

This flavor-packed appetizer is a sweet, smoky, savory sensation! If you are traveling with this pizza, parbake the crust and assemble the pizza at home, then finish the baking on-site. When that's not possible, it is still delicious at room temperature! If you're not a seafood fan, substitute chicken for the shrimp.
—Jamie Miller, Maple Grove, MN

PREP: 40 MIN. + MARINATING
BAKE: 20 MIN. + STANDING
MAKES: 24 SERVINGS

2   sheets frozen puff pastry, thawed
1   lb. uncooked shrimp (31-40 per lb.), peeled and deveined
1   can (8 oz.) unsweetened pineapple tidbits, drained and juice reserved
6   thick-sliced bacon strips, apple- or maple-smoked
1   small green pepper, diced
¼   tsp. salt
¼   tsp. pepper
¼   cup hoisin sauce
1   carton (8 oz.) spreadable chive and onion cream cheese
1   cup shredded Parmesan cheese, plus more for topping

1. Preheat oven to 400°. On a lightly floured surface, unfold pastry sheet; cut in half. Roll each half into a 10x6-in. rectangle. Place on a baking sheet. Fold under ¼ in. of the edges to form a rim. Prick center of pastry with a fork. Repeat with remaining pastry sheet. Bake until crust is golden, about 12 minutes. While pastry is baking, marinate shrimp in the juice from pineapple tidbits.

2. Meanwhile, in a large skillet, cook bacon, stirring occasionally, over medium-low heat until crisp, about 12 minutes. Remove with a slotted spoon; drain on paper towels. Reserve 1½ Tbsp. of the drippings.

3. Heat 1 tsp. of the drippings in the same skillet over medium-high heat;

cook pepper until crisp-tender, about 4 minutes. Remove from skillet. Drain shrimp; add to skillet with the remaining bacon drippings. Sprinkle with salt and pepper. Cook and stir until shrimp turn pink, about 2 minutes. Remove from heat; stir in hoisin sauce.

4. Spread cream cheese over puff pastries. Scatter shrimp evenly over cream cheese. Sprinkle bacon and green pepper over shrimp. Using paper towels, squeeze pineapple tidbits dry; scatter over pizza. Sprinkle with Parmesan.

5. Bake until crust is browned and cheese has melted, about 10 minutes. Let stand briefly before cutting each pastry into six rectangles. If desired, top with additional Parmesan cheese.

"There are endless flavor possibilities for this cocktail!"
—CHRISTINE HAIR

CALANDRIA

A friend and I invented this perfect-anytime drink. It's similar to a caipirinha, Brazil's national cocktail, but is vodka-based. Of course, there are endless flavor possibilities for this drink!
—Christine Hair, Odessa, FL

TAKES: 5 MIN. • **MAKES:** 1 SERVING

- 4 orange wedges or slices, divided
- 1 Tbsp. superfine sugar
  Ice cubes
- 4 Tbsp. orange-flavored vodka

1. Place three orange wedges or slices in a rocks or old-fashioned glass. Add sugar; mash with a muddler or wooden spoon. Fill glass with ice; add vodka.
2. Place a cocktail shaker securely over glass and shake well. Pour contents of the shaker into glass. Serve with the remaining orange wedge or slice.

MINI BEEF TOURTIERES

These are a slight twist on the conventional tourtiere recipe. Ground beef replaces the traditional pork for a subtler taste, and cream cheese pastry takes the place of pie pastry, so they melt in your mouth.
—Cheryl Bruneau, Winnipeg, MB

PREP: 1¼ HOURS + CHILLING
BAKE: 15 MIN.
MAKES: ABOUT 2½ DOZEN

- ½ cup butter
- 4 oz. cream cheese, softened
- 1½ cups all-purpose flour
  FILLING
- 1 Tbsp. canola oil
- 1 lb. lean ground beef (90% lean)
- 1 medium onion, minced
- 2 garlic cloves, chopped
- 2 Tbsp. chopped fresh parsley
- 1 Tbsp. Dijon mustard
- 1 tsp. dried savory or sage
- 1 tsp. poultry seasoning
- ½ tsp. dried thyme
- ½ tsp. celery salt
  Dash salt
  Dash pepper
- ½ cup soft bread crumbs
  Chopped tomatoes plus additional minced fresh parsley, optional

1. Cream butter and cream cheese. Add flour, a little at a time, until a dough forms. Shape dough into a ball; wrap in plastic. Refrigerate 1 hour.
2. Meanwhile for filling, heat oil in a large skillet over medium-high heat. Add the ground beef and onion; cook, crumbling meat, until beef is no longer pink, about 5 minutes. Add garlic; cook 1 minute more. Add the next eight ingredients. Stir in bread crumbs to absorb meat juices. Let stand about 10 minutes.
3. On a lightly floured surface, roll out dough to ⅛-in. thickness. Cut with a floured 2¾-in. round biscuit or cookie cutter. Press dough circles onto the bottom and up the sides of 30 ungreased mini muffin cups, re-rolling the dough as needed.
4. Preheat oven to 375°. Spoon 1 Tbsp. filling into prepared mini muffin cups. Bake until the crust is golden, about 15 minutes. If desired, top with tomatoes and fresh parsley.
NOTE To make soft bread crumbs, tear bread into pieces and place in a food processor or blender. Cover and pulse until crumbs form. One slice of bread yields ½ to ¾ cup crumbs.

remaining bread crumbs in a shallow bowl. Gently coat patties on both sides. Place on two baking sheets lightly sprayed with cooking spray. Lightly spray tops of cakes.

4. Bake for 15 minutes or until lightly browned. Keep warm. Serve with spicy aioli sauce. Garnish with thinly sliced green onions if desired.

CLASSIC SWEDISH MEATBALLS

I'm a Svenska flicka (Swedish girl) from northwest Iowa, where many Swedes settled at the turn of the century. This recipe, given to me by a Swedish friend, is a 20th-century version of a 19th-century favorite—back then they didn't have bouillon cubes or evaporated milk! These modern-day kottbullar are very tasty.
—Emily Gould, Hawarden, IA

PREP: 15 MIN. + CHILLING • **COOK:** 20 MIN.
MAKES: 3½ DOZEN

- 1⅔ cups evaporated milk, divided
- ⅔ cup chopped onion
- ¼ cup fine dry bread crumbs
- ½ tsp. salt
- ½ tsp. allspice
  Dash pepper
- 1 lb. lean ground beef (90% lean)
- 2 tsp. butter
- 2 tsp. beef bouillon granules
- 1 cup boiling water
- ½ cup cold water
- 2 Tbsp. all-purpose flour
- 1 Tbsp. lemon juice
  Canned lingonberries, optional

1. Combine ⅔ cup evaporated milk with the next five ingredients. Add beef; mix lightly. Refrigerate until chilled.

2. With wet hands, shape the meat mixture into 1-in. balls. In a large skillet, heat butter over medium heat. Brown meatballs in batches. Dissolve bouillon in boiling water. Pour over meatballs; bring to a boil. Cover; simmer for 15 minutes.

3. Meanwhile, stir together cold water and flour. Remove meatballs from skillet; skim fat, reserving juices. Add flour mixture and the remaining evaporated milk to pan juices; cook, uncovered, over low heat, stirring until the sauce thickens.

4. Return meatballs to skillet. Stir in lemon juice. If desired, top with lingonberries.

SHRIMP CAKES WITH SPICY AIOLI

I made these for our staff Christmas party last year; they were such a hit that I was flooded with requests for the recipe the next day. This year's party is coming up, and I'm already being asked if I'm bringing the shrimp cakes—I guess I am!
—Linda Zilar, Kennewick, WA

PREP: 1¼ HOURS • **BAKE:** 15 MIN.
MAKES: ABOUT 2 DOZEN

- ⅔ cup reduced-fat mayonnaise
- 2 garlic cloves, crushed
- 1 Tbsp. lemon juice
- 1 tsp. Dijon mustard
- ¼ to ½ tsp. cayenne pepper
SHRIMP CAKES
- 3 large eggs, lightly beaten
- ½ cup reduced-fat mayonnaise
- ⅓ cup chopped green onions
- ⅓ cup chopped sweet red pepper
- 2 tsp. garlic paste
- 1 tsp. Dijon mustard
- ½ tsp. salt
- ¼ tsp. cayenne pepper
- 2½ cups panko (Japanese) bread crumbs, divided
- 2 lbs. uncooked shrimp (26-30 per lb.), peeled, deveined and coarsely chopped
- ¼ cup thinly sliced / chopped green onions, optional

1. To make the aioli sauce, combine first five ingredients. Refrigerate, covered, until serving.

2. For shrimp cakes, combine the next eight ingredients; add ½ cup bread crumbs. Stir in shrimp. Form by ¼ cupfuls into fifteen 2-in.-thick patties. Arrange in a single layer, cover and chill 2 hours.

3. Preheat oven to 400°. Place the

FLORENTINE ALMOND ARTICHOKE MOUNDS

I always enjoyed traditional artichoke cheese dip, and for a drinks and appetizer party, wanted to create a new appetizer that was a spin on that. This original creation is a bit reminiscent of the dip recipe, and works well on a buffet.
—*Sherry Johnston, Green Cove Springs, FL*

PREP: 20 MIN. • **BAKE:** 20 MINUTES • **MAKES:** 8 SERVINGS

- 2 cans (14 oz. each) artichoke bottoms, drained
- 1 pkg. (16 oz.) frozen leaf spinach, thawed and squeezed dry
- ¾ cup heavy whipping cream
- ¾ cup shredded Swiss cheese
- ¾ cup chopped or sliced almonds, divided
- 2 large garlic cloves, minced
- 2 tsp. prepared horseradish
- ½ tsp. salt
- ¼ tsp. coarsely ground pepper

1. Preheat oven to 400°. Rinse artichoke bottoms; pat dry with paper towels. Combine spinach with cream, Swiss cheese and ½ cup almonds; mix in garlic, horseradish, salt and pepper. Place artichoke bottoms on a parchment-lined baking sheet. Mound spinach mixture on artichokes; sprinkle with remaining almonds.
2. Bake until almonds turn golden brown, 20-25 minutes. Serve hot or at room temperature.

HERBED POTATO WEDGES

I used to make these potatoes as a side dish and one day tried them out as an appetizer for a party. What a hit! They are great finger food and taste good at room temperature, and the herbs can be varied however you like. The convenience of these easy, inexpensive appetizers is awesome.
—*Amy Eyler, Ellisville, MO*

PREP: 15 MIN. • **BAKE:** 45 MIN. • **MAKES:** ABOUT 4 DOZEN

- 6 large russet potatoes, cut into 8 wedges each
- ¼ cup olive oil
- 4 tsp. minced fresh rosemary
- 4 tsp. minced fresh thyme
- 1½ tsp. sea salt
- ¾ tsp. pepper
- 1½ cups sour cream
- ⅓ cup grated Parmesan cheese
- 2 garlic cloves, minced

Preheat oven to 425° Combine first six ingredients; toss to coat. Transfer potato wedges to baking sheets or a cooking stone. Bake for 40-45 minutes or until browned on bottom, turning once. Meanwhile, to make sauce, mix sour cream, Parmesan cheese and garlic in a small bowl; refrigerate until serving.

MAKE-AHEAD BREAKFAST

If you want to treat family and friends to a morning celebration, but don't want to spend all morning in the kitchen, here are great dishes you can prepare in advance.

AMISH APPLE SCRAPPLE

Just the aroma of this cooking at breakfast takes me back to my days growing up in Pennsylvania. This recipe, a homemade variation on traditional Amish scrapple, was a favorite at home and at church breakfasts.
—Marion Lowery, Medford, OR

PREP: 1 HOUR 20 MIN. + CHILLING
COOK: 10 MIN. • **MAKES:** 8 SERVINGS

- ¾ lb. bulk pork sausage
- ½ cup finely chopped onion
- 4 Tbsp. butter, divided
- ½ cup diced apple, unpeeled
- ¾ tsp. dried thyme
- ½ tsp. ground sage
- ¼ tsp. pepper
- 3 cups water, divided
- ¾ cup cornmeal
- 1 tsp. salt
- 2 Tbsp. all-purpose flour
  Maple syrup

1. In a large skillet, cook sausage and onion over medium-high heat until the sausage is no longer pink and the onion is tender. Remove from skillet; set aside.
2. Discard all but 2 Tbsp. of the drippings. Add 2 Tbsp. butter, apple, thyme, sage and pepper to drippings; cook over low heat until apple is tender, about 5 minutes. Remove from heat; stir in the sausage mixture. Set aside.
3. In a large heavy saucepan, bring 2 cups of water to a boil. Combine cornmeal, salt and the remaining water; slowly pour into the boiling water, stirring constantly. Return to a boil. Reduce heat; simmer, covered, for 1 hour, stirring occasionally. Stir in the sausage mixture. Pour into a greased 8x4-in. loaf pan. Refrigerate, covered, for 8 hours or overnight.
4. Slice ½ in. thick. Sprinkle flour over both sides of each slice. In a large skillet, heat the remaining butter over medium heat. Add scrapple slices; cook until both sides are browned. Serve with syrup.

SAUSAGE CRESCENT ROLLS

I love pigs in a blanket and thought I could turn it into an amazing breakfast dish. Boy, was I right! These are now on the menu for every family gathering.
—Jimmie Harvey, Bedias, TX

PREP: 25 MIN. + RISING • **BAKE:** 15 MIN.
MAKES: 3 DOZEN

- 36 frozen fully cooked breakfast sausage links
- 1 pkg. (¼ oz.) active dry yeast
- 1 cup warm water (110° to 115°)
- ½ cup sugar
- ½ cup butter, melted
- 3 large eggs
- 1 tsp. salt
- 5½ to 6 cups all-purpose flour, divided

TOPPING
- 1 large egg white
- 1 Tbsp. water
- 3 Tbsp. sesame seeds, toasted

1. In a large skillet, cook sausage over medium heat just until browned, turning frequently. Cool slightly; refrigerate.
2. Dissolve yeast in warm water. Add sugar, butter, eggs, salt and 2 cups of flour. Beat on medium speed until smooth. Stir in enough of the remaining flour to form a soft dough. Refrigerate, covered, overnight.
3. Turn the dough onto a lightly floured surface; divide into six portions. Roll each portion into a 10-in. circle; cut each circle into six wedges. Place a sausage link at the wide end of each wedge; roll up from wide ends. Place point sides down, 2 in. apart, on greased baking sheets. Cover with a kitchen towel; let rise in a warm place until doubled, about 1 hour.
4. Preheat oven to 350°. Beat egg white and water; brush over rolls. Sprinkle with sesame seeds. Bake until lightly browned, 12-14 minutes. Serve warm.

MAPLE BACON FRENCH TOAST BAKE

Each season I try to bring a little different flavor to the table; this blending of maple and bacon is perfect for fall and winter occasions. Whole or 2% milk works best. Regular almond milk also works for those who can't have dairy.
—Peggie Brott, Colorado Springs, CO

PREP: 35 MIN. + CHILLING
BAKE: 50 MIN. + STANDING
MAKES: 12 SERVINGS

- 8 cups cubed bread
- 8 large eggs
- 2 cups 2% milk
- ½ cup packed brown sugar
- ⅓ cup maple syrup
- ½ tsp. ground cinnamon
- 1 lb. bacon strips, cooked and crumbled

1. Place bread in a greased 13x9-in. baking dish. In a large bowl, whisk eggs, milk, brown sugar, syrup and cinnamon. Pour over the bread. Sprinkle with bacon. Refrigerate, covered, for 4 hours or overnight.
2. Remove casserole from refrigerator 30 minutes before baking. Preheat oven to 350°. Bake, uncovered, until a knife inserted in the center comes out clean, 50-60 minutes. Let stand 5-10 minutes before serving.

"This dish is a winner with little kids!"
—KERI COTTON

MOUNTAIN HAM SUPREME

This dish is a winner with little kids—they think it's really neat how the bread makes mountains in the pan! Very tasty, too.
—Keri Cotton, Lakeville, MN

PREP: 20 MIN. + CHILLING • **BAKE:** 45 MIN.
MAKES: 12 SERVINGS

- 12 slices bread
- 1 lb. ground fully cooked ham
- 2 cups shredded cheddar cheese
- ½ cup mayonnaise
- 1 tsp. ground mustard
- 6 large eggs
- 2¼ cups 2% milk
- ¼ tsp. salt
- ¼ tsp. pepper

1. Toast bread. Mix the ham, cheese, mayonnaise and mustard. Spread ham mixture over 6 slices of bread; top with remaining slices to make 6 sandwiches. Cut sandwiches into triangles.

2. In a greased 13x9-in. baking dish, arrange the sandwich triangles with points facing up, pressing together as needed to fit in two rows. Whisk eggs, milk, salt and pepper until well blended. Pour over the sandwich triangles. Refrigerate, covered, overnight.

3. Remove from refrigerator 30 minutes before baking. Preheat oven to 300°. Bake, uncovered, until a knife inserted in center comes out clean, 45-50 minutes.

Holiday Helper
You can use prepared mustard in this recipe if you don't have ground (or dry) mustard in your spice rack. Use 1 Tbsp. of prepared mustard, preferably Dijon, in place of 1 tsp. of dry, then reduce the liquid—in this case, mayonnaise—by 1 tsp.

SWEET ORANGE CROISSANT PUDDING

Time-crunched cooks are sure to appreciate the make-ahead convenience of this delightful dish. Feel free to replace the orange marmalade with any jam or jelly that suits your taste.
—Mary Gabriel, Las Vegas, NV

PREP: 15 MIN. + CHILLING • **BAKE:** 40 MIN. + COOLING
MAKES: 8 SERVINGS

    4 croissants, split
    1 cup orange marmalade, divided
    3 large eggs
  1¼ cups whole milk
    1 cup heavy whipping cream
    ½ cup sugar
    ½ tsp. almond extract
    1 tsp. grated orange zest, optional

1. Spread croissant bottoms with 3 Tbsp. marmalade; replace tops. Cut each croissant into five slices; place in a greased 11x7-in. baking dish.
2. Whisk together the next five ingredients and, if desired, the orange zest. Pour egg mixture over croissants. Refrigerate, covered, overnight.
3. Remove from refrigerator 30 minutes before baking. Preheat oven to 350°. Place dish in a larger baking dish. Fill the larger dish with 1 in. of boiling water.
4. Bake, uncovered, until a knife inserted in the center comes out clean, 40-45 minutes. Remove pan from water bath; cool on a wire rack 10 minutes. Brush the remaining marmalade over top. Cut and serve warm.

GRAIN-FREE APPLE PIE GRANOLA

Because of food allergies, I've learned to swap ingredients. There are no grains in this granola but loads of nuts and apples. Try it with yogurt or milk.
—Courtney Stultz, Weir, KS

PREP: 10 MIN. • **COOK:** 15 MIN. + COOLING • **MAKES:** 2 CUPS

    2 Tbsp. coconut oil
    ½ cup finely chopped almonds
    ½ cup sweetened shredded coconut
    ¼ cup pine nuts
    ¼ cup chopped walnuts
    ¼ cup chopped pecans
    1 tsp. ground cinnamon
    ¼ tsp. ground cloves
    ¼ tsp. ground nutmeg
    1 tsp. vanilla extract
    2 Tbsp. maple syrup
    ¼ cup chopped dried apples

1. Preheat oven to 350°. In a large skillet, heat coconut oil over medium heat. Add the next 10 ingredients. Stir until coated in oil; add chopped apple.
2. Transfer mixture to a foil-lined 15x10x1-in. pan. Bake, stirring occasionally, until golden brown, 12-15 minutes (do not burn).
3. Cool for 10 minutes. Break into pieces; store in a sealed container up to a week.

3 Tbsp. olive oil, divided
1½ cups shredded part-skim
   mozzarella cheese, divided
¾ lb. sliced baby portobello
   mushrooms
¾ tsp. garlic powder
¾ tsp. dried rosemary, crushed
½ tsp. pepper
¼ tsp. salt
2 cups pizza sauce
1 Tbsp. white vinegar
9 large eggs
2 oz. fresh goat cheese, crumbled
½ cup French-fried onions
   Fresh basil leaves

1. Preheat oven to 400°. Grease a 15x10x1-in. baking pan and sprinkle with cornmeal. Unroll pizza dough and press onto bottom of pan. Brush dough with 1 Tbsp. oil; sprinkle with ¾ cup mozzarella cheese. Bake for 8 minutes.
2. Meanwhile, in a large skillet, heat the remaining oil over medium-high heat. Add mushrooms; cook and stir until tender. Stir in garlic powder, rosemary, pepper and salt. Stir pizza sauce into the mushrooms; spread mushroom mixture over the crust.
3. Fill a large skillet with high sides with 2-3 in. of water; add vinegar and bring to a boil. Reduce heat to maintain a gentle simmer. Break cold eggs, one at a time, into a small bowl; holding bowl close to the surface of water, slip eggs into water.
4. Cook, uncovered, 3-5 minutes or until whites are completely set and yolks begin to thicken but are not hard. Using a slotted spoon, remove the eggs; place over the mushroom mixture in baking pan. Sprinkle goat cheese and the remaining mozzarella over top. Refrigerate, covered, overnight.
5. Remove pan from the refrigerator 30 minutes before baking. Preheat oven to 400°. Sprinkle onions over top. Bake, uncovered, until golden brown and heated through, 10-15 minutes. Top with basil just before serving.

GREEN CHILI QUICHE SQUARES

Chilies add spark to this cheesy quiche. You can vary the flavor based on the kind of croutons you buy. I like to serve fresh fruit on the side.
—Connie Wilson, Huntington Beach, CA

PREP: 15 MIN. + CHILLING
BAKE: 40 MIN. + STANDING
MAKES: 12 SERVINGS

3 cups salad croutons
4 cups shredded cheddar cheese
1 can (4 oz.) chopped green chilies
6 large eggs
3 cups whole milk
2 tsp. ground mustard
1 tsp. salt
¼ tsp. garlic powder

1. Arrange croutons in a greased 13x9-in. baking dish. Sprinkle with cheese and chilies. In a bowl, beat the remaining ingredients. Pour over top. Refrigerate, covered, 8 hours or overnight.
2. Remove dish from the refrigerator 30 minutes before baking. Preheat oven to 350°. Bake, uncovered, until a knife inserted in the center comes out clean, 40-45 minutes. Let stand 10 minutes before cutting.

OVERNIGHT BAKED EGGS BRUSCHETTA

I like to spend as much time as I can with family and guests during the holidays, so I rely on make-ahead recipes. I was looking for something a little different for brunch, and came up with this breakfast bruschetta.
—Judi Berman-Yamada, Portland, OR

PREP: 45 MIN. + CHILLING ● **BAKE:** 10 MIN.
MAKES: 9 SERVINGS

1 Tbsp. cornmeal
1 tube (13.8 oz.) refrigerated
   pizza crust

OVERNIGHT PANCAKES

I keep a big batch of this pancake batter in the fridge to ease the morning rush. The golden, fluffy pancakes are delicious, and it's wonderful to be able to serve up a special breakfast without getting up extra early.
—Lisa Sammons, Cut Bank, MT

PREP: 10 MIN. + CHILLING • **COOK:** 10 MIN.
MAKES: 30 PANCAKES

 1 pkg. (¼ oz.) active dry yeast
 ¼ cup warm water (110° to 115°)
 4 cups all-purpose flour
 1 Tbsp. baking powder
 2 tsp. baking soda
 2 tsp. sugar
 1 tsp. salt
 6 large eggs
 4 cups buttermilk
 ¼ cup canola oil

1. Dissolve yeast in warm water; let stand for 5 minutes. Meanwhile, in another bowl, combine the next five ingredients. Whisk eggs, buttermilk and oil; stir into flour mixture just until moistened. Stir in yeast mixture. Refrigerate, covered, for 8 hours or overnight.
2. To make pancakes, lightly grease griddle and preheat over medium heat. Pour batter by ¼ cupfuls onto griddle; cook until the bubbles on top begin to pop and the bottoms are golden brown. Turn; cook until the second side is golden brown.
NOTE Warmed buttermilk will appear curdled.

BROCCOLI-CHICKEN STRATA

On our dairy farm, chores have to come first. That's why this strata comes in handy. I'll prepare it beforehand and pop it in the oven so it's ready when we are.
—Margery Moore, Richfield Springs, NY

PREP: 15 MIN. + CHILLING • **BAKE:** 1 HOUR. + STANDING
MAKES: 8 SERVINGS

 12 slices bread
 2¼ cups shredded cheddar cheese, divided
 3 cups frozen chopped broccoli, thawed and drained
 2 cups diced cooked chicken
 1 Tbsp. butter, melted
 6 large eggs
 3 cups whole milk
 2 Tbsp. finely chopped onion
 ¾ tsp. salt
 ½ tsp. ground mustard
 ¼ tsp. pepper

1. Using a doughnut cutter, cut 12 rings and holes in bread; set aside. Tear remaining bread scraps and place in a greased 13x9-in. baking dish. Sprinkle with 2 cups cheese, the broccoli and chicken. Arrange rings and holes on top; brush bread with melted butter.
2. Beat next six ingredients; pour over top. Refrigerate, covered, 8 hours or overnight.
3. Remove from refrigerator 30 minutes before baking. Bake, uncovered, at 325° for 55-60 minutes. Sprinkle with remaining cheese; bake until a knife inserted in center comes out clean, about 5 minutes longer. Let stand 5-10 minutes before cutting.

EGGS A LA TRISH

By using English muffins instead of bread or rolls, this overnight breakfast dish becomes just a little bit heartier. I'll often switch it up and use different cheeses or meats and it always comes out perfect.
—Mark Bohlke, Rosemount, MN

PREP: 15 MIN. + CHILLING
BAKE: 55 MIN. + STANDING
MAKES: 8 SERVINGS

- 4   English muffins, split and toasted
- 8   slices cheddar cheese
- 8   slices Canadian bacon
- 3¼ cups whole milk
- 6   large eggs
- 1   Tbsp. dried minced onion
- ½   tsp. salt
- ½   tsp. ground mustard

1. In a greased 13x9-in. baking dish, arrange six English muffin halves cut sides up. Cut the remaining muffins in half; fill in spaces in dish with muffin pieces. Top with cheese and Canadian bacon. Whisk the remaining ingredients; pour over the muffins. Refrigerate, covered, overnight.
2. Remove dish from the refrigerator 30 minutes before baking. Preheat oven to 325°. Bake, uncovered, until a knife inserted in center comes out clean, 55-60 minutes. Let stand 5 minutes before cutting.

Holiday Helper
Canadian bacon isn't really bacon—it's smoked pork tenderloin, and unlike tradiitonal bacon, it has very little fat. The best substitute for Canadian bacon is ham.

TOPPINGS

- ½ cup finely chopped walnuts, toasted
- ½ cup finely chopped pecans, toasted
- 2 medium bananas, sliced
- 1 cup sweetened whipped cream

1. Grease and preheat waffle maker. Whisk together first five ingredients. In a separate bowl, whisk together eggs, milk, oil and vanilla until blended. Add to the dry ingredients; stir just until moistened. Cook six waffles according to manufacturer's directions until golden brown.

2. For butterscotch syrup, combine sugar, water and corn syrup in a small heavy saucepan; stir gently to moisten all the sugar. Cook over medium-low heat, gently swirling pan occasionally, until sugar is dissolved. Cover; bring to a boil over medium-high heat. Cook 1 minute. Uncover; continue to boil and gently swirl until syrup turns a medium amber color, 3-4 minutes. Immediately remove from heat, and gradually stir in remaining syrup ingredients. Cool.

3. Combine walnuts and pecans. To assemble, place a waffle on a serving plate. Spoon some butterscotch syrup over it; layer with some of each of the following: banana slices, nut mixture and whipped cream. Repeat layers four times. Top with remaining waffle and syrup; sprinkle with remaining nut mixture.

NOTE: To toast nuts, bake in a shallow pan in a 350° oven for 5-10 minutes or cook in a skillet over low heat until lightly browned, stirring occasionally.

Holiday Helper
Whole wheat flour adds a nutty flavor, firmer texture and rich brown color to waffles and pancakes, quick and yeast breads and other baked goods. Because it's denser and contains less gluten, whole wheat flour will yield disapointing results if used alone. If you have only one flour to use for these waffles, make it all-purpose.

BANANA-NUT WAFFLE CAKE

This tower of waffles is served cool, not warm, so it's a cross between breakfast and dessert. The waffles can be wrapped and stored in the fridge until you're ready to assemble the "cake."
—HomeChef3, TasteOfHome.com

PREP: 25 MIN. • **COOK:** 20 MIN.
MAKES: 6 SERVINGS

- ½ cup whole wheat flour
- ½ cup all-purpose flour
- 2 Tbsp. cornstarch
- 1½ tsp. baking powder
- ¼ tsp. salt
- 2 large eggs
- ½ cup plus 2 Tbsp. whole milk
- 1 Tbsp. canola oil
- 1 tsp. vanilla extract

BUTTERSCOTCH SYRUP

- ¾ cup sugar
- 2 Tbsp. water
- 1 Tbsp. light corn syrup
- ¼ cup heavy whipping cream
- 1 Tbsp. unsalted butter
- 1 tsp. ground cinnamon
- ½ tsp. vanilla extract
- Dash salt

REUBEN BRUNCH BAKE

I created this when I wanted something different for a graduation brunch for our sons. I had most of the ingredients on hand for my usual Reuben dip, so I used them in a casserole instead!
—Janelle Reed, Merriam, KS

PREP: 15 MIN. + CHILLING
BAKE: 40 MIN. + STANDING
MAKES: 8 SERVINGS

- 8   large eggs, lightly beaten
- 1   can (14½ oz.) sauerkraut, rinsed and well drained
- 2   cups shredded Swiss cheese
- ½   cup chopped green onions
- ½   cup whole milk
- 1   pkg. (2 oz.) thinly sliced deli corned beef, cut into 1-in. pieces
- 1   Tbsp. Dijon mustard
- ¼   tsp. salt
- ¼   tsp. pepper
- 3   slices rye bread, toasted and coarsely chopped
- ¼   cup butter, melted

1. Combine the first nine ingredients. Pour into a greased 11x7-in. baking dish. Refrigerate, covered, overnight.

2. Remove casserole from refrigerator 30 minutes before baking. Preheat oven to 350°. Toss bread crumbs and butter; sprinkle over casserole. Bake, uncovered, until a knife inserted in center comes out clean, 40-45 minutes. Let stand for 10 minutes before serving.

TIPS FOR HOSTING THE PERFECT HOLIDAY BRUNCH

PLAN A MIX OF DISHES
Offer both savory and sweet items. Supplement homemade dishes with bakery delicacies.

KEEP THE FOOD WARM
Casseroles, pastries and other hot items can be kept warm in a 200° oven until you're ready to serve. Most guests like to chat and have a drink before they sit down to eat.

OFFER DRINK CHOICES
The mimosa—champagne and OJ—is classic and convenient; you can offer either a morning cocktail or straight juice. Have other juices on hand, too.

SET UP A COFFEE STATION
A coffee station lets everyone fix their coffee just how they like it. Stock with essentials like sugar and cream, then add flavored syrups and spices like cinnamon and nutmeg.

DECORATE LIGHTLY
This quote from the 1964 *Joy of Cooking* holds true: "Don't make your effects so stagey that your guests' reactions will be 'She went to a lot of trouble.' Make them rather say, 'She had a lot of fun doing it.'"

SET UP THE NIGHT BEFORE
Lay out the place settings, decorate, and make sure there are enough seats. Jot down reminders about reheating muffins, brewing coffee, cleaning last-minute dishes and more.

RELAX!
Remember, the whole point of a party is to enjoy the company of your loved ones. Everything else is just details.

SPICY BREAKFAST LASAGNA

It's fun to cook up something new for family and friends—especially when it gets rave reviews. When I brought this dish to a work breakfast, people said it really woke up their taste buds!
—Guthrie Torp Jr., Highland Ranch, CO

PREP: 20 MIN. + CHILLING
BAKE: 35 MIN. + STANDING
MAKES: 16 SERVINGS

- 3 cups 4% cottage cheese
- ½ cup minced chives
- ¼ cup sliced green onions
- 18 large eggs
- ⅓ cup whole milk
- ½ tsp. salt
- ¼ tsp. pepper
- 1 Tbsp. butter
- 8 lasagna noodles, cooked and drained
- 4 cups frozen shredded hash browns, thawed
- 1 lb. bulk pork sausage, cooked and crumbled
- 8 oz. sliced Monterey Jack cheese with jalapeno peppers
- 8 oz. sliced Muenster cheese

1. Combine cottage cheese, chives and onions; set aside. In another bowl, whisk eggs, milk, salt and pepper until blended. In a large skillet, heat butter over medium heat. Pour in egg mixture; cook and stir until eggs are thickened and no liquid egg remains. Remove from heat; set aside.

2. Place four lasagna noodles in a greased 13x9-in. baking dish. Layer with 2 cups hash browns, scrambled eggs, sausage and half of the cottage cheese mixture. Cover with Monterey Jack cheese. Top with the remaining lasagna noodles, hash browns and the cottage cheese mixture. Cover with Muenster cheese. Refrigerate, covered, 8 hours or overnight.

3. Remove baking dish from refrigerator 30 minutes before baking. Preheat oven to 350°. Bake, uncovered, until a knife inserted in center comes out clean, 35-40 minutes. Let stand for 5 minutes before cutting.

CRANBERRY CREAM CHEESE FRENCH TOAST

For a special brunch, my friend made this French toast with blueberries, but I make mine with cranberry sauce. Either way, it's divine!
—Sandie Heindel, Liberty, MO

PREP: 25 MIN. + CHILLING • **BAKE:** 50 MIN. + STANDING
MAKES: 12 SERVINGS

- 12 cups cubed French bread (about 12 oz.)
- 2 pkg. (8 oz. each) cream cheese, cubed
- 1 can (14 oz.) whole-berry cranberry sauce
- 12 large eggs, lightly beaten
- 2 cups 2% milk
- ⅓ cup maple syrup
- 2 tsp. ground cinnamon
  Dash ground nutmeg
  Additional maple syrup

1. Arrange half of the bread in a single layer in a greased 13x9-in. baking dish; top with cream cheese and spoonfuls of cranberry sauce. Top with the remaining bread.
2. In a large bowl, whisk eggs, milk, ⅓ cup of syrup, the cinnamon and nutmeg until blended. Pour over casserole. Refrigerate, covered, overnight.
3. Remove casserole from refrigerator 30 minutes before baking. Preheat oven to 350°. Bake, uncovered, until a knife inserted in center comes out clean, 50-60 minutes. Let stand 10 minutes before serving. Serve with additional maple syrup.

OVERNIGHT SAUSAGE & GRITS

This recipe is so appealing because all the preparation can be done the night before; just pop it into the oven an hour before you want to eat. This hearty dish works well as a side with pancakes or waffles, but also can be served as the main course.
—Susan Ham, Cleveland, TN

PREP: 10 MIN. + CHILLING • **BAKE:** 1 HOUR + STANDING
MAKES: 12 SERVINGS

- 3 cups hot cooked grits
- 2½ cups shredded cheddar cheese
- 1 lb. bulk pork sausage, cooked and crumbled
- 3 large eggs
- 1½ cups whole milk
- 3 Tbsp. butter, melted
- ¼ tsp. garlic powder

1. Mix grits, cheese and sausage. Beat eggs and milk; stir into grits. Add butter and garlic powder. Transfer to a greased 13x9-in. baking dish. Refrigerate, covered, 8 hours or overnight.
2. Remove dish from refrigerator 30 minutes before baking. Preheat oven to 350°. Bake, uncovered, until a knife inserted in the center comes out clean, about 1 hour. Let stand 5 minutes before cutting.

HOLIDAY FEASTS

*The heart of a Christmas celebration is the feast,
when family and friends gather around the table in
fellowship. Create a meal to match the occasion!*

Prime Rib

MUSTARD-CRUSTED PRIME RIB WITH MADEIRA GLAZE

This juicy prime rib is spectacular on its own, but the rich Madeira wine glaze takes it up a notch for special dinners. The roast shares the oven with a pan of tender veggies, so you'll have your main course and a side covered when the timer goes off. If you like, use the leftover fennel fronds and more pink peppercorns as a garnish.
—Kathryn Conrad, Milwaukee, WI

PREP: 20 MIN.
BAKE: 2½ HOURS + STANDING
MAKES: 8 SERVINGS

- 1   bone-in beef rib roast (about 5 lbs.)
- ½   cup stone-ground mustard
- 6   small garlic cloves, minced
- 1   Tbsp. brown sugar
- ½   tsp. salt
- ½   tsp. coarsely ground pink peppercorns, optional

VEGETABLES

- 2   lbs. medium Yukon Gold potatoes, cut into eighths (about 2-in. chunks)
- 4   medium carrots, halved lengthwise and cut into 2-in. pieces
- 1   medium red onion, cut into eighths (with root end intact)
- 1   medium fennel bulb, cut into eighths
- 3   Tbsp. olive oil
- 1   Tbsp. balsamic vinegar
- 1   tsp. brown sugar
- ¾   tsp. salt
- ½   tsp. pepper

MADEIRA GLAZE

- 1   cup balsamic vinegar
- ½   cup Madeira wine
- 1   tsp. brown sugar

1. Let roast stand at room temperature for 1 hour. Preheat oven to 450°. Combine mustard, garlic, brown sugar, salt and, if desired, peppercorns; brush evenly over top and sides of roast but not over bones (mixture may seem loose but will adhere). Place roast bone-side down on a rack in a shallow roasting pan. Place pan on middle oven rack; immediately reduce heat to 350°. Roast 1 hour.

2. Toss potatoes, carrots, onion and fennel with the next five ingredients.

Arrange vegetables in a single layer in a 15x10x1-in. baking pan on the lowest rack of the oven. Roast, stirring vegetables midway through baking, until the meat reaches desired doneness (a thermometer should read 135° for medium-rare, 140° for medium and 145° for medium-well), about 1½ hours. Cover roast loosely with foil during the last 30 minutes to prevent overbrowning. Let stand 15 minutes before carving.

3. Meanwhile, for glaze, combine balsamic vinegar, Madeira wine and brown sugar in a small saucepan. Bring to a boil over medium-high heat; cook until reduced to ½ cup, about 15 minutes. Let glaze cool to room temperature. Serve roast with vegetables and glaze.

CORN & ONION SOUFFLE

I swapped out my old cheese souffle for one with corn. If you're souffle-challenged, it helps to use smaller ramekins instead of one big dish.
—Lily Julow, Lawrenceville, GA

PREP: 25 MIN. • **BAKE:** 45 MIN.
MAKES: 10 SERVINGS

- 6   large eggs
- 2   Tbsp. plus ½ cup cornmeal, divided
- 2   cups fresh or frozen corn (about 10 oz.), thawed
- 2   cups 2% milk
- 1   Tbsp. sugar
- ¾   cup heavy whipping cream
- ½   cup butter, melted
- 1   Tbsp. canola oil
- 1   cup chopped sweet onion
- 3   oz. cream cheese, softened
- 1   tsp. plus ⅛ tsp. salt, divided
- ½   tsp. freshly ground pepper
- ⅛   tsp. baking soda

1. Separate eggs; let stand at room temperature for 30 minutes. Grease a 2½-qt. souffle dish; dust lightly with 2 Tbsp. cornmeal.

2. Preheat oven to 350°. Place corn, milk and sugar in a blender; cover and process until smooth. Add cream and melted butter; cover and process 15-30 seconds longer.

3. In a large saucepan, heat oil over medium heat. Add onion; cook and stir 4-6 minutes or until tender. Stir in corn mixture, cream cheese, 1 tsp. salt, pepper and the remaining cornmeal until heated through. Remove to a large bowl.

4. Whisk a small amount of the hot mixture into the egg yolks; return all to bowl, whisking constantly.

5. In a large bowl, beat the egg whites with baking soda and the remaining salt on high speed until stiff but not dry. With a rubber spatula, gently stir a fourth of the egg whites into corn mixture. Fold in the remaining egg whites. Transfer to the prepared dish.

6. Bake 45-50 minutes or until the top is deep golden brown and puffed and the center appears set. Serve immediately.

CAULIFLOWER WITH ROASTED ALMOND & PEPPER DIP

This side is great any day of the year but shines at Christmas when paired with turkey and dressing or just about any main dish. The festive orange sauce takes some time, but it tastes incredible.
—Lauren Knoelke, Milwaukee, WI

PREP: 40 MIN. • **BAKE:** 35 MIN.
MAKES: 10 SERVINGS (2¼ CUPS DIP)

- 10 cups water
- 1 cup olive oil, divided
- ¾ cup sherry or red wine vinegar, divided
- 3 Tbsp. salt
- 1 bay leaf
- 1 Tbsp. crushed red pepper flakes
- 1 large head cauliflower
- ½ cup whole almonds, toasted
- ½ cup soft whole wheat or white bread crumbs, toasted
- ½ cup fire-roasted crushed tomatoes
- 1 jar (8 oz.) roasted sweet red peppers, drained
- 2 Tbsp. minced fresh parsley
- 2 garlic cloves
- 1 tsp. sweet paprika
- ½ tsp. salt
- ¼ tsp. freshly ground pepper

1. In a 6-qt. stockpot, bring water, ½ cup oil, ½ cup sherry, salt, bay leaf and pepper flakes to a boil. Add cauliflower. Reduce heat; simmer, uncovered, until a knife easily inserts into center of cauliflower, 15-20 minutes, turning halfway through cooking.

Remove with a slotted spoon; drain well on paper towels.
2. Preheat oven to 450°. Place cauliflower on a greased wire rack in a 15x10x1-in. baking pan. Bake on a lower oven rack until dark golden, 35-40 minutes.
3. Meanwhile, place almonds, bread crumbs, tomatoes, roasted peppers, parsley, garlic, paprika, salt and pepper in a food processor; pulse until finely chopped. Add remaining sherry; process until blended. Continue processing while gradually adding remaining oil in a steady stream. Serve with cauliflower.

ICY HOLIDAY PUNCH

Pull out the punchbowl for this rosy thirst-quencher that dazzles at Christmas parties. This fun prep-ahead beverage makes any occasion a bit more special. It's delicious with apricot gelatin, too.
—Margaret Matson, Metamora, IL

TAKES: 10 MIN. + FREEZING • **MAKES:** 30 SERVINGS (5¾ QT.)

- 1 pkg. (6 oz.) cherry gelatin
- ¾ cup sugar
- 2 cups boiling water
- 1 can (46 oz.) unsweetened pineapple juice
- 6 cups cold water
- 2 liters ginger ale, chilled

In a 4-qt. freezer-proof container, dissolve gelatin and sugar in boiling water. Stir in pineapple juice and cold water. Cover and freeze overnight. Remove 2 hours before serving. Place in a punch bowl; stir in ginger ale just before serving.

TUSCAN TRUFFLES

For holiday potlucks, I make an appetizer truffle out of prosciutto, figs and toasted pine nuts. The creaminess comes from mascarpone and goat cheese.
—Roxanne Chan, Albany, CA

TAKES: 25 MIN. + CHILLING
MAKES: 3 DOZEN

- 2 logs (4 oz. each) fresh goat cheese
- 1 carton (8 oz.) mascarpone cheese
- 6 Tbsp. grated Parmesan cheese
- 3 garlic cloves, minced
- 1½ tsp. olive oil
- 1½ tsp. white balsamic vinegar
- ¾ tsp. grated lemon zest
- 3 oz. (6 Tbsp.) chopped prosciutto
- 3 oz. (6 Tbsp.) finely chopped dried figs
- 3 Tbsp. minced fresh parsley
- ¼ tsp. pepper
- 1 cup pine nuts, toasted and chopped

Combine the first 11 ingredients until well blended. Shape into 36 balls; roll in pine nuts. Refrigerate, covered, until serving.
NOTE To toast nuts, bake in a shallow pan in a 350° oven for 5-10 minutes or cook in a skillet over low heat until lightly browned, stirring occasionally.

Holiday Helper

White balsamic vinegar is produced with the same method and ingredients as the better-known dark version. Because it isn't caramelized, it remains a light golden color instead of turning a dark, rich brown; because it's aged for less time, it has a lighter taste. As with regular balsamic, some white balsamics have a slightly syrupy viscosity.

BROWN SUGAR POUND CAKE

This tender pound cake is the first one I mastered. You'll want to eat the browned butter icing by the spoonful—it tastes like pralines.
—Shawn Barto, Winter Garden, FL

PREP: 20 MIN. • **BAKE:** 55 MIN. + COOLING
MAKES: 16 SERVINGS

- 1½ cups unsalted butter, softened
- 2¼ cups packed brown sugar
- 5 large eggs, room temperature
- 2 tsp. vanilla extract
- 3 cups all-purpose flour
- 1 tsp. baking powder
- ¼ tsp. salt
- 1 cup sour cream

GLAZE

- 3 Tbsp. unsalted butter
- ¼ cup chopped pecans
- 1 cup confectioners' sugar
- ¼ tsp. vanilla extract
  Dash salt
- 2 to 3 Tbsp. half-and-half cream

1. Preheat oven to 350°. Grease and flour a 10-in. fluted tube pan.
2. Cream butter and brown sugar until light and fluffy. Add eggs, one at a time, beating well after each addition. Beat in vanilla. In another bowl, whisk flour, baking powder and salt; add to the creamed mixture alternately with sour cream, beating after each addition just until combined.
3. Transfer batter to prepared pan. Bake until a toothpick inserted in center comes out clean, 55-65 minutes. Cool in pan for 10 minutes before removing to a wire rack to cool completely.
4. For glaze, combine butter and pecans in a small saucepan over medium heat, stirring constantly, until butter is light golden brown, 4-5 minutes. Stir in confectioners' sugar. Add vanilla, salt and enough cream to reach a drizzling consistency. Drizzle glaze over cake, allowing some to drip down sides. Let stand until set.

ROASTED TATER ROUNDS WITH GREEN ONIONS & TARRAGON

I am crazy for potatoes, especially when they're roasted and toasted. Toss them with fresh herbs and green onions for a bold finish.
—Ally Phillips, Murrells Inlet, SC

PREP: 25 MIN. • **BROIL:** 10 MIN.
MAKES: 8 SERVINGS

- 4 lbs. potatoes (about 8 medium), sliced ¼ in. thick
  Cooking spray
- 2 tsp. sea salt
- 1 tsp. coarsely ground pepper
- 6 green onions, thinly sliced (about ¾ cup)
- 3 Tbsp. minced fresh parsley
- 2 Tbsp. minced fresh tarragon
  Olive oil, optional

1. Preheat broiler. Place potatoes in a large microwave-safe bowl; spritz with cooking spray and toss to coat. Microwave, covered, on high for 10-12 minutes or until almost tender, stirring halfway through cooking.
2. Spread the potatoes into greased 15x10x1-in. baking pans. Spritz with additional cooking spray; sprinkle with salt and pepper.
3. Broil 4-6 in. from heat 10-12 minutes or until golden brown, stirring halfway through cooking time. In a small bowl, mix green onions, parsley and tarragon. Sprinkle over potatoes; toss to coat. If desired, drizzle with olive oil.

CROWN ROAST OF PORK WITH MUSHROOM DRESSING

It looks so elegant that everyone thinks I really fussed over this delicious roast. But it's easy—the biggest challenge is to remember to order the crown roast from the meat department ahead of time!
—Betty Claycomb, Alverton, PA

PREP: 15 MIN. • **BAKE:** 2 HOURS
MAKES: 10 SERVINGS

- 1   pork loin crown roast (10 to 12 ribs, about 6 to 8 lbs.)
- ½   tsp. seasoned salt

MUSHROOM DRESSING
- ¼   cup butter, cubed
- 1   cup sliced fresh mushrooms
- ½   cup diced celery
- 3   cups cubed day-old bread
- ¼   tsp. salt
- ¼   tsp. pepper
- ⅓   cup apricot preserves
- 1   cup whole fresh cranberries, optional

1. Preheat oven to 350°. Place roast, rib ends up, in a shallow roasting pan; sprinkle with seasoned salt. Cover rib ends with foil. Bake, uncovered, for 1¼ hours.
2. Meanwhile, melt the butter over medium-high heat. Add mushrooms and celery; saute until tender. Stir in bread cubes, salt and pepper. Spoon around the roast. Brush the sides of the roast with preserves. Bake until a thermometer inserted into meat between ribs reads 145°, 45-60 minutes. Remove foil; let meat stand 10 minutes before slicing.
3. If desired, thread cranberries on a 20-in. string or thread. Transfer roast to a serving platter. Loop the cranberry string in and out of the rib ends. Slice between ribs to serve.

PANCETTA, PEAR & PECAN PUFFS

I recently attended a wedding reception where the menu was all small bites. I thought the little pear pastries would be great for the holidays, so I created my own version. They're the perfect combination of savory and sweet.
—Arlene Erlbach, Morton Grove, IL

PREP: 25 MIN. • **BAKE:** 10 MIN. + COOLING
MAKES: 2 DOZEN

- 1 sheet frozen puff pastry, thawed
- 6 oz. cream cheese, softened
- 2 Tbsp. honey
- ⅛ tsp. salt
- ⅛ tsp. pepper
- ¼ cup (1 oz.) crumbled fresh goat cheese
- 3 Tbsp. crumbled crisp pancetta or crumbled cooked bacon
- 3 Tbsp. finely chopped peeled ripe pear
- 2 Tbsp. finely chopped pecans, toasted

1. Preheat oven to 400°. On a lightly floured surface, unfold pastry dough. Using a 1¾-in. round cookie cutter, cut dough into 24 circles. Transfer to parchment paper-lined baking sheets. Bake until golden brown, 10-12 minutes. Cool completely on a wire rack.
2. Beat cream cheese, honey, salt and pepper until well blended. Fold in goat cheese, pancetta, pear and pecans.
3. Halve each cooled pastry. Spoon cream cheese mixture over the bottom halves; cover with the top halves. Serve at room temperature.
NOTE To toast nuts, bake in a shallow pan in a 350° oven for 5-10 minutes or cook in a skillet over low heat until lightly browned, stirring occasionally.

BRUSSELS SPROUTS & QUINOA SALAD

With Brussels sprouts for the green and cranberries for the red, I make a cheery Christmastime salad. Refreshing and versatile, it works with any kind of nut or dried fruit.
—Cameron Stell, Los Angeles, CA

PREP: 15 MIN. • **COOK:** 20 MIN. + CHILLING
MAKES: 6 SERVINGS

- 3 Tbsp. olive oil, divided
- 3 shallots, minced
- 3 garlic cloves, minced
- 2 cups plus 2 Tbsp. water, divided
- 1 cup quinoa, rinsed
- 1 cup fresh Brussels sprouts
- ½ cup dried cranberries
- ½ cup chopped walnuts, toasted
- 2 Tbsp. chopped fresh parsley
- ¼ cup lemon juice
- ½ tsp. salt
- ⅛ tsp. pepper

1. In a small saucepan, heat 1 Tbsp. olive oil over medium heat. Add shallots; cook and stir 3 minutes. Add garlic; cook 1 minute longer. Remove from pan.
2. Add 2 cups water to the same saucepan; bring to a boil. Add quinoa. Reduce heat; simmer, covered, until liquid is absorbed, 12-15 minutes. Remove from heat; fluff with a fork. Cool.
3. Meanwhile, microwave Brussels sprouts with the remaining water, covered, on high until tender, 6-8 minutes, stirring every 2 minutes. Drain. When cool enough to handle, remove leaves from sprouts. Discard the cores.
4. Combine the cooled quinoa, Brussels sprouts leaves, cranberries, walnuts and parsley. Whisk together lemon juice, salt, pepper and the remaining olive oil. Stir in the shallots and garlic. Toss with the quinoa mixture. Refrigerate, covered, 20 minutes.

AUNT MARGARET'S SWEET POTATO CASSEROLE

My great-aunt made an incredible sweet potato casserole for our holiday dinners. I've lightened it up a bit, but we love it just the same.
—Beth Britton, Fairlawn, OH

PREP: 50 MIN. • **BAKE:** 50 MIN.
MAKES: 12 SERVINGS

> 3 lbs. sweet potatoes (about 3 large), peeled and cubed
>
> **TOPPING**
> ¾ cup all-purpose flour
> ¾ cup packed brown sugar
> ¾ cup old-fashioned oats
> ⅛ tsp. salt
> ⅓ cup cold butter, cubed
>
> **FILLING**
> ½ cup sugar
> ½ cup 2% milk
> 2 large eggs, lightly beaten
> ¼ cup butter
> 1 tsp. vanilla extract
> 2 cups miniature marshmallows

1. Preheat oven to 350°. Place sweet potatoes in a 6-qt. stockpot; add water to cover. Bring to a boil. Reduce heat; cook, uncovered, 10-12 minutes or until tender.
2. Meanwhile, make topping by combining flour, brown sugar, oats and salt; cut in butter until crumbly.
3. Drain potatoes; return to pan; mash. Add sugar, milk, eggs, butter and vanilla; beat until combined. Transfer to a broiler-safe 13x9-in. baking dish. Sprinkle topping over the potato mixture.
4. Bake, uncovered, until the topping is golden brown, 40-45 minutes; let stand 10 minutes. Sprinkle with marshmallows. If desired, broil 4-5 inches from heat, 30-45 seconds or until marshmallows are puffed and golden.

CHOCOLATE & CARDAMOM COCONUT TART

This holiday-worthy tart is my nod to our family's Scandinavian heritage. The filling is rich in all the right ways, with coconut, cranberries and chocolate.
—Carole Holt, Mendota Heights, MN

PREP: 20 MIN. + CHILLING
BAKE: 50 MIN. + COOLING
MAKES: 16 SERVINGS

- 1⅓ cups butter, softened
- 1⅓ cups sugar
- 4 tsp. grated orange zest, divided
- 1 large egg
- 2⅔ cups all-purpose flour
- ¾ tsp. ground cardamom
- ¾ cup pistachios
- ½ cup fresh cranberries
- ¾ cup sweetened shredded coconut
- ⅓ cup plus ½ cup 60% cacao bittersweet chocolate baking chips, divided
- ⅔ cup sweetened condensed milk
- ½ cup white baking chips

1. Preheat oven to 325°. Cream butter, sugar and 2 tsp. orange zest until light and fluffy. Beat in egg. Add the flour and cardamom, mixing well. Refrigerate dough for 30 minutes.
2. Meanwhile, pulse pistachios in a food processor until finely chopped; remove. Repeat with cranberries. Mix together ⅓ cup pistachios, the cranberries, coconut, ⅓ cup bittersweet chocolate chips and the milk.
3. Press half the dough onto the bottom and ¼ in. up sides of a greased 9-in. springform pan. Spread the pistachio mixture over dough. Between sheets of waxed paper, roll the remaining dough into a 9-in. circle. Remove top sheet of paper. Gently flip dough and place over pistachio filling; remove remaining paper. Press dough around edge to seal. Place pan on a 15x10-in. rimmed baking pan.
4. Bake until golden brown, 50-60 minutes. Cool in pan for 15 minutes. Loosen sides from pan with a knife; cool completely. Remove rim from pan.
5. Microwave white baking chips on high until melted, stirring every 30 seconds; remove. Repeat with the remaining bittersweet chips. Drizzle tart with the melted white and bittersweet chocolate. Sprinkle with the remaining pistachios and orange zest.
FREEZE OPTION Cover and freeze unbaked tart. Remove from freezer 30 minutes before baking (do not thaw). Preheat oven to 325°. Place tart on a baking sheet; cover edge loosely with foil. Bake as directed, increasing time as necessary. Cool and top as directed.

ROSEMARY BEETS

We're a family of beet eaters. For a simple side dish, I use a slow cooker and let the beets mellow with rosemary and thyme.
—Nancy Heishman, Las Vegas, NV

PREP: 20 MIN. • **COOK:** 6 HOURS
MAKES: 8 SERVINGS

- ⅓ cup honey
- ¼ cup white balsamic vinegar
- 1 Tbsp. minced fresh rosemary or
- 1 tsp. dried rosemary, crushed
- 2 tsp. minced fresh thyme or ¾ tsp. dried thyme
- 1 Tbsp. olive oil
- 2 garlic cloves, minced
- ¾ tsp. salt
- ½ tsp. Chinese five-spice powder
- ½ tsp. coarsely ground pepper
- 5 large fresh beets (about 3½ lbs.), peeled and trimmed
- 1 medium red onion, chopped
- 1 medium orange, peeled and chopped
- 1 cup crumbled feta cheese

1. In a small bowl, whisk the first nine ingredients until blended. Place beets in a greased 4-qt. slow cooker. Add onion and orange. Pour honey mixture over top.
2. Cook, covered, on low 6-8 hours or until beets are tender. Remove beets; cut into wedges. Return to slow cooker. Serve warm or refrigerate and serve cold. Serve with a slotted spoon; sprinkle with cheese.

BEST-EVER CRESCENT ROLLS

My daughter and I have cranked out dozens of homemade crescent rolls. It's a real team effort and a family tradition! I cut the dough into pie-shaped wedges; she rolls.
—Irene Yeh, Mequon, WI

PREP: 40 MIN. + CHILLING
BAKE: 10 MIN/BATCH
MAKES: 32 ROLLS

3¾ to 4¼ cups all-purpose flour
2 pkg. (¼ oz. each) active dry yeast
1 tsp. salt
1 cup whole milk
½ cup butter, cubed
¼ cup honey
3 large egg yolks
2 Tbsp. butter, melted

1. Combine 1½ cups flour, yeast and salt. In a small saucepan, heat milk, cubed butter and honey to 120°-130°. Add to dry ingredients; beat on medium speed 2 minutes. Add egg yolks; beat on high 2 minutes. Stir in enough remaining flour to form a soft dough (the dough will be sticky).
2. Turn dough onto a floured surface; knead until smooth and elastic, about 6-8 minutes. Place dough in a greased bowl, turning once to grease the top. Cover with plastic wrap and let rise in a warm place until doubled, about 45 minutes.
3. Punch down dough; place in a resealable plastic bag. Seal and refrigerate overnight.
4. To bake, turn dough onto a lightly floured surface; divide in half. Roll each portion into a 14-in. circle; cut each circle into 16 wedges. Lightly brush wedges with melted butter. Roll each wedge up from the wide end, pinching the pointed end to seal. Place 2 in. apart on parchment paper-lined baking sheets, point side down. Cover with lightly greased plastic wrap; let rise in a warm place until doubled, about 45 minutes.
5. Preheat oven to 375°. Bake until golden brown, 9-11 minutes. Remove from pans to wire racks; serve warm.
FREEZE OPTION Immediately after shaping, freeze unbaked rolls on parchment paper-lined baking sheets until firm. Transfer to a resealable plastic bag; return to freezer. Freeze up to 4 weeks. To use, let rise and bake as directed, increasing rise time to 2½-3 hours.

TRIM YOUR TABLE

Want to add a bit of cheer to your holiday place settings? Fold your way to a perfect Christmas tree napkin! This basic origami fold is simple to do, looks elegant, and makes a great addition to any holiday table.

1. Start with a clean, pressed square napkin. Fold the napkin in half and then in half again, so you have a square a quarter of the original size.

2. Place the napkin so all the loose edges face toward you. Take the first flap and bring it up to the top of your diamond.

3. Repeat this with the other layers, staggering them slightly.

4. Flip the napkin over so the folds are against your work surface. The point of the (former) diamond should be facing toward you.

5. Fold the sides inward toward the middle. At the center top, a point should form (this is the tip of the tree).

6. Turn the napkin back over. You can tell it's starting to get its tree shape!

7. Take those flaps and turn them under. This will help form the layers of the tree.

8. Continue all the way to the bottom, turning every flap under so you have a tree with a classic triangular shape.

Feast of the Seven Fishes

TUNA STEAK ON FETTUCCINE

For something new to do with tuna, this tangy dish is a delicious option. I prefer the marinade on tuna or mahi mahi, but it's good on any fish—grilled, baked or broiled.
—Caren Stearns, Austin, TX

PREP: 10 MIN. + MARINATING
COOK: 20 MIN. • **MAKES:** 2 SERVINGS

- 8 Tbsp. white wine or chicken broth, divided
- 3 Tbsp. olive oil, divided
- 1 tsp. dried basil, divided
- 1 tsp. dried oregano, divided
- ¼ tsp. salt, divided
- ⅛ tsp. pepper, divided
- 1 tuna, swordfish or halibut steak (about 10 oz.), cut in half
- ½ cup thinly sliced sweet onion
- 1 cup canned diced tomatoes, undrained
- ¼ tsp. brown sugar
- 3 oz. uncooked fettuccine

1. In a resealable plastic bag, combine 2 Tbsp. wine, 2 Tbsp. oil, ¼ tsp. basil, ¼ tsp. oregano, and half the salt and pepper; add tuna. Seal bag and turn to coat; refrigerate 1 hour.
2. In a large skillet, saute onion in the remaining oil until tender. Add tomatoes, brown sugar and the remaining wine, basil, oregano, salt and pepper. Bring to a boil. Reduce heat; simmer, uncovered, until bubbly and slightly thickened, 4-6 minutes. Meanwhile, cook the fettuccine according to the package directions.
3. Drain tuna, discarding marinade. Place tuna over the tomato mixture; return to a boil. Reduce heat; simmer, covered, until fish just begins to flake easily with a fork, about 6 minutes. Remove tuna and keep warm. Drain fettuccine; add to the tomato mixture and toss to coat. Divide between two plates; top with tuna.

SMOKED TROUT PATÉ

My tasty spread is easy to make in a food processor, and it's a guaranteed winner at any party. The recipe is versatile, so feel free to substitute other favorite smoked fish.
—Judy Walle, Toledo, OH

TAKES: 15 MIN. + CHILLING • **MAKES:** 2⅔ CUPS

- 1 lb. flaked smoked trout
- 3 oz. reduced-fat cream cheese
- ½ cup half-and-half cream
- 1 Tbsp. horseradish sauce
- 1 Tbsp. lemon juice
- ⅛ tsp. pepper
- 2 tsp. minced fresh parsley
  Cucumber slices
  Assorted crackers

Pulse the first seven ingredients in a food processor until blended. Refrigerate, covered, until serving. Serve with cucumber slices and assorted crackers.

MANHATTAN CLAM CHOWDER

This classic chowder makes a great soup course as part of a large dinner, or can be its own light meal with a tossed salad and hot rolls on a cold winter evening. My family's enjoyed it for over 30 years.
—Joan Hopewell, Columbus, NJ

PREP: 10 MIN. • **COOK:** 40 MIN.
MAKES: 8 SERVINGS (ABOUT 2 QT.)

- 2 Tbsp. butter
- 1 cup chopped onion
- ⅔ cup chopped celery
- 2 tsp. minced green pepper
- 1 garlic clove, minced
- 2 cups hot water
- 1 cup cubed peeled potatoes
- 1 can (28 oz.) diced tomatoes, undrained
- 2 cans (6½ oz. each) minced clams, undrained
- 1 tsp. salt
- ½ tsp. dried thyme
- ¼ tsp. pepper
  Dash cayenne pepper
- 2 tsp. minced fresh parsley

1. In a large saucepan, heat butter over low heat. Add onion, celery, green pepper and garlic; cook, stirring frequently, for 20 minutes. Add water and potatoes; bring to a boil. Reduce heat; simmer, covered, until potatoes are tender, about 15 minutes.
2. Add tomatoes, clams, salt, thyme, pepper and cayenne; heat through. Stir in parsley. Serve immediately.

CALAMARI SALAD

This is one of the seven fish dishes we serve every Christmas. It is easy to make and quite delicious either warm or cold. The recipe has been passed down to me through my grandparents, who were excellent cooks.
—Paul Rinaldi, Easton, PA

TAKES: 25 MIN. • **MAKES:** 6 SERVINGS

2½ lbs. cleaned fresh or frozen
     calamari (squid), thawed
½ cup olive oil
3 anchovy fillets, minced, optional
2 tsp. minced fresh Italian parsley
1 garlic clove, minced

½ cup dry white wine or dry vermouth
1 can (8 oz.) mushroom stems
    and pieces, drained, optional
¼ tsp. salt
¼ tsp. pepper
½ cup chopped celery
½ cup pitted Italian olives, sliced
3 Tbsp. lemon juice

1. Chop calamari tentacles; cut body into ½-in. rings.
2. In a large saucepan, heat oil over medium heat. Add anchovies if desired; stir in parsley and garlic. Cook 1 minute. Add wine; stir in mushrooms, if desired, and seasonings. Add calamari; bring to a boil. Reduce heat; simmer, covered, until calamari is tender, 2-3 minutes. Remove pan from heat; cool slightly.
3. In a serving bowl, toss celery, olives, lemon juice and calamari mixture. Serve warm, or refrigerate and serve cold.

 Holiday Helper
If your grocery store doesn't carry either fresh or frozen calamari, you can request it in advance from the fish counter. If you do special-order calamari, be sure to ask them to clean it for you; it's a messy job!

OYSTER FRICASSEE

I oversee the gardens at Colonial Williamsburg, and I love this special dish from our holiday recipe collection. The colonists had a ready source of oysters from Chesapeake Bay, so a rich, creamy casserole would have been a good way to present that fresh seafood.
—Susan Dippre, Williamsburg, VA

PREP: 20 MIN. • **BAKE:** 25 MIN. + STANDING
MAKES: 6 SERVINGS

1	qt. shucked oysters
¾	cup butter, divided
2	medium onions, chopped
1½	cups chopped celery
½	cup all-purpose flour
2	cups half-and-half cream
2	tsp. minced fresh parsley
1	tsp. salt
1	tsp. minced fresh thyme or ½ tsp. dried thyme
¼	tsp. pepper
⅛	tsp. cayenne pepper
4	large egg yolks, lightly beaten
2	cups crushed butter-flavored crackers (about 50 crackers)
	Lemon slices
	Fresh thyme sprigs

1. Preheat oven to 400°. Drain oysters, reserving the oyster liquor; set aside. In a large saucepan, heat ½ cup butter over medium heat. Add onions and celery; cook and stir until tender, 4-6 minutes. Stir in flour until blended; gradually whisk in the cream. Bring to a boil, whisking constantly; cook until thickened, about 2 minutes.

2. Reduce heat; add next five ingredients and the reserved oyster liquor. Cook and stir until smooth, about 2 minutes. Remove from heat. Stir a small amount of the hot liquid into egg yolks; return all to the pan, stirring constantly.

3. Pour half of the sauce into a greased 13x9-in. baking dish. Top with half of the oysters; sprinkle with half of the cracker crumbs. Repeat layers. Melt the remaining butter; drizzle over top.

4. Bake, uncovered, until golden brown, 23-28 minutes. Let stand 10 minutes. Serve with lemon slices and thyme sprigs.

CREAMY TIRAMISU CHEESECAKE

The Italian word tiramisu *means "pick-me-up" and refers to a dessert of ladyfinger sponge cake dipped in coffee and layered with mascarpone cheese. Cross it with a cheesecake and you have a guaranteed picker-upper that redefines a classic—the perfect finishing touch to an Italian meal.*
—*Priscilla Gilbert, Indian Harbour Beach, FL*

PREP: 30 MIN.
BAKE: 70 MINUTES + CHILLING
MAKES: 12 SERVINGS

- 1 Tbsp. butter, melted
- ⅓ cup chocolate graham cracker crumbs (about 2 whole crackers)
- 2 Tbsp. plus 2 tsp. instant coffee granules
- 1 Tbsp. hot water
- ⅓ cup strong brewed coffee
- 1 tsp. rum extract
- 1 pkg. (3 oz.) ladyfingers, split
- 4 pkg. (8 oz. each) cream cheese, softened
- 1⅓ cups sugar
- ⅓ cup heavy whipping cream
- ⅓ cup sour cream
- 2 tsp. vanilla extract
- 4 large eggs, lightly beaten
  Baking cocoa

1. Preheat oven to 325°. Brush bottom of a 9-in. springform pan with butter; sprinkle evenly with cracker crumbs. Securely wrap a double thickness of heavy-duty foil (about 18 in. square) under and around the pan.

2. Dissolve coffee granules in hot water; cool and set aside. Combine the brewed coffee and rum extract; brush over the flat sides of the split ladyfingers. Arrange ladyfingers, rounded sides out, along the sides of the prepared pan.

3. Beat cream cheese and sugar until smooth. Beat in cream, sour cream, vanilla and reserved dissolved coffee. Add eggs; beat on low speed just until combined. Pour into prepared pan. Place springform pan in a larger baking pan; add 1 in. of hot water to larger pan.

4. Bake until the center is just set and the top appears dull, 70-80 minutes. Remove the springform pan from water bath; remove foil. Cool cheesecake on a wire rack for 10 minutes; loosen sides from pan with a knife. Cool 1 hour longer. Refrigerate overnight, covering when completely cooled.

5. Remove rim from the pan. Just before serving, dust cheesecake with cocoa.

MARINATED SHRIMP & OLIVES

This colorful dish is my favorite appetizer to serve party guests. The flavors blend beautifully, and the shrimp are tender and tasty.
—*Carol A. Gawronski, Lake Wales, FL*

PREP: 10 MIN. • **COOK:** 5 MIN. + CHILLING
MAKES: 20 SERVINGS

- 1½ lbs. peeled and deveined cooked shrimp (31-40 per lb.)
- 1 can (6 oz.) pitted ripe olives, drained
- 1 jar (5¾ oz.) pimiento-stuffed olives, drained
- 2 Tbsp. olive oil
- 1½ tsp. curry powder
- ½ tsp. ground ginger
- ¼ tsp. salt
- ¼ tsp. pepper
- 2 Tbsp. lemon juice
- 1 Tbsp. minced fresh parsley or 1 tsp. dried parsley flakes

1. Combine shrimp and olives; set aside.

2. In a small saucepan, heat oil over medium heat. In a small bowl, combine curry, ginger, salt and pepper; whisk into hot oil. Cook and stir 1 minute. Remove from heat; stir in lemon juice and parsley. Immediately drizzle over the shrimp mixture; toss gently to coat.

3. Refrigerate, covered, up to 6 hours, stirring occasionally. Serve with toothpicks.

ROASTED HERBED SQUASH WITH GOAT CHEESE

Cooking is a hobby I'm happy to share with my toddler, who's already fascinated with the process. She (and all our Christmas Eve party guests) heartily approved this new potluck favorite. Any type of winter squash works here.
—Lindsay Oberhausen, Lexington, KY

PREP: 25 MIN. • **COOK:** 30 MIN.
MAKES: 10 SERVINGS

- 2 medium acorn squash (about 1½ lbs. each), peeled and cut into 2-in. cubes
- 1 large butternut squash (5 to 6 lbs.), peeled and cut into 2-in. cubes
- 3 Tbsp. olive oil
- 2 Tbsp. minced fresh thyme
- 2 Tbsp. minced fresh rosemary
- 1 Tbsp. kosher salt
- 1 tsp. coarsely ground pepper
- 1 log (11 oz.) fresh goat cheese, crumbled
- 2 Tbsp. coarsely chopped fresh parsley
- 1 Tbsp. maple syrup, warmed slightly

1. Preheat oven to 425°. Toss squashes with oil and seasonings. Transfer to two foil-lined 15x10-in. rimmed pans. Roast squash, stirring once, until soft and some pieces are caramelized, 30-35 minutes. Switch position of pans midway through roasting to ensure even doneness. If a darker color is desired, broil 3-4 in. from the heat for 2-4 minutes.

2. Cool slightly. To serve, add goat cheese to squash; gently toss. Sprinkle with parsley; drizzle with maple syrup.

Holiday Helper

To peel acorn squash, place the whole squash in gently boiling water for 15 minutes; pour off water and chill in cold water for 5 minutes. When cool enough to handle, slice off peel from peaks or ridges with a knife; use a spoon to dig out the peel from the valleys. Slice squash in half and remove seeds and stem; then cut into chunks.

ORANGE-GLAZED CARROTS, ONIONS & RADISHES

Carrots and radishes give color and crunch to this sweet, spicy side dish. We never have leftovers. If you make it ahead of time, don't add the walnuts until you've reheated it and are ready to serve.
—Thomas Faglon, Somerset, NJ

PREP: 15 MIN. • **COOK:** 20 MIN. • **MAKES:** 8 SERVINGS

- 1 lb. fresh pearl onions
- ¼ cup butter, cubed
- 2 lbs. medium carrots, thinly sliced
- 12 radishes, thinly sliced
- ½ cup dark brown sugar
- 4 tsp. grated orange zest
- ½ cup orange juice
- 1 cup chopped walnuts, toasted

1. In a large saucepan, bring 4 cups water to a boil. Add pearl onions; boil 3 minutes. Drain and rinse with cold water. Peel.
2. In a large skillet, heat butter over medium heat. Add carrots, pearl onions, radishes, brown sugar, orange zest and juice; cook, covered, 10-15 minutes or until vegetables are tender, stirring occasionally. Cook, uncovered, 5-7 minutes longer or until slightly thickened. Sprinkle with walnuts.
NOTE To toast nuts, bake in a shallow pan in a 350° oven for 5-10 minutes or cook in a skillet over low heat until lightly browned, stirring occasionally.

EPIPHANY HAM

I wanted to cook a ham but didn't have the ingredients for my usual glaze recipe, so I made substitutions, and it turned out beautifully. Feel free to experiment—try a different flavored soda, or use sweet-and-sour sauce in place of duck sauce.
—Edith Griffith, Havre de Grace, MD

PREP: 10 MIN. • **BAKE:** 3 HOURS • **MAKES:** 12 SERVINGS

- 1 fully cooked bone-in ham (8 to 10 lbs.; not spiral cut)
- 1 can (12 oz.) black cherry soda
- 2 tsp. Chinese five-spice powder
- ⅔ cup duck sauce

1. Preheat oven to 350°. Place ham on a rack in a baking pan or dish; pour soda over ham. Sprinkle with five-spice powder. Cover with aluminum foil; bake 30 minutes.
2. Remove foil and discard. Baste with duck sauce; return to oven and bake, uncovered, until a thermometer reads 140°, about 2½ hours, basting again halfway through baking.

HERB-BRINED CORNISH GAME HENS

Instead of a turkey or a big roast, why not serve individual Cornish game hens for the holidays? They cook in just a fraction of the time and are guaranteed to impress all your guests.
—Shannon Roum, Cudahy, WI

PREP: 35 MIN. + MARINATING
BAKE: 3¾ HOURS + STANDING
MAKES: 8 SERVINGS

⅔ cup kosher salt
¼ cup packed brown sugar
12 whole peppercorns
5 fresh sage leaves
2 garlic cloves
1 fresh thyme sprig
1 fresh rosemary sprig
1 qt. water
1½ qt. cold water

2 large turkey-size oven roasting bags
4 Cornish game hens (20 oz. each)
HERB BUTTER
14 whole peppercorns
2 garlic cloves
¾ cup butter, softened
3 Tbsp. plus 1 tsp. olive oil, divided
⅓ cup packed fresh parsley sprigs
3 Tbsp. fresh sage leaves
1 Tbsp. fresh rosemary leaves
2 Tbsp. fresh thyme leaves
2 lbs. fresh Brussels sprouts, trimmed and halved
2 small red onions, cut into wedges
½ tsp. kosher salt
½ tsp. coarsely ground pepper

1. In a saucepan, combine the salt, brown sugar, peppercorns, sage, garlic, thyme, rosemary and 1 qt. water. Bring to a boil. Cook and stir until salt and sugar are dissolved. Remove from the heat. Add the cold water to cool the brine to room temperature.

2. Place a turkey-size oven roasting bag inside a second roasting bag; add the hens. Carefully pour the cooled brine into the bag. Squeeze out as much air as possible; seal both bags and turn to coat. Place in a roasting pan. Refrigerate for 1-2 hours, turning occasionally. Drain, discard the brine and pat the hens dry.

3. Meanwhile, place peppercorns and garlic in a food processor; cover and pulse until coarsely chopped. Add butter, 3 Tbsp. of olive oil, and the herbs; cover and process until smooth. With fingers, carefully loosen skin from hens; rub half of the butter mixture under skin. Secure skin to the underside of breast with toothpicks; tie drumsticks together. Rub remaining butter mixture over the skin.

4. Preheat oven to 450°. On a 15x10x1-in. baking pan, toss Brussels sprouts and onions with the remaining olive oil, salt and pepper. Arrange in a single layer. Place hens, breast side up, on top of the vegetables. Bake until thermometer reads 165°, 35-40 minutes. Cover loosely with foil if hens brown too quickly.

5. Remove hens and vegetables to a serving platter; cover and let stand for 10 minutes before carving. If desired, garnish with additional herbs.

MOM'S APPLE CORNBREAD STUFFING

My speedy recipe is the end-all be-all stuffing in our family. We never have leftovers.
—Marie Forte, Raritan, NJ

PREP: 15 MIN. • **BAKE:** 35 MIN.
MAKES: 16 SERVINGS

6 large Granny Smith apples, peeled and chopped
1 pkg. (14 oz.) crushed cornbread stuffing
½ cup butter, melted
1 can (14½ oz.) chicken broth

1. Preheat oven to 350°. Grease a 13x9-in. baking dish and set aside. Combine apples, stuffing and melted butter. Add broth; mix well.

2. Transfer to greased baking dish. Bake until golden brown, 35-40 minutes.

FESTIVE RICE

My mom and I transformed plain rice by adding feta, cranberries, pumpkin seeds and cayenne. We wound up with a sweet and spicy crowd-pleaser.
—Lisa de Perio, Dallas, TX

PREP: 20 MIN. • **BAKE:** 30 MIN.
MAKES: 6 SERVINGS

2¼ cups water
¼ cup butter, cubed
1 tsp. salt

1 tsp. white vinegar
½ tsp. garlic powder
1 cup uncooked jasmine rice
¼ cup salted pumpkin seeds or pepitas
2 tsp. brown sugar
¼ to ½ tsp. cayenne pepper
¼ cup crumbled feta cheese
¼ cup chopped fresh mint
¼ cup dried cranberries

1. Preheat oven to 325°. In a small saucepan, bring the first five ingredients to a boil. Remove from heat. Pour over rice in a greased 8-in. square baking dish. Bake, covered, until all liquid is absorbed, 30-35 minutes.

2. Meanwhile, in a small nonstick skillet over medium-high heat, cook pumpkin seeds, brown sugar and cayenne pepper, stirring constantly until the sugar melts and cayenne coats the pumpkin seeds, about 4-5 minutes. Remove from heat; transfer to a plate, spreading out the seeds to cool. Sprinkle cooked rice with feta, mint, cranberries and the spiced pumpkin seeds.

FILLING

    3 pkg. (8 oz. each) cream
       cheese, softened
    ½ cup packed brown sugar
    ⅓ cup granulated sugar
    ¼ cup maple syrup
    3 large eggs, room temperature
    1 can (15 oz.) solid-pack pumpkin
    2 Tbsp. cornstarch
    3 tsp. vanilla extract
 1½ tsp. pumpkin pie spice
TOPPING
    1 cup heavy whipping cream
    ¾ cup maple syrup
    ½ cup chopped pecans, toasted

1. Preheat oven to 325°. Wrap a double thickness of heavy-duty foil (about 18 in. square) around a greased 9-in. springform pan. Mix cracker crumbs and granulated sugar; stir in butter. Press onto bottom of prepared pan.

2. Beat cream cheese, sugars and maple syrup until smooth. Add eggs; beat on low just until blended. Whisk in pumpkin, cornstarch, vanilla and pumpkin pie spice; pour over crust. Place springform pan in a larger baking pan; add 1 in. of hot water to larger pan.

3. Bake until the center is just set and the top appears dull, 70-80 minutes. Remove springform pan from water bath. Cool cheesecake on a wire rack 10 minutes. Loosen the sides from the pan with a knife; remove foil. Cool 1 hour longer. Refrigerate overnight, covering when completely cooled.

4. For topping, combine whipping cream and maple syrup in a small saucepan over medium heat; bring to a boil. Continue boiling, stirring occasionally, until slightly thickened, 15-20 minutes. Stir in toasted pecans. Refrigerate until cold.

5. Remove rim from pan. Stir topping; spoon over chilled cheesecake.

NOTE To toast nuts, bake in a shallow pan in a 350° oven for 5-10 minutes or cook in a skillet over low heat until lightly browned, stirring occasionally.

GREEN BEANS IN RED PEPPER SAUCE

For easy and delicious green beans, I make a simple sauce of sweet red peppers, almonds and parsley. It dresses up other veggies, too—we love it with zucchini or roasted cauliflower.
—Elisabeth Larsen, Pleasant Grove, UT

TAKES: 30 MIN. • **MAKES:** 6 SERVINGS

    1 lb. fresh green beans, trimmed
    ½ cup roasted sweet red peppers
    ¼ cup sliced almonds
    2 Tbsp. olive oil
    2 Tbsp. minced fresh parsley
    2 Tbsp. lemon juice
    2 garlic cloves, halved
    ½ tsp. salt

Place beans in a large saucepan; add water to cover. Bring to a boil. Cook, covered, until crisp-tender, 2-4 minutes. Drain. Pulse remaining ingredients in a food processor until smooth. Toss with beans.

PECAN PUMPKIN CHEESECAKE

I love to play with cheesecake by mixing and matching flavors. This one with pumpkin and maple is the star of our holiday spread.
—Sue Gronholz, Beaver Dam, WI

PREP: 30 MIN. • **BAKE:** 70 MIN. + CHILLING
MAKES: 16 SERVINGS

    1 cup graham cracker crumbs
    3 Tbsp. granulated sugar
    2 Tbsp. butter, melted

FESTIVE
SIDES & BREADS

Even when the main dish is exquisite, a great side dish can steal the show! These supporting dishes and breads are worthy of a spotlight of their own.

CHERRY ALMOND MINI LOAVES

Plenty of good things come in these little loaves. There are golden raisins and cherries in the dough and a luscious surprise—the creamy almond filling—in every scrumptious bite.
—Connie Simon, Reed City, MO

PREP: 45 MIN. + RISING • **BAKE:** 20 MIN.
MAKES: 12 MINI LOAVES

- ¾ cup whole milk
- ¾ cup butter, divided
- ½ cup sugar
- 1 tsp. salt
- 2 pkg. (¼ oz. each) active dry yeast
- ¼ cup warm water (110° to 115°)
- 2 large eggs
- 1 large egg yolk
- 5½ to 6 cups all-purpose flour
- 1½ cups golden raisins
- 1⅓ cups candied cherry halves
- 1 tsp. grated orange zest

FILLING
- 1 pkg. (8 oz.) almond paste
- ½ cup sugar
- 1 large egg white
  Confectioners' sugar

1. In a large saucepan, combine milk, ½ cup butter, sugar and salt. Cook over low heat until butter is melted; stir until smooth. Cool to lukewarm (110°-115°).

2. In a large bowl, dissolve yeast in water. Stir in the milk mixture, eggs and yolk. Gradually beat in 2 cups flour. Stir in raisins, cherries and orange zest. Add enough of the remaining flour to form a soft dough. Turn onto a floured surface; knead until smooth and elastic, about 6-8 minutes.

3. Place in a large greased bowl, turning once to grease the top of the dough. Cover and let rise in a warm place until doubled, about 1½ hours.

4. Punch down dough; divide into 12 portions. Shape each portion into a 6x4-in. oval. Place 2 in. apart on greased baking sheets.

5. For filling, crumble almond paste in a small bowl; stir in sugar and egg white until smooth. Divide the filling into 12 portions; roll each into a 5-in. log. Flatten slightly; place off-center on each oval. Fold dough over filling; pinch edges to seal. Cover with a kitchen towel; let rise until doubled, about 45 minutes.

6. Preheat oven to 350°. Melt remaining butter; brush over each loaf. Bake until golden brown, about 20 minutes. Dust with confectioners' sugar.

BEST-EVER BREADSTICKS

Present these long, thin breadsticks in a tall clear glass. They're an attractive and edible addition to any table setting!
—Carol Wolfer, Lebanon, OR

PREP: 20 MIN. + RISING • **BAKE:** 10 MIN. + COOLING
MAKES: ABOUT 18 BREADSTICKS

- 3 to 3¼ cups all-purpose flour
- 1 pkg. (¼ oz.) quick-rise yeast
- 1 Tbsp. sugar
- 1 tsp. salt
- ¾ cup whole milk
- ¼ cup plus 1 Tbsp. water, divided
- 1 Tbsp. butter
- 1 large egg white
  Coarse salt

1. Combine 1½ cups flour, yeast, sugar and salt. In a small saucepan, heat milk, ¼ cup water and butter to 120°-130°. Add to dry ingredients; beat on medium speed just until moistened. Stir in enough remaining flour to form a stiff dough.
2. Turn dough onto a lightly floured surface; knead until smooth and elastic, 6-8 minutes. Place in a greased bowl, turning once to grease top. Cover with plastic and let rise in a warm place until doubled, about 30 minutes.
3. Punch down dough. Pinch off golf ball-size pieces. On a lightly floured surface, roll into pencil-size strips. Place on greased baking sheets 1 in. apart. Cover and let rise for 15 minutes.
4. Preheat oven to 400°. Beat egg white and the remaining water; brush over the breadsticks. Sprinkle with coarse salt. Bake until golden, about 10 minutes. Remove from pans to wire racks to cool.

EASY POTATO ROLLS

After I discovered this recipe, it became a mainstay for me. I make the dough ahead of time when company is coming, and try to keep some in the refrigerator to bake for our ranch hands. Leftover mashed potatoes are almost sure to go into these rolls.
—Jeanette McKinney, Belleview, MO

PREP: 20 MIN. + RISING • **BAKE:** 20 MIN. • **MAKES:** 45 ROLLS

- 2 pkg. (¼ oz. each) active dry yeast
- 1⅓ cups warm water (110° to 115°), divided
- 1 cup warm mashed potatoes (without added milk and butter)
- ⅔ cup sugar
- ⅔ cup shortening
- 2 large eggs
- 2½ tsp. salt
- 6 to 6½ cups all-purpose flour

1. In a small bowl, dissolve yeast in ⅔ cup warm water. In a large bowl, combine mashed potatoes, sugar, shortening, eggs, salt, remaining ⅔ cup water, yeast mixture and 2 cups of flour; beat until smooth. Stir in enough of the remaining flour to form a soft dough.
2. Do not knead. Shape dough into a ball; place in a greased bowl, turning once to grease the top. Cover and let rise in a warm place until doubled, about 1 hour.
3. Punch down dough; divide into thirds. Divide and shape one portion into 15 balls; place in a greased 9-in. round baking pan. Cover with a kitchen towel. Repeat with the remaining dough. Let rise in a warm place until doubled, about 30 minutes.
4. Preheat oven to 375°. Bake rolls until golden brown, 20-25 minutes. Remove from pans to wire racks to cool slightly. Serve warm.

ROYAL BROCCOLI SOUFFLE

Talk about impressive! This side dish never fails to impress even the toughest of critics—my family.
—Linda Evancoe-Coble, Leola, PA

PREP: 30 MIN. • **BAKE:** 30 MIN.
MAKES: 6 SERVINGS

- 4 large egg whites
- 2 cups chopped fresh broccoli florets
- ¼ cup water
- 2 Tbsp. butter
- 3 Tbsp. all-purpose flour
- ¼ tsp. cayenne pepper
- ¾ cup fat-free milk
- 2 Tbsp. grated Parmesan cheese
- 1 tsp. ground mustard
- ½ tsp. salt
- ¼ tsp. pepper
- 1 large egg yolk, beaten
- ¼ tsp. cream of tartar

1. Let the egg whites stand at room temperature for 30 minutes. Grease a 1½-qt. souffle dish; dust lightly with flour.
2. Preheat oven to 350°. Microwave broccoli and water, covered, on high until broccoli is tender, 2-3 minutes. Let stand for 5 minutes; drain. Pulse broccoli in a food processor until blended.
3. In a small saucepan, melt butter over medium heat. Stir in flour and cayenne pepper until smooth. Gradually whisk in milk. Bring to a boil, stirring constantly; cook and stir until thickened, 1-2 minutes. Transfer to a large bowl; stir in cheese, mustard, salt, pepper and broccoli. Whisk a small amount of the hot mixture into the egg yolk; return all to bowl, whisking constantly. Cool slightly.
4. In another bowl, beat the egg whites with cream of tartar until stiff but not dry. With a rubber spatula, gently stir a fourth of the egg whites into the broccoli mixture until no white streaks remain. Fold in the remaining egg whites. Transfer to the prepared dish. Bake until top is puffed and center appears set, 30-35 minutes. Serve immediately.

SWEET POTATO CARROT CRISP

Sweet potatoes take a different twist in this whipped side dish that pairs them with carrots. It's subtly sweet and has just a hint of garlic, while the nut and crumb topping adds a fun crunch to the holiday meal.
—Diane Molberg, Calgary, AB

PREP: 25 MIN. • **BAKE:** 45 MIN.
MAKES: 16 SERVINGS

- 4 medium sweet potatoes, peeled and cubed
- 2 lbs. carrots, cut into ½-in. chunks
- ¾ cup orange juice
- 2 Tbsp. honey
- 2 Tbsp. butter
- 2 garlic cloves, minced
- 1 tsp. salt
- 1 tsp. ground cinnamon

TOPPING
- ¾ cup soft bread crumbs
- ¼ cup chopped pecans
- 2 to 3 Tbsp. butter, melted
- 2 tsp. minced fresh parsley

1. Preheat oven to 350°. Place sweet potatoes and carrots in a large saucepan; add enough water to cover. Bring to a boil. Reduce heat; cook, covered, just until tender, 10-20 minutes. Drain, then transfer to a blender or food processor. Working in batches, pulse with the next six ingredients until smooth. Pour into a greased 2½-qt. baking dish.
2. Combine the topping ingredients; sprinkle over the sweet potato mixture. Bake, covered, for 30 minutes. Uncover; bake until heated through, 15-20 minutes longer.

2. Turn onto a floured surface; knead until smooth and elastic, 6-8 minutes. Place in a greased bowl, turning once to grease the top. Cover and let rise in a warm place until doubled, about 1 hour.

3. For the filling, crumble the mincemeat in a small saucepan; add water. Bring to a boil. Reduce heat; cook over medium-low heat until thickened, 20-25 minutes. Set aside to cool.

4. Punch down dough. Turn onto a lightly floured surface; divide into thirds. Roll each into a 14x4-in. strip. Spread a third of the filling down the center of each strip; bring the sides of each strip together over the filling. Pinch seams to seal. Place strips, seam side down, on a greased baking sheet and braid. Pinch the ends to seal; tuck under. Cover and let rise in a warm place until doubled, about 1 hour.

5. Preheat oven to 350°. Bake until golden brown, 20-25 minutes. Remove from pan to a wire rack to cool.

6. Combine the icing ingredients; drizzle over braid.

NOTE We tested this recipe with a 9-oz. package of Nonesuch Classic Original Condensed Mincemeat, ordered online.

Holiday Helper

You can also use a bread machine for this recipe. Place the first nine ingredients in the machine pan in the order suggested by manufacturer. Select dough setting (check after 5 minutes of mixing; add 1-2 Tbsp. of water or flour if needed). For the filling, combine mincemeat and water in a small saucepan and bring to a boil. Reduce heat; cook over medium-low until thickened, then set aside. When the bread machine cycle is completed, turn the dough onto a lightly floured surface. Divide into thirds. Roll and fill as directed. Preheat oven to 350°. Bake and cool as directed. Combine icing ingredients; drizzle over the braid.

MINCEMEAT-FILLED BRAID

Raisins, currants and other dried fruit, richly spiced and soaked in brandy...what's not to love? My family and I love it tucked inside this gorgeous-looking bread. It's perfect for breakfast or with dinner.
—Loraine Steinfort, Shelbyville, IN

PREP: 35 MIN. + RISING • BAKE: 20 MIN.
MAKES: 1 LOAF (16 SLICES)

1 pkg. (¼ oz.) active dry yeast
1 cup warm water (110° to 115°)
1 large egg
¼ cup butter, softened
¼ cup sugar
3 Tbsp. buttermilk blend powder
1 tsp. salt
¼ tsp. baking soda
3 to 3½ cups bread flour
FILLING
1 pkg. (9 oz.) condensed mincemeat
1 cup water
ICING
⅓ cup confectioners' sugar
2 tsp. water
⅛ tsp. almond extract

1. Dissolve yeast in warm water. In a large bowl, combine the next six ingredients, the yeast mixture and 1½ cups flour; beat on medium speed 2 minutes. Stir in enough of the remaining flour to form a soft dough (dough will be sticky).

CAULIFLOWER AU GRATIN

This dish will make a vegetable lover out of anyone. Whenever I serve it, everyone just raves about it and asks for the recipe. Sometimes I substitute broccoli for all or half of the cauliflower; it tastes just as good!
—*Jacki Ricci, Ely, NV*

TAKES: 30 MIN. • **MAKES:** 8 SERVINGS

- 6 Tbsp. butter, cubed
- 4 oz. cooked ham, chopped
- 1 to 2 garlic cloves, minced
- 1 head cauliflower, broken into florets
- 1½ cups heavy whipping cream
- 2 Tbsp. all-purpose flour
- ¼ tsp. salt
- ¼ tsp. pepper
  Dash cayenne pepper
- 1½ cups shredded Swiss cheese
- 2 to 3 Tbsp. minced fresh parsley

1. Preheat broiler. Meanwhile, in a large skillet, heat butter over medium heat. Add ham and garlic; saute for 2 minutes. Add cauliflower, and cook just until crisp-tender. Combine cream and flour; stir into skillet, and blend well. Add salt, pepper and cayenne pepper. Cook and stir until thickened and bubbly; cook and stir 1 minute longer.

2. Pour into a 2-qt. baking dish. Sprinkle with cheese. Broil until lightly browned, 2-4 minutes. Sprinkle with parsley. Serve immediately.

ORANGE-CRANBERRY NUT BREAD

Classic flavors of the season come together in this delicious quick bread. Orange, nuts and cranberries make this the perfect start to the morning, a tasty afternoon snack or a sweet late-night indulgence. This recipe doubles well, so give a loaf as a gift!
—*Marilyn Ellis, Canyon Lake, PA*

PREP: 10 MIN. • **BAKE:** 55 MIN. + COOLING
MAKES: 1 LOAF (16 SLICES)

- 2 cups all-purpose flour
- 1 cup sugar
- 1½ tsp. baking powder
- ½ tsp. baking soda
- ¼ tsp. salt
- ½ cup orange juice
- 1 large egg, lightly beaten
- 2 Tbsp. hot water
- 2 Tbsp. melted butter
- 8 oz. fresh cranberries, halved
- ½ cup chopped pecans
- 4 tsp. grated orange zest

1. Preheat oven to 325°. Whisk together first five ingredients. In another bowl, whisk orange juice, egg, water and butter. Stir into the dry ingredients just until moistened. Fold in cranberries, nuts and orange zest.

2. Bake in a greased 9x5-in. loaf pan until a toothpick inserted in center comes out clean, 55-60 minutes. Cool for 10 minutes before removing from the pan to a wire rack.

CARDAMOM HOLIDAY BREAD

I have fond memories of coming home from school to find this bread cooling on a wire rack. I could hardly wait for a warm savory slice.
—Sheryl Olstad, Rochester, NH

PREP: 35 MIN. + RISING
BAKE: 20 MIN. + COOLING
MAKES: 3 LOAVES (16 SLICES EACH)

- 2 pkg. (¼ oz. each) active dry yeast
- ¾ cup warm water (110° to 115°)
- 1 can (12 oz.) evaporated milk
- 4 large eggs, beaten
- 1 cup sugar
- ½ cup butter, softened
- 1 to 1½ tsp. ground cardamom
- 1 tsp. salt
- 7½ to 8 cups all-purpose flour
- 2 cups confectioners' sugar
- 3 to 4 Tbsp. 2% milk
  Halved candied cherries
  Toasted sliced almonds

1. Dissolve yeast in warm water. Add milk, eggs, sugar, butter, cardamom, salt and 2 cups of flour; beat until smooth. Add enough of the remaining flour to form a soft dough.
2. Turn dough onto a floured surface; knead until smooth and elastic, 6-8 minutes. Place in a greased bowl, turning once to grease top. Cover with plastic and let rise in a warm place until doubled, about 1½ hours.
3. Punch down dough. Turn onto a lightly floured surface; divide into nine portions. Roll each into a 12-in. rope. Place ropes on greased baking sheets. Working with three at a time, braid ropes. Pinch ends to seal; tuck under.
4. Cover with kitchen towels; let rise in a warm place until almost doubled, about 45 minutes. Preheat oven to 375°. Bake until golden, 20-25 minutes. Cool.
5. Meanwhile, make a glaze by mixing confectioners' sugar and enough milk to reach desired consistency. Drizzle the glaze over the loaves; decorate as desired with cherries and almonds.

CHEESY BACON RANCH POTATO STUFFING

Every family seems to have a favorite stuffing recipe. My family and I have been making this one for many years. It's so delicious that no gravy is required!
—Sandra Dombek, Camillus, NY

PREP: 25 MIN. • **BAKE:** 40 MIN.
MAKES: 16 SERVINGS

- 3⅓ cups cubed potato dinner rolls, divided
- ⅔ envelope ranch salad dressing mix
- 6 cups mashed potatoes (with added milk and butter)
- 2 medium celery ribs, finely chopped
- 1 cup sliced baby portobello mushrooms
- 5 bacon strips, cooked and crumbled
- 1⅓ cups shredded Monterey Jack cheese
  Chopped green onions, optional

1. Preheat oven to 350°. On an ungreased 15x10x1-in. baking pan, bake cubed rolls until toasted, 7-10 minutes. Meanwhile, stir dressing mix into mashed potatoes.
2. Fold in 2 cups of the cubed rolls, the celery, mushrooms and bacon. Transfer to a greased 13x9-in. baking dish; top with the remaining cubed rolls. Place pan on a baking sheet. Bake, uncovered, for 35 minutes. Sprinkle with cheese; bake until cheese is melted and top is golden brown, 5-10 minutes longer. If desired, top with green onions.

SPICY SAUSAGE, KALE & SQUASH BREAD PUDDING

Whoever said bread pudding has to be for dessert? I love to serve this slow-cooked dish for brunch or with a special dinner when I want a side dish that's hearty and a little bit unusual.
—Lauren Knoelke, Milwaukee, WI

PREP: 10 MIN. • **COOK:** 3 HOURS
MAKES: 8 SERVINGS

- 1   lb. bulk spicy pork sausage
- 1½ cups chopped sweet onion
     (about 1 medium)
- 3   garlic cloves, minced
- ½   cup white wine
- 1   loaf sourdough bread (about
     1 lb.), lightly toasted and cubed
- 4   cups chopped fresh kale
- 3   cups cubed peeled
     butternut squash
- 1   cup shredded Gruyere
     or Swiss cheese
- 1   cup chicken broth
- 4   large eggs
- ½   cup heavy whipping cream
- 1   Tbsp. minced fresh thyme
- 1   tsp. salt
- ½   tsp. coarsely ground pepper

1. In a large skillet, cook and crumble sausage over medium heat until no longer pink, 6-8 minutes. Remove with a slotted spoon; drain on paper towels.
2. In same skillet, cook and stir onion over medium-low heat until just softened, 2-3 minutes. Add garlic; cook 1 minute longer. Add wine, stirring to loosen any browned bits from the pan. Cook until liquid is almost evaporated, 2-4 minutes. Transfer to a large bowl. Add sausage, bread, kale, squash, cheese and broth; toss to combine.
3. In another bowl, whisk eggs, cream, thyme, salt and pepper until blended. Pour over the bread mixture; toss to coat. Transfer to a greased 6-qt. slow cooker. Cook, covered, on low until the squash is tender, 3-4 hours. Serve warm.

ICEBOX ROLLS

I remember my mom making these rolls on Saturdays so they would be ready to bake on Sunday for company or someone just dropping by. Of course, we'd get to enjoy them, too! Although they take a little time to prepare, they're not difficult to make. And there's nothing in the stores that can compare with them!
—Jean Fox, Welch, MN

PREP: 30 MIN. + RISING • **BAKE:** 15 MIN.
MAKES: 36 ROLLS

- 1   pkg. (¼ oz.) active dry yeast
- 2½ cups water, divided
- ½   cup shortening
- 2   large eggs, beaten
- 1½ tsp. salt
- ½   cup sugar
- 8½ to 9 cups all-purpose flour
- ⅓   cup butter, melted

1. Dissolve yeast in ½ cup warm water (110°-115°). In a separate bowl, combine 1 cup boiling water and shortening. Add the remaining water, the eggs, salt, sugar and yeast mixture.
2. Stir in 1 cup of flour at a time, mixing well after each addition, until a soft dough forms. Turn the dough onto a floured surface; knead until smooth and elastic, 6-8 minutes. Place in a greased bowl, turning once to grease top. Cover and refrigerate overnight.
3. Turn dough onto a lightly floured surface; divide into nine portions. Divide and shape each portion into 12 balls. Place three balls in each greased muffin cup. Cover with kitchen towels; let rise in a warm place until doubled, about 1 hour.
4. Preheat oven to 375°. Brush rolls with half of the melted butter; bake until golden brown, 15-20 minutes. Remove from oven; brush with remaining butter.

CHARD WITH BACON-CITRUS SAUCE

Chard is a leafy veggie often used in Mediterranean cooking. I dress it with orange juice and bacon, and the family gobbles it up.
—Teri Rasey, Cadillac, MI

TAKES: 25 MIN. • **MAKES:** 6 SERVINGS

- ½ lb. thick-sliced peppered bacon strips
- 2 lbs. rainbow Swiss chard, chopped
- 1 cup orange juice
- 2 Tbsp. butter
- 4 tsp. grated orange zest
- ⅛ tsp. salt
- ⅛ tsp. pepper

1. In a large skillet, cook bacon over medium heat until crisp; drain on paper towels. Discard all but 1 Tbsp. of the drippings. Cut bacon into small pieces.
2. Add chard to the drippings; cook and stir just until wilted, 5-6 minutes. Add the remaining ingredients; cook 1-2 minutes, stirring occasionally. Top with the bacon.

PUMPKIN MASHED POTATOES

Last year, I added pumpkin to leftover mashed potatoes—it was so good, I'll be doing it on the first go-round this year! Sweet potatoes would also work well.
—Pamela Shank, Parkersburg, WV

PREP: 25 MIN. • **COOK:** 20 MIN.
MAKES: 10 SERVINGS

- 12 medium Yukon Gold potatoes, peeled and cubed (about 4 lbs.)
- 1 can (15 oz.) pumpkin
- ½ cup half-and-half cream
- ½ cup butter, cubed
- 2 Tbsp. honey
- 1¾ tsp. salt
- 1 tsp. pepper
- ¼ tsp. ground cinnamon

Place potatoes in a Dutch oven; add water to cover. Bring to a boil. Reduce heat; cook, covered, until tender, 10-15 minutes. Drain; return to pan and stir over low heat 1 minute to dry. Mash potatoes, gradually adding remaining ingredients, until light and fluffy.

NUTTY MAPLE ROASTED GREEN BEANS

These roasted green beans taste extra special thanks to the addition of pure maple syrup and salted peanuts. It's an excellent side dish that goes with everything!
—Nancy Heishman, Las Vegas, NV

TAKES: 25 MIN. • **MAKES:** 4 SERVINGS

- 1 Tbsp. maple syrup
- 1 tsp. minced fresh thyme or ¼ tsp. dried thyme
- 1 Tbsp. peanut oil or canola oil
- 1½ tsp. sesame seeds
- ¼ tsp. salt
- ⅛ tsp. pepper
- ⅛ tsp. garlic powder
- 1 lb. fresh green beans
- ¼ cup chopped salted peanuts
- 4 maple-flavored bacon strips, cooked and crumbled

Preheat oven to 425°. Line a baking pan with foil and grease the foil. Mix the first seven ingredients. Place the green beans in the prepared pan. Drizzle with maple mixture; toss to coat. Roast, stirring occasionally, until crisp-tender, 15-20 minutes. Sprinkle with peanuts and bacon.

1 tsp. garlic powder
1 tsp. seasoned salt
½ tsp. onion powder
½ tsp. ground turmeric
½ tsp. pepper
½ cup uncooked whole wheat orzo pasta

In a Dutch oven, heat oil over medium heat. Add rice and onion; saute until rice is lightly browned, 8-10 minutes. Add broth; stir in the next six ingredients. Bring to a boil. Reduce heat; simmer, covered, for 35 minutes. Add orzo. Cook, covered, until orzo is tender, 10-15 minutes longer.

MUSHROOM PEA CASSEROLE

This is one of my go-to side dishes that my whole family loves. It's great with chicken, ham, beef and pork; in fact, I haven't found anything it isn't delicious with.
—Lisa Lyons, Westerville, OH

PREP: 10 MIN. • **BAKE:** 25 MIN. • **MAKES:** 10 SERVINGS

1 Tbsp. butter
1 lb. sliced fresh mushrooms
6 cups frozen peas, thawed (about 2 lbs.)
1 can (10½ oz.) condensed cream of celery soup, undiluted
½ cup whole milk
1 pkg. (2.80 oz.) french-fried onions

Preheat oven to 350°. In a large skillet, heat butter over medium heat. Add mushrooms; saute until tender. Stir in peas, soup and milk. Transfer to a greased 11x7-in. baking dish. Sprinkle with onions. Bake, uncovered, until heated through, 25-30 minutes.

SEASONED BROWN RICE PILAF

For white-rice lovers, this pilaf might just sway us all to brown rice! Everyone takes seconds; it is that good. It's easy to prepare, and simple to convert for vegetarians (just substitute veggie broth). If there are any leftovers, they're just as good the next day.
—Amy Berry, Poland, ME

PREP: 10 MIN. • **COOK:** 55 MIN. • **MAKES:** 10 SERVINGS

1 Tbsp. olive oil
2 cups uncooked brown rice
1 small onion, finely chopped
5 cups reduced-sodium beef broth
1 Tbsp. dried parsley flakes

A STEP UP FROM TRADITION

Not everyone can have a Christmas tree every year... but there's no reason you can't still celebrate in style by creating a bright and festive substitute for an evergreen from a wooden ladder. If the ladder is too shiny and new, use a foam brush or rag to apply wood stain to give it a vintage look. When the stain is dry, wrap twinkle lights around the legs and up the sides of the ladder. String clear fishing line between the rungs to suspend all your ornaments. Set an illuminated star on the very top step and plug it into the end of the strand of lights.

"This salad tastes even better when you chill it overnight."
—MARGARET ALLEN

MANDARIN BROCCOLI SALAD

Sweet, crunchy and colorful, with a fresh mix of textures and flavors, this salad tastes even better when you chill it overnight, if you can wait that long!
—Margaret Allen, Abingdon, VA

TAKES: 25 MIN. + CHILLING
MAKES: 9 SERVINGS

- ¾ cup mayonnaise
- ¼ cup sugar
- 4 tsp. cider vinegar
- 4 cups fresh broccoli florets
- 1 small red onion, halved and sliced
- ½ cup raisins
- ½ cup pecan halves, toasted
- 1 can (11 oz.) mandarin oranges, drained

Whisk mayonnaise, sugar and vinegar; set aside. In a salad bowl, combine broccoli, onion, raisins and pecans. Drizzle with dressing; toss to coat. Gently stir in oranges. Refrigerate, covered, at least 3 hours before serving.

BACON & CHEDDAR WHIPPED POTATOES

Bacon and cheese are an easy way to add zest to mashed potatoes. These go so well with practically any main dish, and make a distinctly fun and delicious alternative to traditional mashed.
—Rebekah Beyer, Sabetha, KS

TAKES: 30 MIN. • **MAKES:** 4 SERVINGS

- 6 medium red potatoes, peeled and quartered
- ½ cup 2% milk
- 1 oz. cream cheese, softened
- 2 Tbsp. butter
- ½ tsp. salt
- ¼ tsp. garlic powder
- ¼ tsp. pepper
- ½ cup shredded sharp cheddar cheese
- ¼ cup crumbled cooked bacon

Place potatoes in a large saucepan; add water to cover. Bring to a boil. Reduce heat; cook potatoes, covered, until tender, 15-20 minutes. Drain; transfer to a large bowl. Beat in next six ingredients until blended. Stir in cheese and bacon.

ROASTED CARROTS WITH CILANTRO-WALNUT PESTO

Lightly baked and lightly flavored, this dish uses cilantro, walnuts, extra virgin olive oil, garlic, parsley, Parmesan and basil. You can also use baby carrots if you prefer.
—Aysha Schurman, Ammon, ID

PREP: 15 MIN. • **BAKE:** 20 MIN.
MAKES: 4 SERVINGS

- 2 Tbsp. chopped walnuts
- 2 Tbsp. fresh cilantro leaves
- 1 Tbsp. grated Parmesan cheese
- 1 garlic clove, chopped
- 1 tsp. fresh parsley leaves
- 1 tsp. chopped fresh basil
- ¼ cup olive oil
- 1 lb. medium carrots, halved lengthwise

Preheat oven to 400°. Pulse the first six ingredients in a small food processor until finely chopped. Continue processing while gradually adding oil in a steady stream. Drizzle carrots wit the herb mixture; toss to coat. Transfer to a greased 15x10x1-in. baking pan. Roast, stirring occasionally, until tender, 20-25 minutes.

Holiday Helper

To keep parsley and cilantro fresh, cut ½ inch off the bottom of the bunch and stand it in a glass of water like a bouquet. Cover with a plastic bag (the ones from the produce department work well for this) and keep it in the fridge. It stays fresh for several days.

NAUGHTY BUT NICE

Where's the fun in holiday eating if you're counting calories? It's in this chapter, where every recipe is light on calories and fat, but tastes like you're breaking the rules!

set aside. In a large bowl, beat egg yolks on high speed for 5 minutes or until thick and lemon-colored. Gradually beat in ⅓ cup sugar. Beat in vanilla. Combine the flour, baking powder and salt; gradually add to the yolk mixture and mix well (batter will be very thick). Stir in walnuts.

2. In a small bowl with clean beaters, beat the egg whites on medium speed until soft peaks form. Gradually beat in the remaining sugar, 1 Tbsp. at a time, on high until stiff peaks form. Gradually fold into the batter. Spread evenly into the prepared pan.

3. Bake at 375° for 10-15 minutes or until cake springs back when lightly touched. Cool in pan for 5 minutes. Invert onto a kitchen towel dusted with confectioners' sugar. Gently peel off waxed paper. Roll up cake in the towel jelly-roll style, starting with a short side. Set on a wire rack to cool completely.

4. Meanwhile, in a small saucepan, combine the sugar, flour, coffee granules, and salt. Stir in milk and chocolate. Bring to a boil. Cook and stir for 2 minutes.

5. Remove from the heat. Stir a small amount of the hot mixture into the egg; return all to pan, stirring constantly. Bring to a gentle boil. Cook and stir 2-3 minutes or until mixture reaches 160°. Remove from heat; gently stir in butter and vanilla. Cool to room temperature.

6. Unroll cake; spread filling evenly over the cake to within ½ in. of edges. Roll up again. Place seam side down on a serving platter. Just before serving, sprinkle with confectioners' sugar and garnish with chocolate curls if desired.

Holiday Helper
For a perfect presentation, use a serrated knife to cut slices for your guests. Wipe the knife clean between cuts. This will prevent the filling from transferring from the knife to the top of the cake roll.

MOCHA NUT ROLL

This tender, impressive cake is the perfect indulgence for coffee and chocolate lovers alike! It never fails to delight.
—Susan Bettinger, Battle Creek, MI

PREP: 35 MIN. • **BAKE:** 10 MIN. + COOLING
MAKES: 12 SERVINGS

    4   large eggs, separated
    ⅓   cup plus ½ cup sugar
    ½   tsp. vanilla extract
    ½   cup all-purpose flour
    1   tsp. baking powder
    ¼   tsp. salt
    ¼   cup finely chopped walnuts

    MOCHA FILLING
    ½   cup sugar
    3   Tbsp. all-purpose flour
    2   tsp. instant coffee granules
    ¼   tsp. salt
    1¼ cups whole milk
    1   oz. unsweetened
        chocolate, chopped
    1   large egg, lightly beaten
    1   Tbsp. butter
    1   tsp. vanilla extract
        Confectioners' sugar and chocolate
        curls, optional

1. Line a greased 15x10x1-in. baking pan with waxed paper; grease the paper and

CHICKEN & BRUSSELS SPROUTS SALAD

My mom made the best salads; that's where my love for them started. I've turned her side salads into awesome meals with protein, veggies, nuts and cranberries.
—*Lindsay Tanner, Cathedral City, CA*

TAKES: 30 MIN. • **MAKES:** 6 SERVINGS

- 3 Tbsp. olive oil
- 20 fresh Brussels sprouts, trimmed and halved
- 2 shallots, sliced
- ½ tsp. salt
- ½ cup balsamic vinegar
- 1 skinned rotisserie chicken, shredded
- 3 cups torn romaine
- ⅔ cup chopped roasted sweet red peppers
- ½ cup chopped sun-dried tomatoes (not oil-packed)
- ½ cup balsamic vinaigrette
- ¾ cup pistachios, toasted
- ¾ cup dried cranberries
  Fresh goat cheese, optional

1. In a large skillet, heat oil over medium heat. Add Brussels sprouts and shallots; cook and stir until browned and tender, 10-12 minutes. Sprinkle with salt; drizzle with balsamic vinegar. Cook 2-3 minutes, reducing liquid and stirring to loosen browned bits from pan.
2. Combine chicken, romaine, red pepper and sun-dried tomatoes. Toss with the Brussels sprouts mixture and balsamic vinaigrette. Top with pistachios and dried cranberries; serve with goat cheese if desired.
NOTE To toast nuts, bake in a shallow pan in a 350° oven for 5-10 minutes or cook in a skillet over low heat until lightly browned, stirring occasionally.

CRAB-STUFFED FLOUNDER WITH HERBED AIOLI

If you like seafood, you'll love this scrumptious flounder. The light and creamy aioli tops it off with fresh tones of chives and garlic.
—*Beverly O'Ferrall, Linkwood, MD*

PREP: 20 MIN. • **BAKE:** 20 MIN. • **MAKES:** 6 SERVINGS

- ¼ cup egg substitute
- 2 Tbsp. fat-free milk
- 1 Tbsp. minced chives
- 1 Tbsp. reduced-fat mayonnaise
- 1 Tbsp. Dijon mustard
  Dash hot pepper sauce
- 1 lb. lump crabmeat
- 6 flounder fillets (6 oz. each)
  Paprika

AIOLI
- ⅓ cup reduced-fat mayonnaise
- 2 tsp. minced chives
- 2 tsp. minced fresh parsley
- 2 tsp. lemon juice
- 1 garlic clove, minced

1. In a small bowl, combine the first six ingredients; gently fold in crab. Cut fillets in half widthwise; place six halves in a 15x10x1-in. baking pan coated with cooking spray. Spoon the crab mixture over fillets; top with the remaining fish. Sprinkle with paprika.
2. Bake at 400° for 20-24 minutes or until fish flakes easily with a fork. Meanwhile, combine the aioli ingredients. Serve with fish.

ARTICHOKE SPINACH CASSEROLE

Although he isn't a fan of spinach, my husband loves this dish. The combination of ingredients may sound unusual, but the flavors meld well. It's an excellent side for a formal dinner.
—Judy Johnson, Missoula, MT

PREP: 25 MIN. • **BAKE:** 25 MIN. • **MAKES:** 14 SERVINGS

- 1 lb. fresh mushrooms, sliced
- ⅓ cup chicken broth
- 1 Tbsp. all-purpose flour
- ½ cup evaporated milk
- 4 pkg. (10 oz. each) frozen chopped spinach, thawed and squeezed dry
- 2 cans (14½ oz. each) diced tomatoes, drained
- 2 cans (14 oz. each) water-packed artichoke hearts, rinsed, drained and thinly sliced
- 1 cup sour cream
- ½ cup mayonnaise
- 3 Tbsp. lemon juice
- ½ tsp. garlic powder
- ¼ tsp. salt
- ¼ tsp. pepper
  Paprika, optional

1. In a large skillet, cook mushrooms and broth over medium heat until tender, about 3 minutes. Remove mushrooms with a slotted spoon and set aside.

2. Whisk flour and milk until smooth; add to skillet. Bring to a boil; cook and stir for 2 minutes. Remove from the heat; stir in spinach, tomatoes and mushrooms.

3. Place half of the artichoke in an ungreased 13x9-in. baking dish. Top with half of the spinach mixture. Repeat the layers. Combine sour cream, mayonnaise, lemon juice, garlic powder, salt and pepper; dollop over casserole. Sprinkle with paprika if desired.

4. Bake, uncovered, at 350° for 25-30 minutes or until bubbly.

OVERNIGHT BRUNCH CASSEROLE

I love to cook for company, and I host brunches frequently. Standing out from most egg bakes, this casserole combines scrambled eggs and a cheese sauce, and it bakes up into a rich, creamy dish.
—Candy Hesch, Mosinee, WI

PREP: 30 MIN. + CHILLING • **BAKE:** 40 MIN. + STANDING
MAKES: 12 SERVINGS

- 3 Tbsp. butter, divided
- 2 Tbsp. all-purpose flour
- ½ tsp. salt
- ⅛ tsp. pepper
- 2 cups fat-free milk
- 5 slices reduced-fat process American cheese product, chopped
- 1½ cups sliced fresh mushrooms
- 2 green onions, finely chopped
- 1 cup cubed fully cooked ham
- 2 cups egg substitute
- 4 large eggs

TOPPING
- 3 slices whole wheat bread, cubed
- 4 tsp. butter, melted
- ⅛ tsp. paprika

1. In a large saucepan, melt 2 Tbsp. butter. Stir in flour, salt and pepper until smooth; gradually add milk. Bring to a boil; cook and stir for 2 minutes or until slightly thickened. Stir in cheese until melted. Remove from heat.

2. In a large nonstick skillet, saute mushrooms and green onions in the remaining butter until tender. Add ham; heat through. Whisk egg substitute and eggs; add to skillet. Cook and stir until almost set. Stir in cheese sauce.

3. Transfer to a 13x9-in. baking dish coated with cooking spray. Toss bread cubes with butter. Arrange over the egg mixture; sprinkle with paprika. Cover and refrigerate overnight.

4. Remove from refrigerator 30 minutes before baking. Preheat oven to 350°. Bake, uncovered, 40-45 minutes or until a knife inserted in the center comes out clean. Let stand 10 minutes before cutting.

SPECIAL OCCASION BEEF BOURGUIGNON

I've found many rich and satisfying variations for Beef Bourguignon; this is the one I pull out for special nights. To make the stew gluten-free, use white rice flour instead of all-purpose.
—*Leo Cotnoir, Johnson City, NY*

PREP: 50 MIN. • **BAKE:** 2 HOURS
MAKES: 8 SERVINGS

- 4 bacon strips, chopped
- 1 beef sirloin tip roast (2 lbs.), cut into 1½-in. cubes and patted dry
- ¼ cup all-purpose flour
- ½ tsp. salt
- ½ tsp. pepper
- 1 Tbsp. canola oil
- 2 medium onions, chopped
- 2 medium carrots, coarsely chopped
- ½ lb. medium fresh mushrooms, quartered
- 4 garlic cloves, minced
- 1 Tbsp. tomato paste
- 2 cups dry red wine
- 1 cup beef stock
- 2 bay leaves
- ½ tsp. dried thyme
- 8 oz. uncooked egg noodles
  Minced fresh parsley

1. Preheat oven to 325°. In a Dutch oven, cook bacon over medium-low heat until crisp, stirring occasionally. Remove with a slotted spoon, reserving drippings; drain on paper towels.

2. In batches, brown beef in drippings over medium-high heat; remove from pan. Toss with flour, salt and pepper.

3. In same pan, heat 1 Tbsp. oil over medium heat; saute onions, carrots and mushrooms until the onions are tender, 4-5 minutes. Add garlic and tomato paste; cook and stir 1 minute. Add wine and stock, stirring to loosen browned bits from the pan. Add herbs, the bacon and beef; bring to a boil.

4. Transfer to oven; bake, covered, until the meat is tender, 2-2¼ hours. Remove bay leaves.

5. To serve, cook noodles according to package directions; drain. Serve stew with noodles; sprinkle with parsley.

FREEZE OPTION Freeze cooled stew in freezer containers. To use, partially thaw stew in refrigerator overnight. Heat through in a saucepan, stirring occasionally and adding a little stock or broth if necessary.

"I wanted to make it lighter, and this was the amazingly tasty result."
—BETTY SELCHOW

MAKEOVER
RED VELVET CAKE

*I've had my beloved red velvet cake recipe
for over 45 years, and it's my family's
favorite cake. I wanted to make it lighter,
and this was the amazingly tasty result!*
—Betty Selchow, White Bear Lake, MN

PREP: 20 MIN. • **BAKE:** 15 MIN. + COOLING
MAKES: 16 SERVINGS

- ¼ cup butter, softened
- 1 cup sugar
- 2 large eggs
- ¼ cup unsweetened applesauce
- 1 bottle (1 oz.) red food coloring
- 1 tsp. white vinegar
- 1 tsp. vanilla extract
- 2¼ cups cake flour
- 2 tsp. baking cocoa
- 1 tsp. baking soda
- 1 tsp. salt
- 1 cup buttermilk

FROSTING
- 4½ tsp. all-purpose flour
- ½ cup fat-free milk
- ½ cup butter, softened
- ½ cup sugar
- ½ tsp. vanilla extract

1. Line two 9-in. round baking pans
with parchment paper; coat paper with
cooking spray and sprinkle with flour.
Set aside.

2. In a large bowl, beat butter and sugar
until well blended. Add eggs, one at a time,
beating well after each addition. Beat in
the applesauce, food coloring, vinegar
and vanilla.

3. Combine flour, cocoa, baking soda and
salt. Add to the butter mixture alternately
with buttermilk. Pour into the prepared
pans. Bake at 350° for 14-18 minutes or
until a toothpick inserted in the center
comes out clean. Cool for 10 minutes
before removing from pans to wire racks
to cool completely.

4. For frosting, in a small saucepan, whisk
flour and milk until smooth. Bring to a boil;
cook and stir for 2 minutes. Cool to room
temperature. In a small bowl, cream
butter and sugar until light and fluffy.
Beat in the flour mixture and vanilla.
Spread between layers and over top
of cake.

STUFFED ASIAGO-BASIL
MUSHROOMS

*Don't like mushrooms? You will once you've
tasted these pretty appetizers—they taste
divine! Double the filling and use large
portobellos and you can serve them as
a main dish.*
—Lorraine Caland, Shuniah, ON

PREP: 25 MIN. • **BAKE:** 10 MIN.
MAKES: 2 DOZEN

- 24 baby portobello mushrooms
  (about 1 lb.), stems removed
- ½ cup reduced-fat mayonnaise
- ¾ cup shredded Asiago cheese
- ½ cup loosely packed basil
  leaves, stems removed
- ¼ tsp. white pepper
- 12 cherry tomatoes, halved
  Sliced Parmesan cheese, optional

1. Preheat oven to 375°. Place mushroom
caps in a greased 15x10x1-in. baking pan.
Bake 10 minutes. Meanwhile, place
mayonnaise, Asiago cheese, basil and
pepper in a food processor; process
until blended.

2. Drain juices from mushrooms. Fill each
with 1 rounded tsp. of the mayonnaise
mixture; top each with a tomato half.

3. Bake for 8-10 minutes or until lightly
browned. If desired, top with a thin slice
of Parmesan cheese.

ITALIAN SAUSAGE MUSHROOMS Omit
filling. Prepare mushrooms as directed.
In a large skillet, cook 1 pound bulk Italian
sausage over medium heat until no longer
pink; drain. In a bowl, mix 6 oz. softened
cream cheese, 3 Tbsp. minced fresh
parsley and sausage; spoon into mushroom
caps. Bake as directed. Sprinkle with an
additional 1 Tbsp. minced fresh parsley.

¼ cup finely chopped walnuts
2 Tbsp. all-purpose flour
½ tsp. ground cinnamon
¼ tsp. maple flavoring
GLAZE
¾ cup confectioners' sugar
⅛ tsp. maple flavoring
2 to 4 tsp. 2% milk
¼ cup maple syrup

1. In a large bowl, dissolve yeast in warm water. Add milk, sugar, butter, egg, salt, maple flavoring, cardamom, wheat flour and 1 cup of the all-purpose flour. Beat until smooth. Stir in enough of remaining all-purpose flour to form a soft dough (dough will be sticky).

2. Turn onto a lightly floured surface; knead dough until smooth and elastic, 6-8 minutes. Place in a bowl coated with cooking spray, turning once to coat the top. Cover and let rise in a warm place until doubled, about 1 hour.

3. Line two greased 8x4-in. loaf pans with 15x4-in. strips of parchment paper, letting ends extend up sides; grease paper. Punch dough down. Turn onto a lightly floured surface; divide dough in half. Roll each portion into a 14-in. circle. In a small bowl, combine filling ingredients; spread half of filling over each circle. Cut each circle into 16 wedges. Roll up wedges from the wide ends and arrange in prepared pans.

4. Cover and let rise in a warm place until doubled, about 30 minutes. Preheat the oven to 350°. Bake until golden brown, 25-30 minutes. Lifting with parchment, remove loaves from the pans. Remove parchment; let cool on a wire rack. Mix together the confectioners' sugar, maple flavoring and enough of the milk to reach drizzling consistency. Drizzle loaves with glaze and maple syrup.

NOTE It's important to line the pans with parchment or nonstick foil or the bread will stick to the bottom of the pan.

MAPLE, NUT & APPLE BREAD

This is everything a decadent holiday bread should be. The flavors of walnut, maple and apple set off by rich spices give it the taste of something far more sinful.
—Katherine Wollgast, Troy, MO

PREP: 45 MIN. + RISING
BAKE: 25 MIN. + COOLING
MAKES: 2 LOAVES (12 SLICES EACH)

1 pkg. (¼ oz.) active dry yeast
¼ cup warm water (110° to 115°)
1 cup warm 2% milk (110° to 115°)
¼ cup sugar
¼ cup butter, melted
1 large egg
1½ tsp. salt
1 tsp. maple flavoring
⅛ tsp. ground cardamom
1½ cups whole wheat flour
2½ to 3 cups all-purpose flour
FILLING
1 cup finely chopped peeled tart apple
¼ cup sugar
¼ cup packed brown sugar

GINGERSNAP CREAM COOKIE CUPS

These little tassies are big on classic gingersnap flavor. The soft cookie cups are topped with velvety cream cheese filling.
—*Rebekah Radewahn, Wauwatosa, WI*

PREP: 35 MIN. • **BAKE:** 10 MIN./BATCH • **MAKES:** 2½ DOZEN

- 1½ cups all-purpose flour
- ½ cup whole wheat flour
- ⅓ cup sugar
- 1½ tsp. ground ginger
- 1 tsp. baking soda
- 1 tsp. ground cinnamon
- ½ tsp. salt
- 1 large egg
- ¼ cup canola oil
- ¼ cup unsweetened applesauce
- ¼ cup molasses

FILLING

- 4 oz. reduced-fat cream cheese
- ½ cup confectioners' sugar
- ¾ tsp. vanilla extract
- ½ cup heavy whipping cream, whipped

1. Combine the flours, sugar, ginger, baking soda, cinnamon and salt. In another bowl, combine the egg, oil, applesauce and molasses; add to the dry ingredients. Stir until dough forms a ball. Roll into 1-in. balls. Press onto the bottoms and up the sides of miniature muffin cups greased with cooking spray.
2. Bake at 350° for 10-12 minutes or until golden brown. Cool for 5 minutes before removing from pans to wire racks to cool.
3. For filling, beat cream cheese, confectioners' sugar and vanilla until smooth; fold in whipped cream. Spoon 2 tsp. into each cup.

CHERRY & SPICE RICE PUDDING

Cinnamon and cherries sweeten the deal in this dessert. If you've never tried rice pudding, this an excellent place to start.
—*Deb Perry, Traverse City, MI*

PREP: 10 MIN. • **COOK:** 2 HOURS • **MAKES:** 12 SERVINGS

- 4 cups cooked long grain rice
- 1 can (12 oz.) evaporated milk
- 1 cup 2% milk
- ⅓ cup sugar
- ¼ cup water
- ¾ cup dried cherries
- 3 Tbsp. butter, softened
- 2 tsp. vanilla extract
- ½ tsp. ground cinnamon
- ¼ tsp. ground nutmeg

1. In a large bowl, combine rice, evaporated milk, milk, sugar and water. Stir in the remaining ingredients. Transfer to a 3-qt. slow cooker coated with cooking spray.
2. Cover and cook on low for 2-3 hours or until the mixture is thickened. Stir lightly before serving. Serve warm or cold. Refrigerate leftovers.

NEVER-FAIL SCALLOPED POTATOES

When you want something special to accompany meaty entrees, this creamy, stick-to-the-ribs, potato and onion side dish is a sure winner. It's the perfect comfort food on a blustery winter day, and a recipe you'll turn to often.
—Agnes Ward, Stratford, ON

PREP: 25 MIN. • **BAKE:** 1 HOUR • **MAKES:** 6 SERVINGS

  2 **Tbsp. butter**
  3 **Tbsp. all-purpose flour**
  1 **tsp. salt**
  ¼ **tsp. pepper**
  1½ **cups fat-free milk**
  ½ **cup shredded reduced-fat cheddar cheese**
  2 **lbs. red potatoes, peeled and thinly sliced (about 4 cups)**
  1 **cup thinly sliced onions, divided**

1. Preheat oven to 350°. In a small saucepan, melt butter; stir in flour, salt and pepper until smooth. Gradually whisk in milk. Bring to a boil, stirring constantly; cook and stir until thickened, about 2 minutes. Remove from heat; stir in cheese until melted.
2. Coat an 8-in. square baking dish with cooking spray. Place half of the potatoes in dish; layer with ½ cup onion and half of the cheese sauce. Repeat layers.
3. Bake, covered, for 50 minutes. Uncover; bake until bubbly and the potatoes are tender, 10-15 minutes..

BAKED CRAB CAKES

Reel in a breezy and light taste of the seashore with these baked, rather than fried, crab cakes. You can serve these as an elegant starter, or in larger sizes as a second course.
—Amelia Sunderland, Nashville, TN

PREP: 15 MIN. + CHILLING • **BAKE:** 25 MIN. • **MAKES:** 2 SERVINGS

  1 **can (6 oz.) crabmeat, drained, flaked and cartilage removed**
  ½ **cup soft bread crumbs**
  ¼ **cup shredded carrot**
  1 **large egg, lightly beaten**
  1 **Tbsp. butter, melted**
  1 **tsp. minced fresh parsley**
  1 **tsp. mayonnaise**
  ¾ **tsp. Worcestershire sauce**
  ¼ **tsp. ground mustard**
  ⅛ **tsp. salt**
  ⅛ **tsp. pepper**
    Tartar sauce, optional

1. In a large bowl, combine the first 11 ingredients. Shape into four patties; cover and refrigerate for at least 30 minutes.
2. Place crab cakes on a baking sheet coated with cooking spray. Bake at 350° for 25 minutes or until golden brown. Serve with tartar sauce if desired.

BANANA PANCAKE SNOWMEN

Kids and adults will love these yummy pancakes. Invite your little ones to help decorate their snowmen and they'll jump out of bed in a hurry!
—Phyllis Schmalz, Kansas City, KS

PREP: 15 MIN. • **COOK:** 5 MIN./BATCH • **MAKES:** 4 SNOWMEN

  1 **cup complete buttermilk pancake mix**
  ¾ **cup water**
  ⅓ **cup mashed ripe banana**
  1 **tsp. confectioners' sugar**
    Pretzel sticks, chocolate chips, dried cranberries and/or halved banana slices

1. In a small bowl, stir the pancake mix, water and banana just until moistened.
2. Pour a scant ½ cup batter onto a greased hot griddle, making three circles to form a snowman. Turn when bubbles form on top. Cook until the second side is golden brown. Transfer to a serving plate. Repeat with remaining batter.
3. Sprinkle with confectioners' sugar. Decorate snowmen with pretzels, chocolate chips, cranberries and/or banana if desired.

ORANGE POUND CAKE WITH CRANBERRY COMPOTE

My husband and I enjoy dessert but not all the fat and calories that go with it. This pound cake is made lighter with Greek yogurt. You will never miss that extra fat in taste or texture.
—Ann Goncheroski, Wilkes-Barre, PA

PREP: 30 MIN. • **BAKE:** 55 MIN. + COOLING
MAKES: 16 SERVINGS (1 CUP COMPOTE)

- ½ cup butter, softened
- 1 cup sugar
- 3 large eggs
- 1 Tbsp. grated orange zest
- 1½ tsp. vanilla extract
- ¾ cup fat-free plain Greek yogurt
- ¼ cup orange juice
- 2 cups all-purpose flour
- 1 tsp. baking powder
- ¼ tsp. salt

COMPOTE

- 1 cup fresh or frozen cranberries
- 1 cup orange juice
- ½ cup sugar
- 2 tsp. grated orange zest
- 1 cinnamon stick (3 in.), optional

1. Preheat oven to 325°. Coat a 9x5-in. loaf pan with cooking spray; set aside.
2. In a large bowl, beat butter and sugar until blended. Add eggs, one at a time, beating well after each addition. Beat in orange zest and vanilla. Mix yogurt and orange juice. In another bowl, whisk flour, baking powder and salt; add to the sugar mixture alternately with the yogurt mixture, beating after each addition just until combined.
3. Transfer to the prepared pan. Bake for 55-65 minutes or until a toothpick inserted in the center comes out clean. Cool in pan 10 minutes before removing to a wire rack to cool completely.
4. Meanwhile, in a small saucepan, combine compote ingredients; bring to a boil. Reduce heat; simmer, uncovered, 12-15 minutes or until slightly thickened, stirring occasionally. Discard cinnamon stick. Serve warm compote with cake.

TURKEY & MUSHROOM POTPIES

I always use the leftovers from our big holiday turkey to prepare this recipe. I think my family enjoys the potpies more than the original feast!
—Lily Julow, Lawrenceville, GA

PREP: 40 MIN. • **BAKE:** 20 MIN.
MAKES: 8 SERVINGS

- 4⅓ cups sliced baby portobello mushrooms
- 1 large onion, chopped
- 1 Tbsp. olive oil
- 2½ cups cubed cooked turkey
- 1 pkg. (16 oz.) frozen peas and carrots
- ¼ tsp. salt
- ¼ tsp. pepper
- ¼ cup cornstarch
- 2½ cups chicken broth
- ¼ cup sour cream

TOPPING

- 1½ cups all-purpose flour
- 2 tsp. sugar
- 1½ tsp. baking powder
- 1 tsp. dried thyme
- ¼ tsp. baking soda
- ¼ tsp. salt
- 2 Tbsp. cold butter
- 1 cup buttermilk
- 1 Tbsp. canola oil

1. Preheat oven to 400°. In a Dutch oven, saute mushrooms and onion in oil until tender. Stir in turkey, peas and carrots, salt and pepper. Combine cornstarch and broth until smooth; gradually stir into pan. Bring to a boil. Reduce heat; cook and stir 2 minutes or until thickened. Stir in sour cream. Transfer to eight greased 8-oz. ramekins.
2. In a large bowl, combine flour, sugar, baking powder, thyme, baking soda and salt. Cut in butter until mixture resembles coarse crumbs. In a small bowl, combine buttermilk and oil; stir into dry ingredients just until moistened. Drop by heaping teaspoonfuls over filling.
3. Bake, uncovered, until topping is golden brown and filling is bubbly, 20-25 minutes. Let stand 5 minutes before serving.

MAKEOVER SAUSAGE PECAN STUFFING

Nothing about this moist, pecan-topped stuffing says "lighter." The fabulous flavors take the spotlight; that it's healthier and lower in calories is just a bonus.
—Taste of Home *Test Kitchen*

PREP: 30 MIN. • **BAKE:** 30 MIN.
MAKES: 12 SERVINGS

- 1 lb. lean ground turkey
- 2 cups sliced fresh mushrooms
- 2 celery ribs, chopped
- 1 medium onion, chopped
- 1 tsp. fennel seed
- ¼ tsp. cayenne pepper
- ⅛ tsp. ground nutmeg
- 3 garlic cloves, minced
- 1 loaf (16 oz.) day-old white bread, cubed
- 1 large tart apple, chopped
- 2 tsp. rubbed sage
- 1½ tsp. salt
- 1½ tsp. poultry seasoning
- ½ tsp. pepper
- 2 large eggs
- 1 cup reduced-sodium chicken broth
- ½ cup chopped pecans

1. In a Dutch oven, cook the turkey, mushrooms, celery, onion, fennel seed, cayenne and nutmeg over medium heat until turkey is no longer pink. Add garlic; cook 1 minute longer. Drain.
2. Transfer to a large bowl. Add bread, apple, sage, salt, poultry seasoning and pepper. Whisk eggs and broth; pour over bread mixture and toss to coat. Transfer to a 13x9-in. baking dish coated with cooking spray; sprinkle with pecans.
3. Bake, uncovered, at 350° until top is lightly browned and a thermometer reads 160°, 30-35 minutes.

Holiday Helper
To shave a few minutes off prep time for this stuffing, try substituting an equivalent amount of prepackaged cubed seasoned stuffing for the day-old bread. Prepackaged stuffings generally are not seasoned heavily, so they won't compete with the flavors in this recipe.

PUMPKIN-CITRUS TUBE CAKE

I was determined to make a healthier version of my favorite pumpkin- and spice-laden cake. Judging by the compliments, it worked. Even a picky 4-year-old eater asked for more!
—Krista Frank, Rhododendron, OR

PREP: 20 MIN. • **BAKE:** 55 MIN. + COOLING
MAKES: 14 SERVINGS

- 2 cups canned pumpkin
- 1⅓ cups sugar
- 1¼ cups fat-free milk
- 2 large eggs
- ½ cup orange juice
- ⅓ cup canola oil
- 1½ tsp. maple flavoring
- 1½ tsp. vanilla extract
- 1½ cups all-purpose flour
- 1½ cups whole wheat flour
- ¼ cup ground flaxseed
- 2 Tbsp. grated orange zest
- 4 tsp. baking powder
- 1 Tbsp. cornstarch
- 1 Tbsp. poppy seeds
- 2 tsp. pumpkin pie spice
- 1 tsp. salt
- ½ tsp. baking soda

GLAZE
- 1 cup confectioners' sugar
- 1 tsp. grated orange zest
- 1 to 2 Tbsp. orange juice

1. Grease and flour a 10-in. fluted tube pan; set aside. Preheat oven to 350°. In a large bowl, beat the pumpkin, sugar, milk, eggs, orange juice, oil, maple flavoring and vanilla until well blended. Combine the flours, flaxseed, orange zest, baking powder, cornstarch, poppy seeds, pie spice, salt and baking soda; gradually beat into pumpkin mixture until blended.
2. Transfer to prepared pan. Bake until a toothpick inserted in the center comes out clean, 55-60 minutes. Cool for 10 minutes before removing from pan to a wire rack to cool completely.
3. Whisk the confectioners' sugar, orange zest and enough juice to achieve desired consistency. Drizzle over cake.

BANANA FRENCH TOAST BAKE

Who says you can't have comfort food and watch your weight, too? Try this make-ahead dish the whole family will love. It's the ultimate special-occasion breakfast—or breakfast for dinner!
—Nancy Zimmerman, Cape May Court House, NJ

PREP: 20 MIN. + CHILLING • BAKE: 55 MIN. + STANDING
MAKES: 8 SERVINGS

- 6 whole wheat hamburger buns
- 1 pkg. (8 oz.) reduced-fat cream cheese, cut into ¾-in. cubes
- 3 medium bananas, sliced
- 6 large eggs
- 4 cups fat-free milk
- ¼ cup sugar
- ¼ cup maple syrup
- ½ tsp. ground cinnamon

1. Preheat oven to 350°. Cut buns into 1-in. cubes; place half in a 13x9-in. baking dish coated with cooking spray. Layer with cream cheese, bananas and remaining cubed buns.
2. In a large bowl, whisk eggs, milk, sugar, syrup and cinnamon; pour over top. Refrigerate, covered, 8 hours or overnight.
3. Remove from refrigerator; let stand 30 minutes. Bake, covered, 30 minutes. Uncover; bake until a knife inserted near the center comes out clean, 25-30 minutes longer. Let stand 10 minutes before serving.

EGGNOG MOUSSE

Guests will always find room for this light, fluffy, mouthwatering mousse. It makes an elegant, refreshing finish for heavier meals— and it's also a great way to use up any extra eggnog in the fridge.
—Taste of Home *Test Kitchen*

TAKES: 15 MIN. + CHILLING • MAKES: 4 SERVINGS

- 2 tsp. unflavored gelatin
- 2 cups reduced-fat eggnog
- 2 Tbsp. sugar
- ⅛ tsp. ground cinnamon
- ⅛ tsp. ground nutmeg
- ½ tsp. vanilla extract
- 1 cup reduced-fat whipped topping, divided
  Additional ground nutmeg, optional

1. In a small saucepan, sprinkle gelatin over eggnog; let stand for 1 minute. Heat over low heat, stirring until gelatin is completely dissolved. Stir in sugar, cinnamon and nutmeg until sugar is dissolved. Transfer to a small bowl; stir in vanilla. Refrigerate until mixture begins to thicken.
2. Beat mixture until light and fluffy. Beat in ¾ cup whipped topping. Divide among four dessert dishes. Refrigerate until firm. Garnish with the remaining whipped topping; sprinkle with additional nutmeg if desired.

MAKEOVER MEATLESS LASAGNA

PICTURED ON PAGE 78

If you don't tell your guests, they'll never know there's tofu in this. It blends with the other ingredients, adding protein without the fat and calories of ground beef.
—Mary Lou Moeller, Wooster, OH

PREP: 30 MIN. • **BAKE:** 45 MIN. + STANDING
MAKES: 12 SERVINGS

- 10 uncooked whole wheat lasagna noodles
- 1½ cups sliced fresh mushrooms
- ¼ cup chopped onion
- 2 garlic cloves, minced
- 1 can (14½ oz.) Italian diced tomatoes, undrained
- 1 can (12 oz.) tomato paste
- 1 pkg. (14 oz.) firm tofu, drained and cubed
- 2 large eggs, lightly beaten
- 3 cups (24 oz.) 2% cottage cheese
- ½ cup grated Parmesan cheese
- ½ cup packed fresh parsley leaves
- ½ tsp. pepper
- 2 cups shredded part-skim mozzarella cheese, divided

1. Preheat oven to 375°. Cook noodles according to package directions for al dente. Meanwhile, in a large saucepan, cook mushrooms and onion over medium heat until tender. Add garlic; cook for 1 minute. Add tomatoes and tomato paste; cook and stir until heated through.
2. Pulse tofu in a food processor until smooth. Add the next five ingredients; pulse until combined. Drain the noodles.
3. Place five noodles into a 13x9-in. baking dish coated with cooking spray, overlapping as needed. Layer with half the tofu mixture, half the sauce and half the mozzarella. Top with the remaining noodles, tofu mixture and sauce.
4. Bake, covered, for 35 minutes. Sprinkle with the remaining mozzarella. Bake, uncovered, until the cheese is melted, 10-15 minutes. Let stand 10 minutes before serving.
NOTE There are many types of tofu on the market; be sure to choose one marked firm and not soft. When it is pureed with cottage cheese, its taste and texture is very similar to ricotta.

CREAMY FETA-SPINACH DIP

Garlic and feta make a powerfully tasty pair in this addictive dip. I first tried it at a party and had to drag myself away from the bowl!
—Elissa Armbruster, Medford, NJ

TAKES: 15 MIN. + CHILLING • **MAKES:** 2 CUPS

- 1 cup fat-free plain yogurt
- ¾ cup crumbled feta cheese
- 2 oz. reduced-fat cream cheese, cubed
- ¼ cup reduced-fat sour cream
- 1 garlic clove, minced
- 1½ cups finely chopped fresh spinach
- 1 tsp. dill weed
- ⅛ tsp. pepper
  Fresh vegetables and/or sliced bread

1. Line a strainer with four layers of cheesecloth or one coffee filter; place over a bowl. Place yogurt in prepared strainer; cover with edges of cheesecloth. Refrigerate for 2 hours or until the yogurt has thickened to the consistency of whipped cream.
2. Transfer the yogurt to a food processor (discard the liquid in the bowl). Add feta cheese, cream cheese, sour cream and garlic; cover and process until smooth.
3. Transfer to a small bowl. Stir in spinach, dill and pepper. Cover and refrigerate until chilled. Serve with vegetables and/or bread as desired.

COMPLETELY CHOCOLATE

Chocolate isn't just for dessert! Serve up an amazing feast with every course containing chocolate—even the salad! And yes, there are decadent desserts to choose from, too.

COCOA-CRUSTED BEEF TENDERLOIN

My family and I have cooking competitions with secret ingredients and a 30-minute time limit. This tenderloin recipe earned me sweet, sweet victory.
—Gina Myers, Spokane, WA

TAKES: 30 MIN. • **MAKES:** 4 SERVINGS

- 4 beef tenderloin steaks
  (1½ in. thick and 6 oz. each)
- ½ tsp. salt
- ½ tsp. coarsely ground pepper
- 3 Tbsp. baking cocoa
- 3 Tbsp. finely ground coffee

1. Preheat broiler. Sprinkle steaks with salt and pepper. In a shallow bowl, mix cocoa and coffee. Dip steaks in cocoa mixture to coat all sides; shake off excess.
2. Place steaks on the rack of a broiler pan. Broil 3-4 in. from heat for 9-11 minutes on each side or until the meat reaches desired doneness (for medium-rare, a thermometer should read 135°; medium, 140°; medium-well, 145°).

A BRIEF HISTORY OF CHOCOLATE

- **1000 B.C.:** In what is now Ecuador, people make a bitter, hot chocolate-type drink.
- **400-900 A.D.:** The Maya use cocoa to barter for goods.
- **1600s:** Cacao spreads to Europe, where machine production begins.
- **1850s:** Englishman Joseph Fry invents the chocolate bar.
- **1879:** Rodolphe Lindt invents a machine to refine cocoa for the creamy texture we know today.
- **1895:** Confectioner Milton Hershey produces the first Hershey's Milk Chocolate Bar.
- **1930:** Nestlé begins making white chocolate.
- **Today:** The U.S. consumes 20% of the world's cocoa. The average American eats about 12 pounds of chocolate a year.

TOASTED HAZELNUT & CHOCOLATE ICE CREAM

I am a big hazelnut fan, and who doesn't like chocolate? I've been caught red-handed eating Nutella out of the jar with a spoon!
—Laura Majchrzak, Hunt Valley, MD

PREP: 25 MIN. + CHILLING
PROCESS: 15 MIN. + FREEZING
MAKES: 8 SERVINGS

- 2 large eggs
- ½ cup sugar
- ½ tsp. salt
- 1 cup whole milk
- 1½ cups heavy whipping cream
- ½ cup Nutella
- 3 oz. semisweet chocolate, chopped
- ½ cup chopped blanched hazelnuts, toasted

1. In a small heavy saucepan, whisk eggs, sugar and salt until blended; stir in milk. Cook over medium-low heat until a thermometer reads at least 160°, stirring constantly. Do not allow to boil. Remove from heat.
2. Strain into a bowl; whisk in cream and Nutella until smooth. Stir in chopped chocolate. Press plastic wrap onto surface of custard. Refrigerate overnight.
3. Pour custard into the cylinder of an ice cream maker; freeze according to manufacturer's directions, adding hazelnuts during the last 2 minutes of processing. Transfer ice cream to freezer containers, allowing headspace for expansion; freeze 2-4 hours or until firm.
NOTE To toast nuts, bake in a shallow pan in a 350° oven for 5-10 minutes or cook in a skillet over low heat until lightly browned, stirring occasionally.

CHOCOLATE BALLOON BOWLS

Enlist the kids to help create these edible DIY dessert bowls. It's a fun project, and an ideal make-ahead treat for holiday dinners and birthday parties.
—Sarah Farmer, Waukesha, WI

TAKES: 20 MIN. + CHILLING
MAKES: 8 BOWLS

  8 small balloons, inflated
24 oz. bittersweet chocolate, chopped, melted and slightly cooled
  6 oz. white baking chocolate, chopped, melted and slightly cooled
     Assorted sprinkles, optional
     Mousse, ice cream, sorbet, assorted fresh fruit and assorted candies, optional

1. Clean balloons with a damp paper towel. Drop chocolate, 1 tablespoonful at a time, 2-3 in. apart on a parchment paper-lined baking sheet to make eight circles. Pour the remaining bittersweet chocolate into a small bowl.
2. Drizzle 1 Tbsp. white chocolate over bittersweet chocolate. Swirl with a toothpick or wooden skewer. Holding the tied end, dip 1 balloon halfway into the bowl of melted chocolate, rolling back and forth to coat; allow excess to drip off.
3. To secure, lightly press the dipped side of the balloon down onto a chocolate circle; wait a few seconds before releasing pressure. Repeat to coat and secure the remaining balloons, adding another 1 Tbsp. white chocolate to the bittersweet chocolate before dipping each balloon.
4. Refrigerate until set, 5-10 minutes. Gently make a hole near the top of each balloon so that it deflates rather than pops; discard balloons. Fill the bowls as desired, with mousse, ice cream, sorbet, fresh fruit or candy.

ORANGE-ANCHO SPICED NUTS

Get ready for a flavor adventure! These nuts offer a tasty combination of orange, ancho chili pepper and chocolate. The pepper gives a warm, smoky taste.
—Leigh Doutt, Pueblo West, CO

PREP: 15 MIN. • **BAKE:** 35 MIN. + COOLING • **MAKES:** 4 CUPS

- 1 large egg white
- 1 Tbsp. water
- 1 pkg. (10 oz.) deluxe mixed nuts
- ½ cup sugar
- 1 tsp. pumpkin pie spice
- ¾ tsp. grated orange zest
- ¾ tsp. ground ancho chili pepper
- ½ cup bittersweet chocolate baking chips

1. Preheat oven to 275°. In a large bowl, beat egg white and water until frothy. Add nuts; stir gently to coat. Combine the sugar, pie spice, orange zest and chili pepper; add to the nut mixture and gently stir to coat.

2. Spread into an ungreased 15x10x1-in. baking pan. Bake for 35-40 minutes or until lightly browned, stirring once. Sprinkle with chips. Cool completely. Break into pieces. Store in an airtight container.

CHOCOLATE MARTINI

The variations on martinis seem endless. But this sweet version is both creative and sophisticated in taste and presentation. It's a great way to finish or even start a meal.
—Taste of Home *Test Kitchen*

TAKES: 5 MIN. • **MAKES:** 1 SERVING

Ice cubes
2 oz. vodka
2 oz. creme de cacao or chocolate liqueur
GARNISH
Chocolate shavings, white chocolate curl or chocolate truffle

Fill a mixing glass or tumbler three-fourths full with ice. Add vodka and creme de cacao; stir until condensation forms on outside of glass. Strain into a chilled cocktail glass. Garnish as desired.

CHOCOLATE PEAR & CHERRY SALAD

I developed this vinaigrette knowing how well chocolate would play with stone fruit, the peppery bite of arugula, and the deep acidic sweetness of balsamic.
—Ryan Christie, Pacheco, CA

PREP: 25 MIN. + CHILLING • **BAKE:** 15 MIN.
MAKES: 2 SERVINGS

- ¾ cup cut French green beans (haricots verts)
- 3 Tbsp. olive oil, divided
- ⅛ tsp. salt
- ⅛ tsp. pepper
- ¼ cup balsamic vinegar
- 1 oz. dark chocolate candy bar, chopped
- 1 Tbsp. red wine vinegar
- 4 cups fresh arugula
- 1 medium pear, peeled and cut into ½-in. cubes
- ½ cup frozen pitted sweet cherries, thawed and halved
- ¼ cup dried cranberries
- 3 Tbsp. coarsely chopped pecans
- 1 Tbsp. minced dried apricots
- 2 tsp. thinly sliced fresh mint leaves

1. Heat oven to 350°. In an 8-in. square baking dish, toss beans with 1 Tbsp. olive oil, salt and pepper. Roast until tender, 12-15 minutes. Remove from oven. Toss with balsamic vinegar; refrigerate, covered, 1½-2 hours.

2. Meanwhile, in a microwave, melt chocolate; stir until smooth. Pulse melted chocolate, red wine vinegar and remaining olive oil in a blender until smooth.

3. Divide arugula evenly between two salad bowls. Drizzle with chocolate mixture. Top with pears, cherries, cranberries and beans; sprinkle with pecans, apricots and mint leaves.

Holiday Helper

This recipe serves two, but salad recipes are a snap to "size up." A little of this rich, sweet dressing goes a long way, though, so you won't need to fully double the dressing ingredients if you're doubling the salad. If you're looking for something a little different, dried currants make a great substitution for the cranberries.

RED WINE & CHOCOLATE CUPCAKES

Red wine and chocolate make an amazing pairing, especially in these rich, elegant cupcakes. I first made them for my mother's birthday—she adores them!
—Candace Cheney, Fort McMurray, AB

PREP: 15 MIN. • **BAKE:** 20 MIN. + COOLING
MAKES: 2 DOZEN

- ½ cup baking cocoa
- 4 oz. bittersweet chocolate, chopped
- ½ cup boiling water
- 1 cup butter, softened
- 1½ cups sugar
- 4 large eggs
- 1¾ cups all-purpose flour
- 1½ tsp. baking powder
- 1 tsp. salt
- ½ cup dry red wine

MASCARPONE ICING
- 2 cartons (8 oz. each) mascarpone cheese
- 2 cups confectioners' sugar
- ½ tsp. vanilla extract

1. Place the cocoa and chocolate in a small bowl; whisk in boiling water until the chocolate is melted and the mixture is blended.
2. In a large bowl, cream butter and sugar until light and fluffy. Add eggs, one at a time, beating well after each addition. Combine flour, baking powder and salt; add to the creamed mixture alternately with wine and the chocolate mixture, beating well after each addition. Fill paper-lined muffin cups three-fourths full of batter.
3. Bake at 350° for 18-22 minutes or until a toothpick inserted in center comes out clean. Cool for 10 minutes before removing from pans to wire racks to cool completely.
4. In a small bowl, beat the mascarpone cheese, confectioners' sugar and vanilla extract until creamy. Frost cupcakes. Store in the refrigerator.

SHORT RIB TACOS

Whenever we visit Houston, we enjoy cabeza—cow's head, cooked slowly, resulting in extremely tender meat that's excellent in tacos. Back in Seattle, it's hard to find, so I use short ribs to replicate the texture. A quick pico de gallo adds freshness to the rich, flavorful meat.
—Anai Yost, Bothell, WA

PREP: 40 MIN. • **BAKE:** 2½ HOURS
MAKES: 6 SERVINGS

- 2 Tbsp. canola oil
- 6 bone-in beef short ribs
- ¼ tsp. salt
- ¼ tsp. pepper
- 2 medium carrots, finely chopped
- 1 small yellow onion, finely chopped
- 2 Tbsp. baking cocoa
- 1 can (15 oz.) tomato sauce
- 1 bottle (12 oz.) dark beer or beef broth
  Water, optional
- 12 corn tortillas (6 in.), warmed
- ¾ cup pico de gallo
- ¾ cup queso fresco or crumbled feta cheese

1. Preheat oven to 325°. In an ovenproof Dutch oven, heat oil over medium-high heat. Sprinkle beef with salt and pepper; brown in batches. Remove with tongs.
2. Reduce heat to medium. Add carrots and onion to drippings; cook, stirring frequently, until vegetables start to brown, 3-5 minutes. Add cocoa; toast, stirring frequently, until aromatic, 1-2 minutes. Add tomato sauce and beer, stirring to loosen browned bits from pot. Bring to a boil; simmer 2-3 minutes.
3. Return ribs to pot; add water, if necessary, to cover. Bake, covered, until meat is tender, 2½-3 hours. Remove from the oven. When cool enough to handle, remove meat from bones; discard bones and reserve juices. Shred meat with two forks. Skim fat from juices. Return meat and juices to Dutch oven; heat through. Serve on tortillas with pico de gallo and queso fresco.

CHOCOLATE MOCHA DUSTED ALMONDS

These nuts are chocolaty with a hint of coffee—elegant and addictive! I give them away as gifts at holidays; I've even made them for wedding favors.
—Annette Scholz, Medaryville, IN

TAKES: 20 MIN. + CHILLING • **MAKES:** 12 SERVINGS

- 1 cup dark chocolate chips
- 2 cups toasted whole almonds
- ¾ cup confectioners' sugar
- 3 Tbsp. baking cocoa
- 4½ tsp. instant coffee granules

1. Microwave chocolate chips, covered, at 50% power, stirring once or twice, until melted, 3-4 minutes. Stir until smooth. Add almonds; mix until coated.

2. Meanwhile, combine the remaining ingredients. Transfer almonds to sugar mixture; toss to coat evenly. Spread over waxed paper-lined baking sheet.

3. Refrigerate until chocolate is set. Store in an airtight container in refrigerator.

Holiday Helper

If you like spice, add ½ tsp. ground chipotle pepper or chili powder to the mix.

DARK CHOCOLATE PANNA COTTA

Everything about this dessert, from the pretty presentation to its silky smooth texture, says special. Sweet, ripe berries accent the rich flavor of chocolate perfectly.
—Susan Asanovic, Wilton, CT

PREP: 25 MIN. • **COOK:** 10 MIN. + CHILLING • **MAKES:** 8 SERVINGS

- 1 can (14 oz.) whole-berry cranberry sauce
- 5 Tbsp. raspberry liqueur, divided
- 1 envelope unflavored gelatin
- 1 cup cold 2% milk
- 4 oz. 53% cacao dark baking chocolate, chopped
- 1½ cups heavy whipping cream
- ½ cup sugar
- ⅛ tsp. salt
- 2 tsp. vanilla extract
  Fresh raspberries and mint leaves, optional

1. Place cranberry sauce in a food processor; cover and process until pureed. Strain and discard pulp. Stir in 3 Tbsp. raspberry liqueur; set aside.

2. In a small bowl, sprinkle the gelatin over the milk; let stand for 1 minute. Meanwhile, place chocolate in another small bowl. In a small saucepan, bring cream, sugar and salt just to a boil. Pour over chocolate; whisk until smooth.

3. Stir a small amount of the chocolate mixture into the gelatin mixture until the gelatin is completely dissolved. Stir in 1 cup of the cranberry puree and the vanilla. Pour into eight 6-oz. custard cups. Cover and refrigerate for 8 hours or overnight.

4. In a small bowl, combine the remaining cranberry puree and liqueur; cover and refrigerate until serving.

5. Unmold onto serving plates. Serve with sauce and garnish with fresh raspberries and mint if desired.

SLOW COOKER BEEF WITH RED SAUCE

A homemade rub spices up this tender beef; vinegar and gingersnaps add depth to the sauce. You can substitute graham crackers for the cookies.
—Laurie Tietze, Longview, TX

PREP: 25 MIN. • **COOK:** 8 HOURS
MAKES: 8 SERVINGS

- 2 Tbsp. canola oil
- 2 Tbsp. baking cocoa
- 1 Tbsp. chili powder
- 2 tsp. dried oregano
- 1 tsp. salt
- 1 tsp. pepper
- 1 tsp. ground cumin
- ½ tsp. ground cloves
- ½ tsp. ground cinnamon
- 1 beef rump roast or bottom round roast (3 lbs.), cut into 1½-in. cubes
- 1 large onion, chopped
- 1 can (28 oz.) whole tomatoes, undrained
- 3 Tbsp. cider vinegar
- 1½ cups crushed gingersnap cookies (about 30 cookies)
- 9 garlic cloves, peeled
- 1 Tbsp. sugar
  Hot cooked noodles, rice or mashed potatoes

1. In a small bowl, combine the first nine ingredients; set aside.
2. Place beef and onion in a 4-qt. slow cooker; rub beef with spice mixture. Pour tomatoes over the top; sprinkle with vinegar, gingersnaps and garlic. Cover and cook on low for 8-10 hours or until meat is tender. Stir in sugar. Serve with noodles, rice or mashed potatoes, as desired.

FUDGE PECAN BROWNIE TART

I love inventing my own recipes and entering contests—I won a blue ribbon at the Iowa State Fair for this one! This pleases the kids, and is elegant enough for company.
—Gloria Kratz, Des Moines, IA

PREP: 30 MIN. **BAKE:** 30 MIN.
MAKES: 12 SERVINGS

- 1 cup all-purpose flour
- ¼ cup packed light brown sugar
- ¼ cup finely chopped pecans
- ½ cup cold butter
- 2 Tbsp. whole milk
- 1 tsp. vanilla extract

BROWNIE FILLING

- 3 oz. unsweetened chocolate
- ½ cup chocolate chips
- ½ cup butter, cut into pieces
- 1½ cups sugar
- 3 large eggs
- 2 tsp. vanilla extract
- ¾ cup all-purpose flour
- 1 cup chopped pecans

FUDGE FROSTING

- 1½ oz. unsweetened chocolate
- ⅔ cup sweetened condensed milk
- ¼ cup butter
- 1 large egg yolk, beaten
- ½ tsp. vanilla extract
  Whipped cream and whole pecans for garnish, optional

1. Preheat oven to 350°. Combine flour, brown sugar and nuts in a large bowl; cut in butter until mixture resembles coarse meal. Mix in milk and vanilla with a fork just until blended. Pat onto bottom and up the sides of an 11-in. tart pan; set aside.
2. For filling, melt chocolate and chips in the top of a double boiler over hot water. Remove from heat and stir in butter. Place in a large bowl and combine with sugar. Add eggs and vanilla; blend well. Gradually add the flour, blending well after each addition. Add nuts. Pour over crust.
3. Bake for 30-35 minutes, or until center is just set and toothpick comes out clean. Cool on wire rack.
4. For frosting, melt chocolate in a small saucepan over low heat. Add milk, butter, yolk and vanilla. Heat, stirring vigorously, until smooth and thick, about 5 minutes. Spread over tart. Garnish with whipped cream and pecans if desired.

BAKED BEANS MOLE

My son and husband love this hearty side dish that is quick and easy to prepare but yet so flavorful. Chocolate, chili and honey mingle to create a rich, savory flavor that's not too spicy and not too sweet.
—Roxanne Chan, Albany, CA

PREP: 25 MIN. • **BAKE:** 40 MINUTES
MAKES: 8 SERVINGS

¼ lb. fresh chorizo, crumbled
½ cup chopped onion
½ cup chopped sweet red pepper
1 large garlic clove, minced

1 can (15 oz.) black beans, rinsed and drained
1 can (15 oz.) pinto beans, rinsed and drained
1 can (15 oz.) black-eyed peas, rinsed and drained
1 cup salsa (medium or hot)
1 cup chili sauce
2 Tbsp. honey
1 Tbsp. instant coffee granules
½ tsp. ground cinnamon
2 oz. chopped bittersweet or semisweet chocolate
Minced fresh cilantro

Preheat oven to 375°. In a large ovenproof skillet with a lid, cook the chorizo, onion, red pepper and garlic over medium heat until the sausage is browned, 4-6 minutes. Add next nine ingredients; mix well. Bake, covered, until thickened and flavors are blended, about 40 minutes. Sprinkle with the cilantro.

Holiday Helper
Although this dish is great with several types of beans you can certainly pick just one. You could also add 2 to 3 cups of broth and make a festive mole chili instead!

CHOCOLATE MOLASSES PORK ROAST

This new twist on pork roast has a rich molasses flavor with a tantalizing hint of chocolate. It's easy to make, yet elegant enough for entertaining. Serve this with mashed potatoes so as not to waste a drop of the delicious gravy.
—Avionne Huppert, Adams, NY

PREP: 20 MIN. • **COOK:** 6 HOURS
MAKES: 10 SERVINGS

- ½ cup packed brown sugar
- ½ cup maple syrup
- ¼ cup beef broth
- ¼ cup Worcestershire sauce
- ¼ cup ketchup
- ¼ cup molasses
- 2 Tbsp. baking cocoa
- 2 tsp. garlic powder
- 2 tsp. onion powder
- ¾ tsp. salt
- ½ tsp. ground ginger
- ½ tsp. ground mustard
- 1 boneless pork loin roast (4 to 5 lbs.)
- 3 Tbsp. cornstarch
- 3 Tbsp. water

1. In a small bowl, mix first 12 ingredients. Cut roast in half; place in a 5- or 6-qt. slow cooker. Pour sauce over top. Cover and cook on low for 6-8 hours or until meat is tender.

2. Remove pork to a serving platter; keep warm. Skim fat from cooking juices. Transfer juices to a small saucepan; bring to a boil. In a small bowl, mix cornstarch and water until smooth; gradually stir into the pan. Return to a boil; cook and stir for 2 minutes or until thickened. Serve with pork.

down. Return to oven, baking until crisp, 6-8 minutes on each side. Remove from pans to wire racks to cool completely. Store in an airtight container.

NOTE To toast whole hazelnuts, bake, stirring occasionally, in a shallow pan in a 350° oven until fragrant and lightly browned, 7-10 minutes. Wrap cooled hazelnuts in a tea towel; rub with towel to loosen skins.

CHOCOLATE-COVERED CHEESE WITH BLACK SEA SALT

Every time I make these for guests or for a cooking demonstration about real food made simply, people rave about them. They're a great, surprising addition to an appetizer table—or even served after dinner paired with a nice cabernet or port.
—*Dorothy McNett, Pacific Grove, CA*

TAKES: 45 MIN. + STANDING
MAKES: 6½ DOZEN

- 8 oz. aged cheddar or Monterey Jack cheese
- 6 oz. bittersweet chocolate, chopped Black sea salt, optional

Cut cheese into ½-in. cubes. In a microwave, melt chocolate; stir until smooth. Dip cheese cubes in chocolate, allowing excess to drip off. Place on waxed paper. If desired, sprinkle with a few grains of salt. Let stand until set.

DOUBLE CHOCOLATE, ORANGE & HAZELNUT BISCOTTI

My family and I love to snack on biscotti. Biscotti is actually very easy to make and is delicious with breakfast or as a snack. It stores well for over a week in a sealed jar or bag. I came up with the recipe when trying to use odds and ends I had in the house. It's delicious with coffee or espresso!
—*Sarah Knoblock, Hyde Park, IN*

PREP: 20 MIN. • **BAKE:** 25 MIN.
MAKES: ABOUT 1½ DOZEN

- ¼ cup whole hazelnuts, toasted and skins removed
- 1 large egg
- ⅓ cup sugar
- ¼ cup 2% milk
- 1 tsp. vanilla extract
- 2 cups all-purpose flour
- ¼ cup baking cocoa
- ¼ tsp. baking soda
  Dash salt
- 2 tsp. grated orange zest
- ½ cup semisweet chocolate chips

1. Preheat oven to 350°. Place hazelnuts in a resealable plastic bag; crush nuts using a mallet or rolling pin.

2. Beat egg, sugar and milk until light and thick; add vanilla. Whisk flour, cocoa, baking soda and salt; stir in orange zest. Gradually beat into egg mixture (dough will be thick). Fold in chocolate chips and crushed hazelnuts by hand.

3. On an ungreased baking sheet, shape dough into a 9x5-in. rectangle. Bake until a toothpick inserted in center comes out clean, about 20 minutes. Cool on pans on wire racks until firm, 5-10 minutes.

4. Reduce oven setting to 325°. Transfer baked rectangle to a cutting board. Using a serrated knife, cut crosswise into ½-in. slices. Place on baking sheet, cut sides

CHOCOLATE CINNAMON ROLLS WITH ICING

These chocolaty treats are a change from ordinary cinnamon rolls...and perfect for coffee breaks!
—Rita Lempka, Sterling, NE

PREP: 30 MIN. + RISING • **BAKE:** 25 MIN.
MAKES: 1 DOZEN

- 1 pkg. (¼ oz.) active dry yeast
- ¾ cup warm water (110° to 115°)
- ¼ cup shortening
- 1 tsp. salt
- ¼ cup plus 3 Tbsp. sugar, divided
- 1 large egg
- ⅓ cup baking cocoa
- 2¼ cups all-purpose flour, divided
- 1 Tbsp. butter, softened
- 1½ tsp. ground cinnamon

QUICK WHITE ICING

- 1 cup confectioners' sugar
- ½ tsp. vanilla extract
- 1½ Tbsp. whole milk

1. In a large bowl, dissolve yeast in warm water; let stand for 5 minutes. Add the shortening, salt, ¼ cup sugar, egg, cocoa and 1 cup flour; beat for 2 minutes. Stir in remaining flour and blend with a spoon until smooth. Cover and let rise in a warm place until doubled, about 1 hour. Stir dough down and turn onto a well-floured surface (dough will be soft). Roll out into a 12x9-in. rectangle. Carefully spread with butter.

2. Combine cinnamon and remaining sugar; sprinkle over butter. Roll up gently, beginning at wide end. Cut into 12 pieces and place in a greased 9-in. square baking pan. Cover and let rise in a warm place until doubled, about 45 minutes. Bake at 375° for 25 minutes.

3. Meanwhile, for icing, cream all the ingredients together in a small bowl until mixture is desired spreading consistency. Frost rolls while still warm.

DOUBLE CHOCOLATE ALMOND CHEESECAKE

This cheesecake is easy to make—but it's definitely not easy to wait till the next day to eat it! The recipe came from a friend and former co-worker.
—Darlene Brenden, Salem, OR

PREP: 25 MIN. + CHILLING
BAKE: 50 MIN. + CHILLING
MAKES: 12-16 SERVINGS

CRUST
- 1 pkg. (9 oz.) chocolate wafer cookies, crushed (about 2 cups)
- ¼ cup sugar
- ¼ tsp. ground cinnamon
- ¼ cup butter, melted

FILLING
- 2 pkg. (8 oz. each) cream cheese, softened
- 1 cup sugar
- 1 cup sour cream
- 8 oz. semisweet chocolate, melted and cooled
- ½ tsp. almond extract
- 2 large eggs, lightly beaten

TOPPING
- 1 cup sour cream
- ¼ tsp. baking cocoa
- 2 Tbsp. sugar
- ½ tsp. almond extract
  Sliced almonds, toasted, optional

1. In a small bowl, combine the crust ingredients; reserve 2 Tbsp. for garnish. Press the remaining crumbs evenly onto the bottom and 2 in. up the sides of a 9-in. springform pan. Chill.

2. For filling, in a large bowl, beat cream cheese and sugar until smooth. Beat in the sour cream, chocolate and extract.

Add eggs; beat on low speed just until combined. Pour into crust.

3. Place pan on a baking sheet. Bake at 350° for 40 minutes (filling will not be set). Remove from oven and let stand for 5 minutes.

4. Meanwhile, combine topping ingredients. Gently spread over filling. Sprinkle with reserved crumbs. Bake 10 minutes longer.

5. Cool on a wire rack for 10 minutes. Carefully run a knife around edge of pan to loosen; cool 1 hour longer. Refrigerate overnight. Garnish with toasted almonds if desired.

DARK CHOCOLATE PUMPKIN TRUFFLES

The combination of pumpkin and dark chocolate is unexpected and delectable. These delicious truffles make a pretty addition to a party plate, a sweet way to finish up a meal, or a gift your friends and family will love.
—Monica Mooney, Roseville, CA

TAKES: 30 MIN. + FREEZING
MAKES: 2½ DOZEN

- ⅔ cup reduced-fat cream cheese
- ½ cup confectioners' sugar
- ⅔ cup canned pumpkin
- 1 tsp. pumpkin pie spice
- 1 tsp. vanilla extract
- 2¼ cups crushed reduced-fat graham crackers
- 1 pkg. (10 oz.) dark chocolate chips

1. In a small bowl, beat cream cheese and confectioners' sugar until blended. Beat in pumpkin, pie spice and vanilla. Stir in cracker crumbs. Freeze, covered, for 20 minutes or until firm enough to shape.
2. Shape pumpkin mixture into 1-in. balls; place on waxed paper-lined baking sheets; freeze 20 minutes or until firm.
3. In a microwave, melt chocolate; stir until smooth. Dip truffles in chocolate; allow excess to drip off. Return to baking sheets; refrigerate until set. Store in airtight containers in the refrigerator.

MAINLY MUSHROOM BEEF CARBONNADE

This is the ultimate comfort food, an earth-and-turf combo that smells delicious and tastes like home. The mushrooms taste so meaty, you can decrease the beef and add more portabellos if you like.
—Susan Asanovic, Wilton, CT

PREP: 45 MIN. • **BAKE:** 2 HOURS
MAKES: 6 SERVINGS

- 2 Tbsp. plus 1½ tsp. canola oil, divided
- 1½ lbs. beef stew meat, cut into 1-in. cubes
- ¾ tsp. salt
- ¼ tsp. plus ⅛ tsp. pepper
- 3 medium onions, chopped
- 1¼ lbs. portobello mushrooms, stems removed, cut into ¾-in. dice
- 4 garlic cloves, minced
- 2 Tbsp. tomato paste
- ½ lb. fresh baby carrots
- 1 thick slice day-old rye bread, crumbled (about 1½ cups)
- 3 bay leaves
- 1½ tsp. dried thyme
- 1 tsp. beef bouillon granules
- 1 bottle (12 oz.) light beer or beef broth
- 1 cup water
- 1 oz. bittersweet chocolate, grated

1. Preheat oven to 325°. In an ovenproof Dutch oven, heat 2 Tbsp. of oil over medium-high heat. Sprinkle beef with salt and pepper; brown in batches. Remove with a slotted spoon.
2. Reduce heat to medium. Add onions to the drippings; cook, stirring frequently, until dark golden brown, about 8 minutes. Stir in the remaining oil; add mushrooms and garlic. Saute until mushrooms begin to brown and release their liquid. Stir in tomato paste.
3. Add carrots, bread, bay leaves, thyme and bouillon. Add beer and water, stirring to loosen browned bits from pan. Bring to a boil; return beef to pan.
4. Bake, covered, until meat is tender, 2-2¼ hours. Remove from oven; discard bay leaves. Stir in chocolate until melted.

Holiday Helper
A light-bodied beer can be replaced with dark beer or red wine in this hearty dish. Serve on top of mashed potatoes, egg noodles or seasoned rice, whichever you prefer.

5-INGREDIENT ENTERTAINING

Planning a holiday party doesn't demand a book-length shopping list! These dishes come together with only five ingredients (not counting water, salt, pepper or oil).

SUN-DRIED TOMATO GOAT CHEESE EMPANADAS

I entertain a lot and am always trying to think of things I can do ahead of time. These empanadas are perfect, because they can be done well in advance and frozen, or made the day before and refrigerated. Whenever I make them, I need to have extras because people love them so much!
—Lynn Scully, Rancho Santa Fe, CA

PREP: 1 HOUR • **BAKE:** 15 MIN.
MAKES: ABOUT 1½ DOZEN

- 1 Tbsp. olive oil
- 1 medium sweet onion, halved and thinly sliced
- 1 log (4 oz.) fresh goat cheese, crumbled
- ¼ cup finely chopped oil-packed sun-dried tomatoes, drained
  Pastry for a single-crust pie (9 in.) or refrigerated pie crust

1. In a large skillet, heat oil over medium heat. Add onion; cook and stir until softened, 4-5 minutes. Reduce heat to medium-low; cook, stirring occasionally, until deep golden brown, 30-40 minutes. Remove from heat. Let cool slightly. Gently stir in goat cheese and tomatoes.
2. Preheat oven to 400°. On a lightly floured surface, roll dough to ¼-in. thickness. Cut with a floured 3-in. round biscuit cutter. Place circles 2 in. apart on baking sheets. Place 1 heaping tsp. filling on one side of each circle. Brush edges of pastry with water; fold circles in half. With a fork, press edges to seal. Bake until golden brown, 15-20 minutes.

PASTRY FOR SINGLE-CRUST PIE (9 IN.)
Combine 1¼ cups all-purpose flour and ¼ tsp. salt; cut in ½ cup cold butter until crumbly. Gradually add 3-5 Tbsp. ice water, tossing with a fork until dough holds together when pressed. Wrap in plastic wrap and refrigerate 1 hour.

CHOCOLATE FRAMBOISE PARFAITS

Having unexpected company? Relieve some of the stress of presenting a beautiful holiday dessert with these quick, tasty parfaits—they're ready in minutes. It doesn't get any easier.
—Charlene Chambers, Ormond Beach, FL

TAKES: 15 MIN. + FREEZING • **MAKES:** 6 SERVINGS

- 6 Tbsp. raspberry liqueur
- 1½ pints vanilla ice cream
- 1½ pints fresh raspberries
- 2¼ cups chocolate wafer crumbs
  Sweetened whipped cream

Layer each of six parfait glasses with 1 tsp. raspberry liqueur, 2½ Tbsp. ice cream, four or five raspberries and 2 Tbsp. chocolate wafer crumbs. Repeat layers twice. Freeze. To serve, top with whipped cream and the remaining raspberries.

MEDITERRANEAN CAULIFLOWER

I adapted a recipe from a friend to make this delicious—and deliciously different—cauliflower dish. It's prepared quickly in a skillet and only uses a handful of ingredients. What a great way to take ordinary cauliflower to a whole new level!
—Valerie G. Smith, Aston, PA

TAKES: 25 MIN. • **MAKES:** 10 SERVINGS

- 1 large head cauliflower, broken into florets
- 2 cans (14½ oz. each) diced tomatoes with basil, oregano and garlic, drained
- ½ cup sliced green olives with pimientos
- 4 green onions, sliced
- ½ tsp. pepper
- ¼ tsp. salt
- 1 cup crumbled feta cheese

1. In a 6-qt. stockpot, place a steamer basket over 1 in. of water. Place cauliflower in basket. Bring to a boil. Reduce heat; steam, covered, until crisp-tender, 4-6 minutes. Drain cauliflower and transfer to a large skillet.
2. Stir in tomatoes, olives, onions, salt and pepper. Bring to a boil. Reduce heat; simmer, uncovered, until cauliflower is tender and tomatoes are heated through, 3-5 minutes. Sprinkle with feta cheese before serving.

ARUGULA PIZZA

We serve this pizza as an appetizer when family or friends get together. My girlfriends and I love it because it has a sophisticated gourmet touch, and it's healthy, too! This also serves four people as a main course.
—Annette Riva, Naperville, IL

TAKES: 20 MIN. • **MAKES:** 16 PIECES

- ½ cup pizza sauce
- 1 prebaked 12-in. pizza crust (14 oz.)
- 1 cup shaved Parmesan cheese
- 3 oz. thinly sliced prosciutto
- 2 cups fresh arugula
  Optional topping: additional fresh arugula

Preheat oven to 425°. Spread sauce over pizza crust. Layer with ½ cup Parmesan cheese, prosciutto and arugula; top with remaining cheese. Bake directly on oven rack until edges are lightly browned, 10-12 minutes. Cut into small squares. If desired, top with more arugula.

CREAMY PARMESAN RICE

This quick and easy side dish can be made with ingredients you probably already have on hand. It's great served with chicken, pork chops or fish.
—Angela McArthur, Snover, MI

TAKES: 30 MIN. • **MAKES:** 4 SERVINGS

- 2 cans (14½ oz. each) chicken broth
- 1 cup uncooked long grain rice
- ¼ tsp. salt
- ⅛ tsp. garlic powder
- ¼ cup grated Parmesan cheese
- 2 tsp. minced fresh parsley

1. In a large saucepan, heat 2 cups of the broth (reserving the remainder) over medium heat. Bring to a boil; stir in the rice, salt and garlic powder. Reduce heat; simmer, covered, until most of the liquid is absorbed, about 20 minutes.
2. Stir in the Parmesan cheese. Add the reserved broth, 2 Tbsp. at a time, stirring constantly. After each addition, wait until the liquid is absorbed before adding more broth. Cook just until creamy and the rice is almost tender, 5-10 minutes. Stir in the parsley. Serve immediately.

WARM CHICKEN TORTELLINI AU GRATIN

I have a number of easy planned-leftover meals in my recipe arsenal, which is especially useful during the holiday season. This is one of my favorites. Pasta from Monday plus roast chicken from Tuesday equals this delicious dish on Wednesday. Paired with a salad and bread, it's a meal fancy enough for company.
—Brenda Cole, Reisterstown, MD

PREP: 15 MIN. • **BAKE:** 30 MIN.
MAKES: 6 SERVINGS

- 2 cans (14 oz. each) water-packed artichoke hearts
- 3 cups shredded cooked chicken
- 3 cups refrigerated spinach tortellini, cooked
- 1½ cups mayonnaise
- 1½ cups grated Asiago cheese, divided

Preheat oven to 350°. Drain artichoke hearts, reserving ¼ cup of juices. Coarsely chop; combine with chicken, tortellini, mayonnaise, 1 cup cheese and reserved artichoke liquid. Place artichoke mixture in a greased 13x9-in. baking dish; sprinkle with remaining cheese. Bake until bubbly and starting to brown, about 30 minutes.

CRANBERRY-APRICOT PORK TENDERLOINS

Stuffing made with cranberries and apricots complements pork tenderloin wonderfully. This is an elegant entree that you can pull together in no time.
—Joann Brown, Los Alamos, NM

PREP: 30 MIN. • **BAKE:** 30 MIN.
MAKES: 6-8 SERVINGS

- 1 cup dried cranberries
- 1 cup chopped dried apricots
- 3 Tbsp. water
- 2 tsp. dried rosemary, crushed
- ½ tsp. salt
- ¼ tsp. pepper
- 2 pork tenderloins (1 lb. each)

1. In a small saucepan, combine the first six ingredients. Bring to a boil. Reduce heat; simmer, covered, until fruit is softened, about 10 minutes. Cool.

2. Preheat oven to 400°. Cut a lengthwise slit down the center of each tenderloin to within ½ in. of bottom. Open tenderloins so they lie flat; cover with plastic wrap. Flatten to ¾-in. thickness; remove plastic. Spread with fruit mixture to within ¾ in. of edges. Roll up jelly-roll style, starting with a long side; tie with kitchen string at 1½-in. intervals.

3. Line a shallow pan with heavy-duty foil. Place meat on a rack in prepared pan. Bake, uncovered, until a thermometer reads 145°, 30-35 minutes. Let stand 5-10 minutes before slicing.

Holiday Helper

To flatten your pork, you can use a meat mallet, a rolling pin or even a cast-iron skillet! Start in the center and work outward, pounding lightly. If using a meat mallet, be sure to use the flat side; the spiky side will tear the meat. Use a lighter touch than for a beef steak; if pounded too hard, the pork will fall apart and be mushy.

ITALIAN STEAK BRUSCHETTA

This recipe combines my favorite things to eat: toast, steak, bruschetta topping and pancetta. It's so pretty on the plate! This five-ingredient appetizer is easy to prepare but will have everyone thinking you spent a long time in the kitchen.
—Devon Delaney, Westport, CT

PREP: 30 MIN. • **BROIL:** 10 MIN.
MAKES: 1 DOZEN

- 4 oz. sliced pancetta or bacon strips, chopped
- 1 beef top sirloin steak (1 lb.)
- ½ tsp. salt
- ¼ tsp. pepper
- 12 diagonally cut French bread slices (½ in. thick)
- 1½ cups prepared bruschetta topping
- 1 cup fresh arugula or baby spinach

1. Preheat broiler. In a large skillet, cook pancetta over medium heat until crisp. Remove to paper towels with a slotted spoon; drain.

2. Meanwhile, sprinkle steak with salt and pepper; place on a 15x10x1-in. baking pan. Broil 3-4 in. from heat for 4-6 minutes on each side until the meat reaches desired doneness (for medium-rare, a thermometer should read 135°; medium, 140°; medium-well, 145°). Let stand for 5 minutes, then cut into thin slices.

3. Place bread on an ungreased baking sheet. Broil 3-4 in. from heat until golden brown, 30-45 seconds on each side. Top with bruschetta topping, arugula, steak and pancetta.

NOTE Look for bruschetta topping in the pasta aisle or your grocer's deli case.

QUICK & EASY BAKLAVA SQUARES

I love baklava but rarely indulged because it takes so much time to make. Then a friend of mine gave me this simple recipe. I've made these squares for family, friends and co-workers—they can't get enough. I'm always asked to bring them to special gatherings and parties, and I even give them as gifts during the holidays.
—Paula Marchesi, Lenhartsville, PA

PREP: 20 MIN. • **BAKE:** 30 MIN. • **MAKES:** 2 DOZEN

- 1   lb. (4 cups) chopped walnuts
- 1½ tsp. ground cinnamon
- 1   pkg. (16 oz., 14x9-in. sheets) frozen phyllo dough, thawed
- 1   cup butter, melted
- 1   cup honey

1. Preheat oven to 350°. Coat a 13x9-in. baking dish with cooking spray. Combine walnuts and cinnamon.

2. Unroll phyllo dough. Layer two sheets of phyllo dough in the prepared pan; brush with butter. Repeat with six more sheets of phyllo, brushing every other one with butter. (Keep the remaining phyllo covered with plastic wrap and a damp towel to prevent it from drying out.)

3. Sprinkle ½ cup of the nut mixture in the pan; drizzle with 2 Tbsp. of honey. Add two more phyllo sheets, brushing with butter; sprinkle another ½ cup of the nut mixture and 2 Tbsp. honey over phyllo. Repeat layers six times. Top with the remaining phyllo sheets, brushing every other one with butter. Using a sharp knife, score the surface to make 24 squares. Bake until golden brown and crisp, 25-30 minutes. Cool on a wire rack for 1 hour before serving.

SWEET & SPICY CHIPOTLE CHICKEN

My husband and I have created many wonderful memories by sharing this meal with our friends. The chicken pretty much cooks itself, leaving you plenty of time to visit with friends and family.
—Ashlie Delshad, West Lafayette, IN

PREP: 15 MIN. + MARINATING
BAKE: 1 HOUR 50 MIN. + STANDING
MAKES: 8 SERVINGS

- 2 chipotle peppers plus 3 Tbsp. adobo sauce
- ¼ cup tomato paste
- 3 Tbsp. honey
- 2 Tbsp. olive oil
- 1 tsp. sea salt
- 1 roasting chicken (6 to 7 lbs.)

1. Pulse chipotle peppers, adobo sauce, tomato paste, honey, olive oil and sea salt in a food processor or blender until smooth. Spread the mixture evenly over chicken. Refrigerate, covered, for at least 1 hour or overnight.
2. Preheat oven to 400°. Place chicken on a rack in a shallow roasting pan, breast side up. Tuck wings under chicken; tie drumsticks together.
3. Roast 20 minutes. Reduce oven setting to 350°. Roast 1½-1¾ hours longer or until a thermometer inserted in thickest part of thigh reads 170°-175°. (Cover loosely with foil if chicken browns too quickly.)
4. Remove chicken from oven; tent with foil. Let stand for 15 minutes before carving. If desired, skim fat from pan drippings and thicken for gravy. Serve with chicken.

SKEWERED LAMB WITH BLACKBERRY-BALSAMIC GLAZE

This dish proves that it only takes a couple of simple, high-quality ingredients to make a phenomenal dinner. I love serving these skewers for parties, but they're also good for a weeknight dinner.
—Elynor Townsend, Summerfield, FL

PREP: 10 MIN. + MARINATING
GRILL: 10 MIN. • **MAKES:** 6 SERVINGS

- ½ cup seedless blackberry spreadable fruit
- ⅓ cup balsamic vinegar
- 1 Tbsp. minced fresh rosemary or 1 tsp. dried rosemary, crushed
- 1 Tbsp. Dijon mustard
- 1½ lbs. lean boneless lamb, cut into 1-in. cubes
- ¼ tsp. salt

1. In a small bowl, combine the spreadable fruit, vinegar, rosemary and mustard. Pour ⅔ cup of the marinade into a large resealable plastic bag; add the lamb. Seal the bag and turn to coat; refrigerate for at least 1 hour. Cover and refrigerate the remaining marinade to use for basting.
2. Drain and discard the marinade in the bag. Thread lamb onto six metal or soaked wooden skewers. Place kabobs on a greased grill rack, covered, over medium heat or broil 4 in. from the heat for 10-12 minutes or until the lamb reaches desired doneness (for medium-rare, a thermometer should read 145°; medium, 160°; well-done, 170°). Turn once while cooking and baste frequently with the reserved marinade. Sprinkle with salt before serving.

SAUSAGE FLORENTINE SHEPHERD'S PIE

In this Italian take on traditional shepherd's pie, sausage takes the place of ground beef (or lamb), and spinach replaces the green veggies. Zesty tomatoes, mixed Italian cheese and garlicky mashed potatoes make this incredibly long on flavor, even though the ingredient list is short.
—Leah Lyon, Ada, OK

PREP: 15 MIN. • **BAKE:** 30 MIN. + STANDING • **MAKES:** 6 SERVINGS

1   lb. bulk mild Italian sausage
1   can (14½ oz.) Italian diced tomatoes, lightly drained
1   pkg. (10 oz.) frozen chopped spinach, thawed and squeezed dry
3   cups shredded Italian cheese blend, divided
1   pkg. (24 oz.) refrigerated garlic mashed potatoes

1. Preheat oven to 375°. In a Dutch oven over medium heat, cook sausage, crumbling the meat, until it is no longer pink, 5-6 minutes; drain. Stir in tomatoes, spinach and 2 cups of the shredded cheese.
2. Pour the sausage mixture into a greased 11x7-in. baking dish; top evenly with mashed potatoes. Bake for 20 minutes; sprinkle with the remaining cheese. Bake until the cheese is melted and the top begins to brown, about 20 minutes longer. Let stand for 10 minutes before serving.
NOTE If you prefer a spicier dish, you can easily substitute hot Italian sausage for the mild version.

SCENTS OF THE SEASON

Our sense of smell is more closely tied to memory than any of our other senses. The aromas of apple cider, gingerbread and—of course!—pine create an immediate and indelible feeling of Christmas. Setting a holiday atmosphere to welcome your guests as they walk in your door is as easy as boiling water.

Fill a saucepan with water and some choice aromatics, leaving about an inch of room at the top. Bring to a simmer and let the aroma fill your house. Don't stray too far from the stove, and remember you can always add more water to keep the scent going. For a low-maintenance version, use an uncovered slow cooker on the low setting.

As for the aromatics, it's easy to create your own custom blend. Save Christmas tree clippings, orange peels, apple peels, stray herbs and spices from your cooking—you can use all these and more to make your home smell incredible. If you're looking for a place to start, though, here are a few stovetop potpourri combinations you can try.

Winter Forest
Pine sprigs • cinnamon sticks • 1-2 bay leaves • lemon peel • orange or grapefruit peel

Cinnamon Bun
Cinnamon sticks • 1 tsp. vanilla extract • 1 tsp. almond extract • whole nutmeg

Warm & Fuzzy
Apple peels • orange peels • cinnamon sticks • whole cloves

Apple Pie
Halved apples • orange peels • star anise • cinnamon sticks • whole allspice • vanilla bean, split • whole cloves

Cozy Cranberry
Fresh cranberries • orange peel • cinnamon sticks • sprigs of fresh rosemary

"This is the only way my kids will eat Brussels sprouts!"
—TERI RASEY

BETTER BRUSSELS SPROUTS

This is the only way my kids will eat Brussels sprouts! It's actually great for me because this dish is fast, easy and healthy, and it makes a lovely side. Quick-cooking Brussels sprout halves are available in the prepackaged salad aisle at the grocery store. They're a timesaver if you can find them, but you can always just buy whole ones and slice them in half.
—Teri Rasey, Cadillac, MI

TAKES: 20 MIN. • **MAKES:** 6 SERVINGS

3 Tbsp. coconut oil
1 pkg. (16 oz.) fresh halved Brussels sprouts
⅓ cup sliced onions
½ cup coarsely chopped cashews
1 tsp. granulated garlic
Salt and pepper to taste

In a large heavy skillet or wok, heat coconut oil over medium heat. Add Brussels sprouts; cook and stir 5 minutes. Add onion slices; cook 3 minutes longer, stirring every 20-30 seconds. Add cashews and garlic; cook 1 minute longer. Sprinkle with salt and pepper.

COCONUT MANGO THAI BEEF CURRY

My recipe provides a lot of sweet heat. The mango and coconut milk taste tropical while the curry paste adds a little fire. It's a great dish to spice up the traditional offerings of the season. To make a milder dish, just reduce the amount of curry paste.
—Terri Lynn Merritts, Nashville, TN

PREP: 10 MIN. • **COOK:** 2¼ HOURS • **MAKES:** 6 SERVINGS

2 Tbsp. peanut oil or canola oil
3 Tbsp. red curry paste
2½ cups coconut milk
2½ lbs. boneless beef chuck roast, cut into 1-in. cubes
1 cup dried mango, chopped
1 tsp. salt
¼ tsp. pepper
Hot cooked rice, optional

In a Dutch oven, heat peanut oil over low heat. Stir in curry paste. Cook and stir 3-5 minutes. Add coconut milk; cook and stir 3-5 minutes longer. Stir in beef, mango, salt and pepper. Increase heat to medium-high; bring to a boil. Reduce heat; simmer, uncovered, stirring occasionally, until meat is tender, about 2 hours. If desired, serve with rice.
NOTE This recipe was tested with regular (full-fat) coconut milk. Light coconut milk contains less fat.

ORANGE POMEGRANATE SALMON

A colorful, festive salmon dish makes an impressive addition to your holiday table—and it's as delicious as it is beautiful. What no one will guess? How easy it is to cook. I serve this with roasted baby potatoes and asparagus for a show-stopping holiday meal.
—Thomas Faglon, Somerset, NJ

PREP: 10 MIN. • **BAKE:** 25 MIN. • **MAKES:** 4 SERVINGS

1 small red onion, thinly sliced
1 skinned salmon fillet (about 2 lbs.)
½ tsp. salt
1 medium navel orange, thinly sliced
1 cup pomegranate seeds
2 Tbsp. extra virgin olive oil
1 Tbsp. minced fresh dill

1. Preheat oven to 375°. Place a 28x18-in. piece of heavy-duty foil in a 15x10x1-in. baking pan. Place onion slices in a single layer on foil. Top with salmon; sprinkle with salt. Arrange orange slices over top. Sprinkle with pomegranate seeds; drizzle with oil. Top with a second piece of foil. Bring edges of foil together on all sides and crimp to seal, forming a large packet.
2. Bake until the salmon just begins to flake easily with a fork, 25-30 minutes. Be careful of escaping steam when opening the packet. Remove to a serving platter; sprinkle with dill.

CRANBERRY BRIE PECAN PINWHEELS

Here's my twist on baked Brie. My family always requests these during the holidays. They are delicious and make the kitchen smell amazing!
—*Jacquie Franklin, Hot Springs, MT*

PREP: 20 MIN. • **BAKE:** 15 MIN. • **MAKES:** ABOUT 2 DOZEN

- 1 lb. Brie cheese, rind removed
- 1 pkg. (17.30 oz.) frozen puff pastry, thawed
- ⅔ cup whole-berry cranberry sauce
- 1 large egg
- 1 Tbsp. water
- ½ cup chopped pecans

1. Preheat oven to 400°. Beat trimmed Brie on medium until smooth and creamy, about 5 minutes.
2. On a lightly floured surface, unfold one sheet of puff pastry; spread half of the Brie to within ½ in. of edges. Spread half the cranberry sauce over the Brie. Starting with a short side, roll up jelly-roll style. Cut crosswise into 12 slices; place slices on parchment paper-lined baking sheets. Whisk egg with water; brush over slices. Sprinkle with chopped pecans. Repeat with the remaining puff pastry. Bake until pinwheels are golden brown, 15-20 minutes.

ROASTED HONEY SWEET POTATOES

Cinnamon and honey bring out the natural earthy sweetness of sweet potatoes in this simple, elegant side dish.
—*Laura Mifsud, Northville, MI*

PREP: 10 MIN. • **BAKE:** 45 • **MAKES:** 12 SERVINGS

- 6 medium sweet potatoes, peeled and cut into 1-in. cubes
- ⅓ cup honey
- ¼ cup olive oil
- 1½ tsp. salt
- 1½ tsp. ground cinnamon
- ½ tsp. pepper

Preheat oven to 375°. Place potatoes in a large bowl. Whisk together honey, oil, salt, cinnamon and pepper; add to the potatoes and toss to coat. Transfer to a greased 15x10x1-in. baking pan. Roast until tender, 45-50 minutes, stirring once.

CREAMY MARINARA GNOCCHI

This recipe has gone through many different trials, but I have come to an easy, tried-and-true method. Whenever I make it for guests, they think I've toiled all day long!
—Darolyn Jones, Fishers, IN

TAKES: 30 MIN. • **MAKES:** 8 SERVINGS

- 2 pkg. (16 oz. each) potato gnocchi
- 1 Tbsp. olive oil
- 3 cups sliced baby portobello mushrooms
- 1 tsp. salt, divided
- ¾ tsp. pepper, divided
- 1 jar (24 oz.) spicy marinara sauce
- 1 carton (15 oz.) whole-milk ricotta cheese
  Minced fresh basil

1. Cook gnocchi according to package directions. Meanwhile, in a large skillet, heat olive oil over medium heat. Add mushrooms, ½ tsp. salt and ½ tsp. pepper; saute 3 minutes. Add marinara sauce. Reduce heat; simmer until slightly thickened, about 10 minutes, stirring frequently. Stir in ricotta cheese and the remaining salt and pepper.
2. Drain the gnocchi; transfer to a serving bowl. Toss with the marinara mixture. Serve with basil.
NOTE Look for potato gnocchi in the pasta or frozen foods section.

Holiday Helper
Gnocchi are Italian dumplings made with potatoes and flour or farina. Eggs and seasonings are added, and the dough is shaped into ropes, cut in pieces and rolled into balls. The balls then are rolled over fork tines, a cheese grater or a special board, making ridges that help the gnocchi cook faster.

CHOCOLATE POMEGRANATE CANDIES

This recipe pairs white and dark chocolate with whole, natural ingredients for an unbelievably delicious treat! These candies are perfect to give as a gift for Christmas.
—Kelly Zdrowak, Orchard Park, NY

TAKES: 10 MIN. + CHILLING
MAKES: ABOUT ½ LB.

- 6 oz. white baking chocolate, coarsely chopped
- ¼ cup flaked coconut, toasted
- ¼ cup pomegranate seeds
- 2 oz. dark chocolate, chopped

1. Line an 8-in. square pan with foil and grease foil with butter; set pan aside. In a microwave, melt white chocolate; stir until smooth. Stir in the coconut and pomegranate seeds.
2. Spread white chocolate mixture into the prepared pan. Melt dark chocolate in the microwave. Drizzle over white chocolate mixture. Refrigerate until chocolate is firm, about 1 hour. Using foil, lift mixture out of pan. Remove foil; break candy into pieces. Store in an airtight container.

SEASONAL
GET-TOGETHERS

*Whether you're gathering for an informal meal,
ringing in the New Year with an elegant dinner party,
or hosting a house full of kids, there's a menu
here that will fit the occasion.*

North Pole Kids' Party

When throwing a party for children, you need food that adds to the fun and that they'll love to eat! From adorable Santa's bellies full of treats to a hot and hearty pizza casserole, these delicious, kid-friendly recipes have you covered!

SANTA'S STUFFED BELLY COOKIES

These surprise-inside cookies are so much fun to give as gifts—just wrap in colored cellophane and tie with a festive ribbon. You can exchange the M&Ms for mini cookies or anything you'd like. If desired, you can color the cookie dough red, too!
—*Crystal Schlueter, Babbitt, MN*

PREP: 1 HOUR • **BAKE:** 10 MIN.
MAKES: 6 STUFFED COOKIES

1½ cups butter, softened
 3 cups sugar
 4 large eggs
 1 tsp. peppermint extract
 1 tsp. vanilla extract
 5 cups all-purpose flour
 2 tsp. baking powder
 1 tsp. salt
ROYAL ICING
3¾ to 4 cups confectioners' sugar
 5 to 6 Tbsp. warm water
   (110° to 115°)
 3 Tbsp. meringue powder
   Red, white, black and gray food
   coloring
   Red and green milk chocolate
   M&M's

1. In a large bowl, cream butter and sugar until light and fluffy. Beat in eggs and extracts. In another bowl, whisk flour, baking powder and salt; gradually beat into the creamed mixture. Divide dough into quarters. Shape each into a disk; wrap in plastic. Refrigerate until firm enough to roll, about 2 hours.
2. Preheat oven to 350°. On a lightly floured surface, roll each portion of dough to ¼-in. thickness. Cut with a floured 4-in. round cutter. Using a floured 3½-in. round cutter, cut centers out of three-fifths of the cookies to make window cookies. (You will need three window cookies for every two solid cookies.) Collect and reroll the dough trimmings to cut more cookies. Place solid and window cookies 2 in. apart on greased baking sheets. Bake until the edges are firm, 8-10 minutes. Remove from pans to wire racks to cool.
3. For royal icing, combine confectioners' sugar, water and meringue powder; beat on low speed just until blended. Beat on

high until stiff peaks form, 4-5 minutes. Separate icing into bowls and tint as desired with red, white, black and gray food coloring. Keep unused icing covered at all times with a damp cloth. If necessary, beat again on high to restore texture.
4. Frost half of the solid cookies with red icing; using a pastry bag, pipe them with black belts, gray buckles and white trim. Pipe white icing around the edges of window cookies and the remaining solid cookies so they will adhere. On each undecorated solid cookie, layer three window cookies; fill the opening with M&M's. Top with a red-frosted cookie. Let stand at room temperature several hours until frosting is dry and firm. Store in an airtight container.

FROTHY FESTIVE PUNCH

If you're looking for something special for those holiday celebrations, this is your punch! The mixture of ice cream and fruit makes a refreshing, delicious treat that the kids will love.
—*Carol Gillespie, Chambersburg, PA*

TAKES: 10 MIN. + STANDING
MAKES: 2½ QT.

1½ qt. vanilla ice cream, softened
 4 cups cold whole milk
 3 cups pineapple juice, chilled
 ½ cup orange juice, chilled
 1 Tbsp. lemon juice
 1 tsp. vanilla extract
 ¼ tsp. almond extract

Combine all ingredients; beat until frothy. Pour into a chilled punch bowl. Let stand for 15-20 minutes or until froth rises to the top.

AMBROSIA FRUIT

You can capture the flavor of fresh fruit any time of year with this recipe. With its combination of canned pineapple, fresh apples and flaky coconut, it brings a bright tropical note to the coldest winter.
—Marsha Ransom, South Haven, MI

TAKES: 15 MIN. + CHILLING
MAKES: 6 SERVINGS

- 1 can (20 oz.) pineapple tidbits
- ¼ cup packed brown sugar
- ½ tsp. grated orange zest
- 2 medium oranges
- 2 medium unpeeled apples, diced
- 1 Tbsp. sweetened shredded coconut

Drain pineapple, reserving ¼ cup of the juice in a saucepan; set pineapple aside. Add brown sugar and orange zest to the juice; heat until the sugar dissolves. Peel and section oranges into a large bowl, reserving any juice; add the apples and pineapple. Add pineapple juice mixture and stir gently. Chill. Just before serving, sprinkle with coconut.

Holiday Helper
Apples freeze well if they are properly prepared. Peel and slice the apples, then drop into Fruit Fresh to keep them from discoloring. Place in boiling water for 2 minutes, then in ice water for 2 minutes. Drain. Pack into plastic freezer bags in premeasured amounts; seal, label and freeze. If you need diced apples, cut the slices after they're defrosted.

HERBED BUBBLE BREAD

It takes just five ingredients to dress up a package of frozen rolls to make this buttery, crusty loaf.
—*Anita Whorton, Powder Springs, GA*

PREP: 10 MIN. + RISING • **BAKE:** 15 MIN. • **MAKES:** 12 SERVINGS

¼ cup butter, melted
1 tsp. garlic powder
1 tsp. dried oregano
½ tsp. dried thyme
1 pkg. (16 oz.) frozen dinner roll dough, thawed

1. In a small bowl, combine butter, garlic powder, oregano and thyme. Cut each roll in half; dip into butter mixture.
2. Arrange cut rolls in a greased 12-cup fluted tube pan. Pour the remaining herb mixture over top. Cover and let rise in a warm place for 1 hour or until doubled.
3. Bake at 350° for 15-20 minutes or until golden brown.

PIZZA LOVER'S CASSEROLE

When you're looking for a surefire crowd-pleaser for a kids' party, it's hard to go wrong with this dish—it delivers the taste of pizza in a convenient and delicious casserole. Pair it with a salad and bread, and you have a great meal for a table full of kids without the pizzeria tab!
—*Jackie Hannahs, Cedar Springs, MI*

PREP: 20 MIN. • **BAKE:** 20 MIN. • **MAKES:** 8 SERVINGS

7 cups uncooked wide egg noodles
1 lb. bulk Italian sausage
2 jars (14 oz. each) pizza sauce
6 oz. sliced pepperoni
2 cups shredded cheddar cheese

1. Preheat oven to 350°. Grease a 13x9-in. baking dish and set aside. Cook noodles according to package directions. Meanwhile, crumble sausage into a large skillet. Cook over medium heat until meat is no longer pink; drain. Add pizza sauce.
2. Drain noodles and add to skillet; toss to coat. Transfer half of the noodle mixture to the prepared baking dish. Layer with half of the pepperoni and cheese. Repeat layers. Bake, uncovered, for 20-25 minutes or until cheese is melted.

HOLIDAY HUMMUS & VEGGIE SANTA TRAY

This festive tray will be the hit of any holiday party and will even get kids to eat their veggies! If your guests don't like cauliflower, substitute crumbled feta and serve pita chips around the platter for dipping.
—*Crystal Schlueter, Babbitt, MN*

TAKES: 15 MIN. • **MAKES:** 12 SERVINGS

- 1 carton (17 oz.) hummus
- 1 medium head cauliflower, broken into florets
- 1½ cups cherry tomatoes
- 2 small sweet red peppers, thinly sliced
- ½ cup ranch salad dressing, optional
- 1 piece string cheese (1 oz.)
- 1 sliced ripe olive
- 1 sweet red pepper strip
- ½ tsp. paprika, optional
  Additional cauliflower florets, cherry tomatoes and sweet red pepper slices

1. Start making a Santa face by spreading hummus in an 8-in. circle over a large platter. For Santa's beard, place several cauliflower florets at the bottom of the hummus circle. For the rim of the stocking cap, place florets at the top of the circle. Use tomatoes and red pepper slices to form the cap; add cauliflower florets to create a pompom for it. (If desired, use a small bowl of ranch dressing instead.)
2. Place one tomato in the center of the hummus circle for the nose. Cut string cheese in half lengthwise, then cut in half crosswise; use two cheese pieces for eyebrows and two for a mustache. For eyes, cut an olive slice in half. Shape a red pepper strip into a smile. Sprinkle paprika across cheeks if desired.
3. Refrigerate until serving. Serve with additional cauliflower, tomatoes and pepper slices for dipping.

RASPBERRY GELATIN JEWELS

Kids love this jiggly gelatin salad, and honestly, so do the adults! It's always going to be on my holiday buffet.
—*Brenda Leonard, APO, AP*

TAKES: 10 MIN. + CHILLING
MAKES: 8 SERVINGS

- 1 pkg. (6 oz.) raspberry gelatin
- 1½ cups boiling water
- 1 can (20 oz.) unsweetened crushed pineapple, drained
- 1 pkg. (12 oz.) frozen unsweetened raspberries

Grease an 11x7-in. dish; set aside. In a large bowl, dissolve the gelatin in boiling water. Stir in fruit. Pour into the prepared dish. Refrigerate for 4 hours or until firm. Cut into squares.

Ornament Exchange

In this special gift exchange, every guest gives and receives
a single ornament to decorate their tree, and the focus is on
fun and fellowship. Make the menu hearty, comforting and casual,
served as a sit-down dinner or a standout buffet!

HONEY-SOY GLAZED PORK ROAST

This succulent pork roast is scented with warm spices and has a tempting dark brown-sugar, honey-glazed lacquered finish. This recipe also works beautifully with lamb.
—Ellen Ottoson, Springfield, OH

PREP: 20 MIN. + STANDING
BAKE: 3¼ HOURS + STANDING
MAKES: 8 SERVINGS

- 1 bone-in pork shoulder butt roast (4 lbs.)
- 1 Tbsp. ground cinnamon
- 1 Tbsp. ground ginger
- 1½ tsp. garlic powder
- ¼ tsp. salt
- 2 tsp. whole cloves

GLAZE
- ¼ cup honey
- ¼ cup packed brown sugar
- 1 Tbsp. soy sauce or reduced-sodium soy sauce
- 1 tsp. ground cinnamon
- 1 tsp. ground ginger
- ¼ tsp. garlic powder

1. Pat meat dry. Combine cinnamon, ginger, garlic powder and salt; sprinkle mixture over meat, patting to adhere. Insert whole cloves into roast about 1 in. apart. Place on a rack in a 15x10x1-in. baking pan lined with foil. Let stand for 30 minutes, then bake at 300° until fork-tender, about 3 hours. Remove from oven; discard the cloves. Increase oven setting to 425°.
2. Microwave glaze ingredients on high until sugar dissolves, about 1 minute. Brush glaze over roast. Return roast to oven until dark brown and caramelized, 12-15 minutes, brushing with the glaze halfway through cooking. Remove from oven; let stand 45 minutes before slicing.

CHIVE BISCUIT ORNAMENTS

We used a star, but you can use any shape of cutter you like to create these tender bites.
—Taste of Home *Test Kitchen*

TAKES: 30 MIN. • **MAKES:** 1 DOZEN

- 3¼ cups biscuit/baking mix
- ½ cup shredded cheddar cheese
- 1 Tbsp. minced chives
- 1 tsp. crushed red pepper flakes
- 1 cup heavy whipping cream
- 12 whole chives

1. Preheat oven to 450°. In a large bowl, combine the biscuit mix, cheese, minced chives and pepper flakes. Stir in cream just until moistened.
2. Turn onto a lightly floured surface; knead 8-10 times. Pat to ½-in. thickness. Cut with a floured 3-in. star-shaped cookie cutter. Using a ½-in. round cookie cutter, cut a hole near top of each biscuit.
3. Place 2 in. apart on ungreased baking sheets. Bake for 8-10 minutes or until golden brown. Remove to wire racks to cool. Thread one whole chive through each biscuit hole; tie a knot. Serve warm.

CARAMEL GLAZE

CARAMEL GLAZE
3 Tbsp. butter
⅓ cup packed brown sugar
2 Tbsp. 2% milk
¾ cup confectioners' sugar
1 tsp. vanilla extract

1. Place egg whites in a large bowl; let stand at room temperature 30 minutes.
2. Meanwhile, preheat oven to 350°. Sift flour, sugar, baking powder, baking soda, cinnamon, salt, cloves and ginger together twice; place in another large bowl.
3. In a small bowl, whisk the egg yolks, coffee, honey and oil until smooth. Add to the flour mixture; beat until well blended.
4. Add cream of tartar to the egg whites; with clean beaters, beat on high speed just until stiff but not dry. Fold a fourth of the whites into batter, then fold in the remaining whites.
5. Gently transfer batter to an ungreased 10-in. tube pan. Bake on the lowest oven rack for 50-60 minutes or until the top springs back when lightly touched. Immediately invert pan; cool completely, about 1½ hours.
6. In a small heavy saucepan, melt butter. Stir in brown sugar and milk. Bring to a boil; cook over medium heat until sugar is dissolved. Stir in confectioners' sugar and vanilla; cook until thickened, about 5 minutes.
7. Run a knife around sides and center tube of pan. Remove to a serving plate.

Holiday Helper
To cut down on the mess of measuring honey—and to improve your measuring accuracy—wipe the inside of your measuring cup with a little bit of oil before filling it with honey. The honey will come out easily, and you'll get the full measure without having to scrape the cup.

HOLIDAY HONEY CAKE

Thirty-five years ago, I gave a friend of mine a platter of home-baked Christmas cookies. The very next day, she brought over this delicious Hannukah cake. Naturally, we exchanged recipes and my family and I have been enjoying this moist and flavorful honey cake ever since!
—Kristine Chayes, Smithtown, NY

PREP: 20 MIN. + STANDING
BAKE: 50 MIN. + COOLING
MAKES: 12 SERVINGS

3 large eggs, separated
3½ cups all-purpose flour
1 cup sugar
2½ tsp. baking powder
1 tsp. baking soda
1 tsp. ground cinnamon
½ tsp. salt
½ tsp. ground cloves
¼ tsp. ground ginger
1⅓ cups brewed coffee
1⅓ cups honey
¼ cup canola oil
¼ tsp. cream of tartar

HOLIDAY POTATO BAKE

I have made this at Thanksgiving and Christmas for the past several years; now my family requests this dish all the time, even when it's not a holiday! Happy, cherished family memories.
—Vickie West, Long Beach, CA

PREP: 25 MIN. • **BAKE:** 15 MIN. • **MAKES:** 12 SERVINGS

- 3   lbs. potatoes, peeled and cut into ½-in. cubes
- 3   medium carrots, shredded
- 3   celery ribs, trimmed and diced
- 1   medium onion, diced
- 2   cups shredded sharp cheddar cheese, divided
- ½   cup butter, cubed
- 4   oz. cream cheese, softened
- ¼   cup plus 1 Tbsp. minced fresh parsley, divided
- ½   tsp. salt
- ½   tsp. pepper
- ¼   cup chopped ripe olives

1. Preheat oven to 350°. Place potatoes, carrots, celery and onion in a Dutch oven; add water to cover. Cook, covered, until vegetables are almost tender, 8-10 minutes. Drain. Return to Dutch oven; toss with 1¾ cups of cheddar cheese, the butter, cream cheese, ¼ cup parsley, salt and pepper.

2. Transfer to a greased 13x9-in. baking dish. Top with olives and the remaining cheese. Bake, uncovered, until bubbly and the cheese is melted, 15-20 minutes. To serve, sprinkle with the remaining parsley.

DAD'S CREAMED PEAS & PEARL ONIONS

When I was growing up, it was a family tradition to make creamed peas with pearl onions for every Christmas dinner. My dad would not be happy if he didn't see this dish on the table...it was his favorite! I made the dish for my own family while our kids were growing up; my daughter now makes this dish for her family.
—Nancy Heishman, Las Vegas, NV

TAKES: 25 MIN. • **MAKES:** 6 SERVINGS

- 5 cups frozen peas (about 20 oz.), thawed and drained
- 2 cups frozen pearl onions (about 9 oz.), thawed and drained
- 2 celery ribs, finely chopped
- ¾ cup chicken broth
- ½ tsp. salt
- ½ tsp. pepper
- ½ tsp. dried thyme
- ½ cup sour cream
- 10 bacon strips, cooked and crumbled
- ¾ cup salted cashews

In a large skillet, combine the first seven ingredients; bring to a boil. Reduce heat to medium; cook, uncovered, 8-10 minutes or until onions are tender and most of liquid is evaporated, stirring occasionally. Remove from heat; stir in sour cream. Top with bacon and cashews.

MAPLE WINTER SQUASH CASSEROLE

This scrumptious casserole combines pumpkin and two different kinds of squash in a creamy, savory mix. It's so good with three kinds of squash, but feel free to use whatever combination you have, or just go with a single variety.
—Joanne Iovino, Kings Park, NY

PREP: 1¼ HOURS • **BAKE:** 35 MIN. • **MAKES:** 12 SERVINGS

- 1 medium pie pumpkin (3 lbs.)
- 1 medium butternut squash (3 lbs.)
- 1 medium acorn squash (1½ lbs.)
- ¼ cup sugar
- ¼ cup maple syrup
- ¼ cup butter, softened
- ½ tsp. salt
- ½ tsp. ground cinnamon

TOPPING
- ½ cup all-purpose flour
- ½ cup packed brown sugar
- ½ cup old-fashioned oats
- ½ cup cold butter, cubed
- ½ cup chopped walnuts

1. Preheat oven to 400°. Grease two 15x10x1-in. baking pans; set aside. Cut pumpkin and squashes in half lengthwise; discard the seeds or save for toasting. Place in prepared pans, cut side down. Bake, uncovered, 40-50 minutes or until tender.
2. Cool slightly; scoop out pulp and place in a large bowl. Mash pulp with sugar, maple syrup, butter, salt and cinnamon. Transfer to a greased 13x9-in. baking dish. In a small bowl, mix flour, brown sugar and oats; cut in butter until crumbly. Stir in walnuts. Sprinkle over the squash mixture. Bake, uncovered, 35-40 minutes or until bubbly and topping is golden brown.

SMOKED PIMIENTO CHEESE CROSTINI

Pimiento cheese has long been a favorite in our family, so these bite-sized appetizers are a treat! I add Worcestershire sauce and hot sauce to give them a little kick. Caramelized onions create another layer of flavor. You can make the cheese and onions three to five days in advance; they store well. If you need to save time, you can use premade jalapeno pimiento cheese.
—Caitlyn Bunch, Trenton, GA

PREP: 50 MIN. • **BAKE:** 10 MIN.
MAKES: 4 DOZEN

48 slices French baguette (¼ in. thick)
CARAMELIZED ONIONS
2 Tbsp. canola oil
2 large onions, chopped
½ cup beef broth
2 Tbsp. balsamic vinegar
1½ tsp. sugar
¼ tsp. salt
¼ tsp. pepper
  Dash dried rosemary, crushed
  Dash dried thyme
PIMIENTO CHEESE
2½ cups shredded smoked
  Gouda cheese
2½ cups shredded sharp
  cheddar cheese
½ cup mayonnaise
2 jars (4 oz. each) diced
  pimientos, drained
1 tsp. Worcestershire sauce
1 tsp. hot pepper sauce
½ tsp. garlic powder
½ tsp. pepper
9 bacon strips, cooked and crumbled

1. Preheat oven to 400°. Place bread slices on baking sheets. Bake for 4-6 minutes or until light brown.

2. In a large skillet, heat oil over medium heat. Add onions; cook and stir for 4-6 minutes or until softened. Stir in broth, vinegar, sugar and seasonings. Reduce heat to medium-low; cook for 12-15 minutes or until the liquid is evaporated, stirring occasionally.

3. In a large bowl, toss cheeses; beat in mayonnaise, pimientos, Worcestershire sauce, pepper sauce and seasonings. Spread 1 tablespoon of the cheese mixture over each baguette slice; top with 2 teaspoons of the onion mixture. Sprinkle with bacon. Bake 3-4 minutes or until the cheese is melted.

Champagne Toast

Look back at the past year and forward to the new
with an elegant dinner party and a glass of bubbly!
Set the tone with a menu that's classic and stylish—
just the thing for a sparkling winter evening celebration.

SPINACH & FETA FLANK STEAK

While this dish may look difficult to pull off, it's actually quite easy to do. It's pretty enough for holiday meals but so simple you can make it for a weeknight dinner.
—Josh Carter, Birmingham, AL

PREP: 15 MIN. • **BAKE:** 40 MIN.
MAKES: 6 SERVINGS

- 1　beef flank steak (1½ to 2 lbs.)
- 1　pkg. (10 oz.) frozen chopped spinach, thawed and squeezed dry
- 1　pkg. (4 oz.) crumbled feta cheese
- ⅓　cup minced fresh parsley
- 3　Tbsp. snipped fresh dill
- 3　Tbsp. chopped green onions
- 1　tsp. salt
- ½　tsp. pepper
- 1　Tbsp. olive oil

1. Preheat oven to 400°. Cut steak horizontally from a long side to within ½ in. of opposite side. Open the steak so it lies flat; cover with plastic wrap. Flatten to ¼-in. thickness. Remove plastic.
2. Combine the spinach, cheese, parsley, dill and onions. Spread over the steak to within 1 in. of edges. Roll up jelly-roll style, starting with a short side; tie with kitchen string. Sprinkle with salt and pepper.
3. In a large skillet, brown meat in oil on all sides; transfer to the greased rack of a shallow roasting pan. Bake until meat reaches desired doneness (for medium-rare, a thermometer should read 135°; medium, 140°; medium-well, 145°), 40-45 minutes. Remove from oven and let stand 15 minutes. To serve, remove string; cut into 1-in.-thick slices.

ROSEMARY ROASTED POTATOES WITH CARAMELIZED ONIONS

Roasted potatoes are amazing on their own, but add some rosemary and caramelized onions and they're over-the-top delicious!
—Mary Jones, Athens, OH

PREP: 15 MIN. • **BAKE:** 45 MIN.
MAKES: 6 SERVINGS

- 2　lbs. small red potatoes, quartered
- 2　garlic cloves, minced
- 1　Tbsp. olive oil
- 2　tsp. minced fresh rosemary or ½ tsp. dried rosemary, crushed
- ½　tsp. minced fresh thyme or ⅛ tsp. dried thyme
- ¼　tsp. salt
- ¼　tsp. pepper

CARAMELIZED ONIONS
- 2　large sweet onions, chopped
- 2　Tbsp. olive oil
- 1　Tbsp. sugar
- 2　tsp. balsamic vinegar

1. Preheat oven to 425°. In a large bowl, combine the first seven ingredients; toss to coat. Transfer to a greased 15x10x1-in. baking pan.
2. Bake for 45-50 minutes or until the potatoes are tender, stirring once.
3. Meanwhile, in a large skillet, saute onions in oil until softened. Stir in sugar. Reduce heat to medium-low; cook for 30-40 minutes or until deep golden brown, stirring occasionally. Stir in balsamic vinegar.
4. Transfer roasted potatoes to a large bowl; stir in caramelized onions.

CREAMY CHICKEN VOL-AU-VENT

My friends and I have been getting together for ladies lunches for years. These pretty vol-au-vents are the perfect no-fuss fancy food. While they may look complicated, they're actually simple and fun to make.
—Shauna Havey, Roy, UT

PREP: 20 MIN. + CHILLING • **BAKE:** 20 MIN.
MAKES: 6 SERVINGS

- 1 pkg. (17.30 oz.) frozen puff pastry, thawed
- 1 large egg
- 1 Tbsp. water
- 6 bacon strips
- 2 medium leeks (white portion only), sliced
- 1 medium sweet yellow pepper, diced
- 1 cup shredded rotisserie chicken
- 8 oz. cream cheese, softened
- ¼ tsp. salt
- ¼ tsp. pepper
  Minced fresh parsley
  Additional ground pepper

1. Preheat oven to 400°. On a lightly floured surface, unfold one puff pastry sheet. Using a 3¼-in. round cutter, cut out six circles. Place on a parchment paper-lined baking sheet.

2. Unfold the remaining pastry sheet. Cut out six more circles with the 3¼-in. cutter; with a 2½-in. round cutter, cut centers out of the circles to make rings. Place rings on top of the circles on the baking sheet. Place the center circles on the baking sheet as well. In a small bowl, whisk egg and water; brush over the pastries. Chill 15 minutes. Bake until dark golden brown, 20-25 minutes. Cool on a wire rack.

3. Meanwhile, in a large skillet, cook bacon over medium heat until crisp. Remove to paper towels to drain. Discard all but 1 Tbsp. of the drippings. Add leeks and pepper to the reserved drippings; cook and stir over medium-high heat until tender, 5-7 minutes. Reduce heat to low; stir in bacon, chicken, cream cheese, salt and pepper. Cook and stir until blended; remove from heat.

4. When cool enough to handle, hollow out pastries with a small knife. Fill with chicken mixture. Sprinkle with parsley and pepper. Serve with the small center pastries on the side.

LEMON-SESAME GREEN BEAN SALAD

There's a kabob shop in Charlottesville, Virginia, called Sticks with wonderful sides, including sesame beans. I love them so much that I had to make my own version. You can use fresh or frozen green beans, and haricots verts (French green beans) work well, too. This salad only gets better as it sits, so it's great (and convenient!) to make a day or two in advance.
—Dyan Carlson, Kents Store, VA

TAKES: 20 MIN. • **MAKES:** 6 SERVINGS

- 1½ lbs. fresh green beans, trimmed and cut into 1-in. pieces
- 3 Tbsp. sesame oil
- 1 Tbsp. lemon juice
- 3 Tbsp. sesame seeds, toasted
- 3 tsp. grated lemon peel
- 2 garlic cloves, minced
- ½ tsp. salt
- ⅛ to ¼ tsp. crushed red pepper flakes
- ⅛ tsp. pepper

1. In a large saucepan, bring 4 cups water to a boil. Add green beans; cook, uncovered, 3-4 minutes or just until crisp-tender. Remove green beans; drain well.
2. Whisk the remaining ingredients until blended. Pour over green beans; toss to coat. Serve hot or at room temperature.

BLOOD ORANGES WITH PROSECCO SABAYON

I love treating my dinner guests to this elegant, unusual dessert. The bright, vivid colors of this dish are perfect for the holidays. Omit the Prosecco when serving to children.
—Jerry Gulley, Pleasant Prairie, WI

TAKES: 25 MIN. • **MAKES:** 6 SERVINGS (¾ CUP SAUCE)

- 6 medium blood oranges, peeled and cut into ¼-in. slices
- 1 vanilla bean, split
- ¼ cup sugar plus 3 Tbsp. sugar, divided
- ½ cup Prosecco or sparkling white wine, divided
  Dash salt
- 3 large egg yolks

1. Arrange orange slices on a serving platter or individual plates. Scrape vanilla bean seeds into a small bowl. Add ¼ cup sugar, ¼ cup Prosecco and salt; combine and drizzle over oranges. Refrigerate until serving.
2. In a double boiler or metal bowl over simmering water, constantly whisk the egg yolks, the remaining sugar and the Prosecco until the mixture reaches 160° and coats the back of a spoon. Drizzle over oranges. Serve immediately.
NOTE With their bright rosy color, blood oranges can make a stunning dessert but they are available for only a short amount of time. Feel free to substitute navel oranges, tangerines or pink grapefruit when the blood orange season is over.

CRAB, GRAPEFRUIT & WATERCRESS SALAD

The flavor of crab is wonderful with grapefruit, avocado and watercress. The addition of a delicious poppy seed dressing makes this simple-to-prepare salad extra special!
—Lisa Speer, Palm Beach, FL

TAKES: 15 MIN. • **MAKES:** 4 SERVINGS

- 3 Tbsp. champagne vinegar
- 3 Tbsp. honey
- 2 Tbsp. chopped sweet onion
- 1 tsp. Dijon mustard
- ½ tsp. sea salt
- ½ cup canola oil
- 1 Tbsp. poppy seeds
- 2 cans (6½ oz. each) jumbo lump crabmeat, drained
- 6 cups watercress
- 2½ cups fresh grapefruit segments
- 12 cherry tomatoes, halved
- 1 medium ripe avocado, peeled, pitted and sliced
- 1½ tsp. white grapefruit juice

1. Process first five ingredients in a blender or food processor until smooth. While processing, gradually add oil in a steady stream until dressing thickens. Pour into a serving bowl; stir in poppy seeds.
2. Transfer ¼ cup salad dressing to a small bowl. Toss with the crabmeat. Add the remaining ingredients to the serving bowl; gently toss until combined. Top with the crab mixture.

Holiday Helper
Be sure to get jumbo lump crabmeat for this recipe. While regular lump crabmeat works well for cooked recipes, the more tender and flavorful jumbo crab is better for a fresh salad.

CREAMY MUSHROOM-THYME SOUP

I pick the mushrooms for this soup in the beautiful forests of the Pacific Northwest. The combination of wild mushrooms, sherry, herbs and shallots make for a sophisticated spin on mushroom soup.
—Kristy Arnett, Stevenson, WA

PREP: 15 MIN. • **COOK:** 40 MIN.
MAKES: 8 SERVINGS

- ¼ cup butter, cubed
- 1 shallot, finely chopped
- 1 lb. fresh chanterelle mushrooms or other wild mushrooms, coarsely chopped
- 1 tsp. minced fresh thyme
- ¼ cup all-purpose flour
- ½ tsp. salt
- ¼ tsp. pepper
- 6 cups chicken stock
- 1 cup heavy whipping cream
- ½ cup cream sherry

1. In a 6-qt. stockpot, melt butter over medium-high heat. Add the shallot; cook and stir for 1-2 minutes or until tender. Add mushrooms and thyme; cook 5 minutes longer.
2. Stir in the flour, salt and pepper until blended; gradually whisk in stock. Bring to a boil. Reduce heat; simmer, uncovered, 15-20 minutes to allow flavors to blend.
3. Puree the soup using an immersion blender. Or, cool soup slightly and puree in batches in a blender; return soup to pan. Add cream and sherry; heat through.

WINTER SALADS

In a season known for rich, hearty and filling foods, a cool salad is a refreshing addition. Let these colorful and delicious seasonal salads dress up your holiday table!

WINTER BEET SALAD

To save time, you can use packaged salad greens in this recipe. The earthy sweetness of the beets, the bright tang of the oranges and the anise-flavored zing of the fennel are the perfect holiday combination, and the simple dressing is easy to assemble.
—Taste of Home *Test Kitchen*

PREP: 20 MIN. • **BAKE:** 1 HOUR + COOLING
MAKES: 4 SERVINGS

- 2 medium fresh beets
- 1 pkg. (5 oz.) mixed salad greens
- 2 medium navel oranges, peeled and sliced
- 1 small fennel bulb, halved and thinly sliced
- ¼ cup chopped hazelnuts, toasted

DRESSING

- 3 Tbsp. olive oil
- 2 Tbsp. orange juice
- 1 Tbsp. balsamic vinegar
- 2 tsp. grated orange zest
- ¼ tsp. onion powder

Preheat oven to 425°. Cut slits in beets; place on a baking sheet. Bake until tender, about 1 hour. When cool enough to handle, peel beets and cut into wedges. Divide greens among salad plates; top with beets, oranges, fennel and hazelnuts. Combine dressing ingredients in a jar with a tight-fitting lid; shake well. Drizzle over salads.

NOTE To toast nuts, bake in a shallow pan in a 350° oven for 5-10 minutes or cook in a skillet over low heat until lightly browned, stirring occasionally.

MARINATED CAULIFLOWER SALAD

I often serve this as an appetizer alongside a meat and cheese tray. But it also works nicely as a side dish.
—Stephanie Hase, Lyons, CO

TAKES: 20 MIN. + MARINATING
MAKES: 12 SERVINGS

- ¼ cup red wine vinegar
- ¼ cup olive oil
- 2 Tbsp. water
- 5 cups fresh cauliflowerets
- 1 bay leaf
- 1 garlic clove, minced
- ¼ tsp. salt
- ¼ tsp. coarsely ground pepper
- 1 medium carrot, shredded
- 1 small red onion, chopped
- ¼ cup minced fresh parsley
- ¼ tsp. dried basil

1. In a small saucepan, bring vinegar, oil and water just to a boil.
2. Meanwhile, place next five ingredients in a large heatproof bowl. Add hot oil mixture; toss to coat. Refrigerate, covered, at least 6 hours or overnight, stirring occasionally.
3. Add carrot, onion, parsley and basil; toss to coat. Refrigerate salad, covered, 2 hours longer. Discard bay leaf. Serve with a slotted spoon.

HOLIDAY RICE SALAD

It's nice to prepare a salad like this when entertaining because it can be made ahead and doesn't take up valuable oven space.
—Debra Walter, Huntington Woods, MI

TAKES: 10 MIN. + CHILLING • **MAKES:** 14 SERVINGS

 7 cups cooked wild rice, cooled
 1 cup chopped pecans, toasted
 1 cup thinly sliced green onions
 ½ cup dried cranberries
 ½ cup dried cherries or additional dried cranberries
 ½ cup golden raisins
 ½ cup minced fresh parsley
 ¼ cup slivered almonds, toasted
 1 Tbsp. chopped fresh mint or 1 tsp. dried mint flakes

DRESSING
 ½ cup orange juice
 ⅓ cup cider vinegar
 ¼ cup olive oil
 1 Tbsp. lime juice
 2 tsp. sugar
 1 tsp. salt
 ⅛ tsp. pepper

Combine the first nine ingredients. In a jar with a tight-fitting lid, combine dressing ingredients; shake well. Pour over rice mixture and toss to coat. Refrigerate, covered, for 2 hours or until serving.

NOTE To toast nuts, bake in a shallow pan in a 350° oven for 5-10 minutes or cook in a skillet over low heat until lightly browned, stirring occasionally.

BRUSSELS SPROUTS SALAD

My husband and I love Brussels sprouts, so I'm always looking for new ways to use them. I most often serve this colorful salad with roast pork or duck.
—Nancy Korondan, Yorkville, IL

TAKES: 20 MIN. • **MAKES:** 8 SERVINGS

 1½ lbs. fresh Brussels sprouts, trimmed and halved
 2 green onions, chopped
 ½ cup olive oil
 2 Tbsp. lemon juice
 1 to 1½ tsp. Dijon mustard
 ½ tsp. salt
 ½ tsp. dried thyme
 ¼ tsp. pepper
 1 large bunch red leaf lettuce or radicchio, torn
 2 Tbsp. slivered almonds, toasted

1. Place Brussels sprouts in a large saucepan; add 1 in. of water. Bring to a boil. Reduce heat; simmer, covered, until tender, 8-10 minutes. Drain; rinse with cold water and pat dry. Combine with green onions.

2. Whisk together next six ingredients. Toss 2 Tbsp. of dressing with lettuce; transfer to a serving bowl. Pour the remaining dressing over the Brussels sprouts and onions; toss to coat. Mound on top of the lettuce. Sprinkle with almonds.

NOTE To toast nuts, bake in a shallow pan in a 350° oven for 5-10 minutes or cook in a skillet over low heat until lightly browned, stirring occasionally.

FENNEL SALAD WITH CITRUS DRESSING

My family really enjoys crunchy fennel, which pairs well with citrus vinaigrette. The salad makes a great addition to any meal. To save time, the dressing can be prepared up to three days ahead.
—Denise Elder, Hanover, ON

TAKES: 20 MIN+ CHILLING • **MAKES:** 5 SERVINGS

1	large fennel bulb, thinly sliced
1	small apple, thinly sliced
¼	cup sliced sweet onion

DRESSING
⅓	cup olive oil
½	tsp. grated lemon zest
2	Tbsp. lemon juice
½	tsp. grated orange zest
2	Tbsp. orange juice
½	tsp. Dijon mustard
½	tsp. salt
⅛	tsp. pepper

Combine fennel, apple and onion. In another bowl, whisk together dressing ingredients. Pour over salad; toss to coat. Refrigerate until serving.

APRICOT SALAD

Colorful gelatin salad adds a spot of brightness to any table and blends well with a holiday feast. As children, we didn't know if it should be a salad or dessert, with its smooth texture and delicate flavor!
—Fae Fisher, Callao, VA

TAKES: 20 MIN. + CHILLING • **MAKES:** 10 SERVINGS

2	pkg. (3 oz. each) apricot gelatin
2	cups boiling water
1	pkg. (8 oz.) cream cheese, softened
1	cup whole milk
1	can (20 oz.) crushed pineapple, undrained
1¾	cups frozen whipped topping, thawed
	Canned apricots and fresh mint leaves, optional

1. Dissolve gelatin in boiling water; set aside. Beat cream cheese until smooth; gradually beat in milk until smooth. Stir in the gelatin. Add pineapple, mixing well. Refrigerate.
2. When the mixture begins to thicken, fold in whipped topping. Pour into a 2½-qt. serving bowl. Refrigerate at least 2 hours. If desired, serve with canned apricots and fresh mint leaves.

JAMBALAYA RICE SALAD

My cold rice salad has a little hint of spice for a classic jambalaya-style kick. Shrimp, tomatoes, ham and peppers give it holiday colors and a delightful texture.
—Karen Rahn, Hixon, TN

PREP: 20 MIN. • **COOK:** 15 MIN. + CHILLING
MAKES: 8 SERVINGS

1⅓ cups uncooked long grain rice
2 Tbsp. olive oil
2 cups cubed fully cooked ham
⅓ cup chopped onion

2 garlic cloves, minced
1 tsp. dried oregano
1 tsp. dried thyme
½ to 1 tsp. salt
¼ to ½ tsp. cayenne pepper
¼ tsp. pepper
⅓ cup red wine vinegar
1½ lbs. peeled and deveined cooked shrimp (31-40 per lb.)
2 celery ribs, thinly sliced
1 small green pepper, julienned
1 small sweet red pepper, julienned
1 pint cherry tomatoes, halved
2 green onions, sliced

1. Prepare rice according to package directions; cool. Heat oil over medium heat. Add ham and onion; cook and stir until onion is tender, about 5 minutes. Add next six ingredients; cook and stir 2 minutes. Remove from heat; stir in vinegar.

2. Combine rice, ham mixture, shrimp, celery and peppers. Refrigerate, covered, at least 2 hours. Add tomatoes; toss to combine. Sprinkle with onions.

PAPER WREATH CENTERPIECE

Simple folded paper fans make a beautiful wreath-themed centerpiece! Cut a doughnut shape out of green foam board to fit around a hurricane candle holder. Cut roughly thirty 1½x10-in. strips of green card stock or patterned craft paper, and fold each strip accordion-style. Fan out each strip and glue it to the wreath base, trimming as needed. Continue to add strips to cover the entire base. (Cut more strips if needed.)

For the bow, cut one 1½-in.-wide and two 1-in.-wide strips of red paper. Bend the ends of the 1½-in.-wide strip to the center, trimming the strip as needed and gluing the ends in place to form the bow loops. Wrap the 1-in. strip around the center of the loops; trim and glue on the back to make the bow knot. Cut the remaining strip into two equal tails; glue them in place and trim the ends in dovetails. Glue the bow to the wreath. Let the glue dry completely before placing the wreath over the candle holder. Remember: Never leave a lit candle unattended!

CITRUS AVOCADO SALAD

This recipe nicely showcases grapefruit and oranges, which are at their peak around the holidays. Citrus fruits pair well with a sweet poppy-seed dressing.
—Sonia Candler, Edmonton, AB

TAKES: 10 MIN. • **MAKES:** 12 SERVINGS

- 12 cups torn salad greens
- 2 medium grapefruit, peeled and sectioned
- 2 medium navel oranges, peeled and sectioned
- 2 medium ripe avocados, peeled, pitted and cut into chunks
- 1 small red onion, thinly sliced and separated into rings

DRESSING
- ½ cup canola oil
- ¼ cup sugar
- 3 Tbsp. lemon juice
- 1½ tsp. poppy seeds
- ½ tsp. salt
- ¼ tsp. ground mustard
- ¼ tsp. grated onion

Gently toss the first five ingredients. In a jar with a tight-fitting lid, combine the dressing ingredients; shake well. Drizzle over the salad; toss to coat.

LOADED BAKED POTATO SALAD

I revamped my mother's potato salad recipe to taste more like baked potatoes with all the fixin's. It's now the most requested dish at family gatherings. Even my mother asked for the recipe!
—Jackie Deckard, Solsberry, IN

PREP: 20 MIN. • **BAKE:** 40 MIN. + COOLING
MAKES: 20 SERVINGS

- 5 lbs. small unpeeled red potatoes, cubed
- 1 tsp. salt
- ½ tsp. pepper
- 8 hard-boiled large eggs, chopped
- 1 lb. sliced bacon, cooked and crumbled
- 2 cups shredded cheddar cheese
- 1 sweet onion, chopped
- 3 dill pickles, chopped
- 1½ cups sour cream
- 1 cup mayonnaise
- 2 to 3 tsp. prepared mustard

1. Preheat oven to 425°. Sprinkle potatoes with salt and pepper; bake, uncovered, in a greased 15x10x1-in. baking pan until tender, 40-45 minutes. Cool in pan on a wire rack.

2. Combine potatoes with the next five ingredients. In another bowl, combine sour cream, mayonnaise and mustard; pour over the potato mixture, tossing to coat. Refrigerate until serving.

Holiday Helper

Very fresh eggs can be more difficult to peel. The American Egg Board recommends storing eggs in the refrigerator for seven to 10 days before cooking. After cooking, crackle the shells by gently tapping on the kitchen counter. Eggshells will come off more easily and without tearing the whites when they're in smaller pieces.

SWEET POTATO WALDORF SALAD

I'd promised to bring a potato salad to a party but had no regular potatoes on hand. The sweet potatoes were there, so I revised my regular recipe and a new dish was born! This version serves two, but you can easily multiply the ingredients to feed more.
—Lois Jeffery, Chesterland, OH

PREP: 10 MIN. • **COOK:** 25 MIN. + CHILLING
MAKES: 2 SERVINGS

- 1 small sweet potato
- 1 medium apple, cubed
- ¼ cup chopped celery
- 2 Tbsp. chopped walnuts
- 2 Tbsp. golden raisins
- 2 Tbsp. miniature marshmallows
- 2 Tbsp. mayonnaise
- 2 Tbsp. sour cream
- ½ tsp. lemon juice
  Leaf lettuce, optional

1. Place sweet potato in a small saucepan; add water to cover. Bring to a boil. Reduce heat; cook, covered, until just tender, about 20 minutes. Drain and cool completely.

2. Peel potato and cube; combine with next five ingredients. In another bowl, combine mayonnaise, sour cream and lemon juice; pour over salad, and gently toss. Refrigerate, covered, for at least 1 hour. If desired, serve on lettuce.

CHRISTMAS BROCCOLI SALAD

What could be more Christmasy than a red and green dish? Once people taste this crisp, lightly dressed salad, I never have to worry about leftovers.
—LuAnn Kessi, Eddyville, OR

TAKES: 10 MIN. + CHILLING
MAKES: 10 SERVINGS

4½ cups fresh broccoli florets
3 cups chopped sweet red pepper
10 bacon strips, cooked and crumbled
⅓ cup sliced green onions
¼ cup chopped pecans
¾ cup mayonnaise
1 Tbsp. cider vinegar
Dash pepper

Combine the first five ingredients. In a small bowl, stir together the remaining ingredients until smooth. Pour over the broccoli mixture; toss to coat. Refrigerate, covered, until serving.

SWEET ORANGE & ALMOND SALAD

As far as I'm concerned, the citrusy aroma of oranges is a must at Christmastime! This dessert salad looks bright and appealing served in a glass bowl, and it's a light and easy way to finish off a hearty holiday meal.
—Billie Moss, Walnut Creek, CA

TAKES: 15 MIN. + CHILLING
MAKES: 8 SERVINGS

8 to 10 large oranges, any variety
¼ cup thawed orange juice concentrate or Triple Sec
½ cup sweetened shredded coconut
½ cup sliced almonds
½ cup confectioners' sugar

1. Peel oranges, removing as much white membrane as possible. Cut into sections or ¼-in. slices. Overlap half of the orange sections or slices on a large platter or in a glass bowl.
2. Sprinkle with orange juice concentrate, coconut, the almonds and half of the confectioners' sugar. Top with remaining oranges; sprinkle with remaining sugar. Refrigerate until serving.

HOT SPINACH APPLE SALAD

This salad is lightly coated in a sweet-tangy dressing so the spinach doesn't wilt and the apples retain their crunch. It's especially good served with a loaf of fresh-baked homemade bread.
—Denise Albers, Freeburg, IL

TAKES: 20 MIN.
MAKES: 10 SERVINGS

6 bacon strips, diced
¼ cup cider vinegar
3 Tbsp. brown sugar
9 cups fresh baby spinach
2 unpeeled large red apples, thinly sliced
1 medium red onion, chopped (about ¾ cup)

1. In a large skillet, cook bacon until crisp. Remove to paper towels. Drain, reserving 2 Tbsp. drippings.
2. In the same skillet, combine vinegar, brown sugar and the reserved drippings. Bring to a boil; cook and stir until the sugar is dissolved. Cool slightly.
3. Meanwhile, in a serving bowl, combine spinach, apples, onion and bacon. Drizzle with warm dressing; toss to coat. Serve immediately.

"Use fruit juice instead for a delicious, kid-friendly version."
—NICOLE NEMETH

SANGRIA GELATIN RING

You just can't go wrong with a gelatin salad with fresh berries—it's sangria on a plate! Use fruit juice instead for a delicious, kid-friendly version.
—Nicole Nemeth, Komoka, ON

TAKES: 15 MIN. + CHILLING
MAKES: 10 SERVINGS

1½ cups boiling white wine
    or white grape juice
2 pkg. (3 oz. each) lemon gelatin
2 cups club soda, chilled
1 cup sliced fresh strawberries
1 cup fresh or frozen blueberries
1 cup fresh or frozen raspberries
½ cup green grapes, halved

In a large heatproof bowl, add boiling wine to gelatin; stir 2 minutes or until gelatin is completely dissolved. Stir in chilled club soda. Refrigerate until thickened but not firm, about 45 minutes. Stir in berries and grapes. Pour into a 6-cup ring mold coated with cooking spray. Refrigerate until set, about 4 hours. Unmold onto a serving platter.

MY FAVORITE AVOCADO SALAD

Tangy lime dressing is the perfect topper for this avocado salad. We love the flavor of toasted walnuts with avocados, but feel free to experiment with whatever kind of nuts you prefer.
—Ilia Kaku, North Richland Hills, TX

TAKES: 25 MIN. • **MAKES:** 9 SERVINGS

1 Tbsp. lemon juice
2 medium avocados,
    peeled and cubed
1 pkg. (5 oz.) spring mix salad greens
5 plum tomatoes, chopped
½ cup chopped red onion
¼ cup chopped walnuts, toasted
LIME DRESSING
3 Tbsp. olive oil
1 Tbsp. minced fresh parsley
1 Tbsp. minced fresh cilantro
1 Tbsp. sour cream
1 Tbsp. lime juice
1 tsp. yellow mustard
⅛ tsp. salt
⅛ tsp. pepper
    Dash sugar

Drizzle lemon juice over avocados. In a serving bowl, combine salad greens, tomatoes, onion, walnuts and avocados. Whisk together the dressing ingredients; pour over salad. Toss to coat.

NOTE To toast nuts, bake in a shallow pan in a 350° oven for 5-10 minutes or cook in a skillet over low heat until lightly browned, stirring occasionally.

EGGNOG FRUIT FLUFF

I regularly include this blend of apples, blueberries and other fruit in my December menus. The eggnog in the dressing suits this sweet salad for Christmas.
—Tami Harrington, Scottsdale, AZ

TAKES: 10 MIN. + CHILLING
MAKES: 12 SERVINGS

1 cup eggnog, chilled
1 envelope whipped topping
    mix (Dream Whip)
¼ tsp. ground nutmeg
1 can (20 oz.) pineapple
    tidbits, drained
1 can (15¼ oz.) sliced
    peaches, drained
2 medium tart apples, chopped
1 cup fresh blueberries
¾ cup halved maraschino cherries
¾ cup chopped walnuts

Beat eggnog, whipped topping mix and nutmeg on high speed until soft peaks form. Combine the remaining ingredients; fold into the eggnog mixture. Refrigerate, covered, until chilled. Gently stir before serving.

Holiday Helper
Fresh blueberries are usually available during the holidays, but they're often pricey. If you don't want to splurge, skip frozen blueberries because they'll be too juicy. Instead, add another apple to this classic fluff salad.

CELERY ROOT & PEAR SLAW

Crunchy celery root is an underappreciated yet completely delicious veggie. It lends a sweetness to this tangy slaw; I like to serve this dish on holidays alongside pork roast or baked ham.
—Roxanne Chan, Albany, CA

TAKES: 40 MIN. • **MAKES:** 16 SERVINGS

    1   medium celery root, peeled and julienned
    3   cups shredded red cabbage
    3   medium pears, thinly sliced
    ⅓   cup golden raisins
    ¼   cup chopped red onion
    ¼   cup minced fresh parsley
    ¼   cup sliced almonds
    ¾   cup sour cream
    ⅓   cup mayonnaise
    4   tsp. poppy seeds
    4   tsp. prepared horseradish
    2   garlic cloves, minced
    1½ tsp. honey
    ¾   tsp. pepper
    ¾   tsp. grated lemon peel
    4   tsp. lemon juice
    ½   cup crumbled blue cheese

In a large bowl, combine the first seven ingredients. In a second bowl, combine the next nine ingredients; pour over slaw, tossing to coat. Sprinkle with blue cheese.

AMBROSIA FRUIT SALAD

One of my most vivid memories as a child growing up in Maine is waking up to hear my mother cooking up a storm in the kitchen. She made all her meals from scratch, and her ambrosia fruit salad is one of our family favorites.
—Colleen Belbey, Warwick, RI

TAKES: 20 MIN. • **MAKES:** 6 SERVINGS

    2   cups cubed fresh pineapple
    2   large navel oranges, peeled and sectioned
    1½ cups green grapes
    1   cup miniature marshmallows
    1   large banana, sliced
    ½   cup sweetened shredded coconut
    ¼   cup chopped almonds
    ¾   cup (6 oz.) vanilla yogurt
        Toasted sweetened shredded coconut, optional

Combine the first seven ingredients; gently fold in yogurt. Refrigerate until serving. If desired, top with toasted coconut. **NOTE** To toast coconut, bake in a shallow pan in a 350° oven for 5-10 minutes or cook in a skillet over low heat until golden brown, stirring occasionally.

MERRY BERRY SALAD

Every fall and winter we go through a cranberry craze and develop recipes that celebrate the season with a subtle twist. Dried cranberries drizzled with a fresh cranberry vinaigrette infuse this salad with the holiday spirit.
—Taste of Home *Test Kitchen*

TAKES: 20 MIN. • **MAKES:** 10 SERVINGS

1 pkg. (10 oz.) mixed salad greens
1 medium red apple, diced
1 medium green apple, diced
1 cup shredded Parmesan cheese
½ cup dried cranberries
½ cup slivered almonds, toasted

DRESSING
1 cup fresh cranberries
½ cup sugar
½ cup cider vinegar
¼ cup thawed apple juice concentrate
1 tsp. salt
1 tsp. ground mustard
1 tsp. grated onion
1 cup canola oil

Combine the first six ingredients. To make dressing, pulse the next seven ingredients in a blender or food processor, covered, until well mixed. While processing, gradually add oil in a steady stream. Drizzle the desired amount of dressing over the salad; toss to coat. Refrigerate any leftover dressing.

NOTE To toast nuts, bake in a shallow pan in a 350° oven for 5-10 minutes or cook in a skillet over low heat until lightly browned, stirring occasionally.

SLOW-COOKED
CHRISTMAS

At the busiest time of year for your kitchen, let your slow cooker shoulder some of the work. For main courses, soups, sides and desserts, the cook's best friend helps make the holidays a little less stressful!

SLOW-COOKED PORK WITH ROOT VEGETABLES

This is truly a one-pot recipe—no need to brown the roast, as the rub gives it great color. As it cooks, it fills the house with a delicious aroma. Use the cooking liquid as a sauce when you're ready to serve.
—Jackie Sharp, Suffolk, VA

PREP: 25 MIN. • **COOK:** 3½ HOURS
MAKES: 10 SERVINGS

- 3 large sweet potatoes (about 2¼ lbs.)
- 2 medium turnips
- 1 tart medium apple
- ¼ cup water
- 1 medium onion, quartered
- 2 Tbsp. packed brown sugar
- 2 tsp. salt
- 1½ tsp. paprika
- ½ tsp. pepper
- 1 boneless pork loin roast (3 to 4 lbs.)
- ½ cup unsweetened apple juice
- 2 Tbsp. cider vinegar
- 1 Tbsp. Worcestershire sauce
- 1 tsp. salt
- 1 tsp. yellow mustard
- ¼ tsp. crushed red pepper flakes

1. Peel and cut the sweet potatoes, turnips and apple into ¾-in. pieces. Microwave sweet potatoes, turnips and water, covered, on high until just slightly tender, 8-10 minutes. Drain; transfer to a 6-qt. slow cooker. Add apple and onion. In a small bowl, mix brown sugar, salt, paprika and pepper; rub over meat and place in slow cooker.

2. Whisk the remaining ingredients; pour around the pork. Cook, covered, on low until a thermometer reads 145° and the meat is tender, 3½-4½ hours.

3. Remove roast from the slow cooker; tent with foil. Let stand for 15 minutes before slicing. Strain the cooking juices; serve pork and vegetables with juices.

FIRE-ROASTED TOMATO MINESTRONE

This soup was created to accommodate special Christmas dinner guests who are vegetarians. It was so good we all enjoyed it. This can also be cooked on the stovetop for two hours at a low simmer.
—Donna_Marie Ryan, Topsfield, MA

PREP: 20 MIN. • **COOK:** 4½ HOURS
MAKES: 8 SERVINGS (ABOUT 3 QT.)

- 1 medium sweet onion, chopped
- 1 cup cut fresh green beans
- 1 small zucchini, cubed
- 1 medium carrot, chopped
- 1 celery rib, chopped
- 2 garlic cloves, minced
- 2 Tbsp. olive oil
- ¼ tsp. salt
- ¼ tsp. pepper
- 2 cans (14½ oz. each) fire-roasted diced tomatoes
- 1 can (15 oz.) cannellini beans, rinsed and drained
- 1 carton (32 oz.) vegetable broth
- 1 cup uncooked small pasta shells
- 1 cup chopped fresh spinach

Combine the first nine ingredients in a 5-qt. slow cooker. Add tomatoes and beans; pour in broth. Cook, covered, on low until the vegetables are tender, 4-6 hours. Stir in pasta; cook, covered, on low until the pasta is tender, 30-40 minutes. Stir in spinach before serving.

CRANBERRY APPLE TOPPING

A generous spoonful of this sweet-tart sauce is a tasty addition to chicken, turkey or pork. The ruby-red color lends a festive look to the meal, perfect for holiday visitors.
—Lise Ode, Delray Beach, FL

PREP: 15 MIN. • **COOK:** 3½ HOURS + COOLING • **MAKES:** 3¾ CUPS

- 4 cups fresh or frozen cranberries
- 2 medium tart apples, peeled and chopped
- 1¼ cups sugar
- ¼ cup orange juice
- 2 tsp. grated orange zest
- ½ tsp. ground cinnamon
- 2 Tbsp. cornstarch
- 2 Tbsp. cold water

In a 3-qt. slow cooker, combine the first six ingredients. Cook, covered, on low until bubbly, 3-4 hours. In a small bowl, combine cornstarch and water until smooth; stir into the cranberry mixture. Cook, covered, until thickened, 30 minutes longer; cool.

SLOW COOKER MIXED FRUIT & PISTACHIO CAKE

This cake is easy to make and a guaranteed-delicious dessert for several days, if you can make it last that long. It's wonderful for the fall and the holidays.
—Nancy Heishman, Las Vegas, NV

PREP: 20 MIN. • **COOK:** 2 HOURS + COOLING
MAKES: 8 SERVINGS

- 1½ cups all-purpose flour
- 1½ tsp. ground cinnamon
- ½ tsp. baking soda
- ½ tsp. baking powder
- ½ tsp. ground allspice
- ¼ tsp. salt
- 1 can (8 oz.) jellied cranberry sauce
- ⅓ cup packed brown sugar
- ⅓ cup buttermilk
- ¼ cup butter, melted
- 2 tsp. grated orange zest
- ½ tsp. orange extract
- 1 large egg
- 1 cup mixed dried fruit bits
- 1 cup pistachios
  Sweetened whipped cream, optional

1. Whisk together the first six ingredients. In another bowl, combine the next seven ingredients. Add the cranberry mixture to the flour mixture; stir until smooth. Add dried fruit and pistachios.

2. Pour batter into a greased 1½-qt. baking dish; place dish in a 6-qt. slow cooker. Lay a 14x12-in. piece of parchment paper over the top of the slow cooker, under the lid. Cook, covered, on high until a toothpick inserted in the center comes out clean, about 2½ hours. Remove dish from the slow cooker to a wire rack. Cool for 30 minutes before inverting onto a serving platter. Cut into wedges with a serrated knife; if desired, serve with sweetened whipped cream.

Holiday Helper
Unsalted pistachios are preferred for baking. If you can't find unsalted, you can buy salted and wipe off most of the salt, or substitute pine nuts or blanched almonds instead.

CHICKEN WITH SUGAR PUMPKINS & APRICOTS

When we have family gatherings, we give the slow cooker kitchen duty. This yummy chicken with pumpkin and apricots has the warm flavors of Morocco.
—Nancy Heishman, Las Vegas, NV

PREP: 20 MIN. • **COOK:** 4 HOURS.
MAKES: 8 SERVINGS

- 3 peeled and cubed fresh Sugar Baby pumpkins (5 to 6 cups each)
- 1 Tbsp. canola oil
- 8 boneless skinless chicken thighs (4 oz. each)
- 1 medium red onion, chopped
- 2 garlic cloves, minced
- ¾ cup dried Turkish apricots, diced
- ½ cup apricot nectar
- ⅓ cup apricot preserves
- 2 Tbsp. lemon juice
- 1 tsp. ground ginger
- 1 tsp. ground cinnamon
- 1 tsp. salt
- ½ tsp. pepper
- 3 Tbsp. minced fresh parsley
  Hot cooked rice
- ½ cup pomegranate seeds, optional

1. Place cubed pumpkin in a 5-qt. slow cooker coated with cooking spray.

2. In a large nonstick skillet, heat oil over medium-high heat; brown chicken thighs on all sides. Transfer the chicken to the slow cooker. In same skillet, saute onions and garlic 1-2 minutes; transfer to the slow cooker.

3. Add the next eight ingredients to the slow cooker. Cook, covered, on low until the meat is tender, 4-5 hours. Top with parsley. If desired, serve with hot cooked rice and sprinkle with pomegranate seeds.

A KICK & A TWIST ARTICHOKE DIP

Some warm cream cheese-based dips are too salty for me. This one has a nice balance. Adding black pepper or lemon pepper can add more zing if you want it.
—Susan Hein, Burlington, WI

TAKES: 25 MIN. • **MAKES:** 8 CUPS

- 1 Tbsp. olive oil
- 10 to 12 green onions, chopped
- 6 garlic cloves, pureed
- 1 jalapeno pepper, seeded and chopped
- ¼ cup minced fresh parsley
- 3 Tbsp. lemon juice
- 4 pkg. (8 oz. each) cream cheese, softened
- 1 cup sour cream
- 1 cup mayonnaise
- 2 tsp. cracked fennel seed
- 1 to 2 tsp. crushed red pepper flakes
- 2 cups shredded Parmesan cheese
- 2 cans (14 oz. each) water-packed artichoke hearts, drained and coarsely chopped
    French bread baguette, sliced

1. In a large skillet, heat oil over medium heat. Add onions, garlic and jalapeno; cook and stir until soft, 4-6 minutes. Reduce heat; stir in the parsley and lemon juice.

2. Add cream cheese and cover, stirring every few minutes, until melted. Stir in sour cream, mayonnaise, fennel and pepper flakes. Remove from heat. Add Parmesan cheese and artichoke hearts, stirring gently to prevent artichokes from breaking up.

3. Transfer to a 3- or 4-qt. slow cooker; turn heat to low. Serve warm on baguette slices. Dip may be made in advance and refrigerated until serving; reheat in slow cooker set to low.

PUMPKIN CRANBERRY BREAD PUDDING

Savor your favorite fall and winter flavors with this scrumptious bread pudding, served warm with a sweet vanilla sauce.
—Judith Bucciarelli, Newburgh, NY

PREP: 15 MIN. • **COOK:** 3 HOURS
MAKES: 8 SERVINGS (1⅓ CUPS SAUCE)

- 8 slices cinnamon bread, cut into 1-in. cubes
- 4 large eggs, beaten
- 2 cups 2% milk
- 1 cup canned pumpkin
- ¼ cup packed brown sugar
- ¼ cup butter, melted
- 1 tsp. vanilla extract
- ½ tsp. ground cinnamon
- ¼ tsp. ground nutmeg
- ½ cup dried cranberries

SAUCE
- 1 cup sugar
- ⅔ cup water
- 1 cup heavy whipping cream
- 2 tsp. vanilla extract
    Vanilla ice cream, optional

1. Place bread in a greased 3- or 4-qt. slow cooker. Combine next eight ingredients; stir in cranberries. Pour over the bread cubes. Cook, covered, on low until a knife inserted in the center comes out clean, 3-4 hours.

2. For sauce, bring sugar and water to a boil in a large saucepan over medium heat. Cook until sugar dissolves and the mixture turns golden amber, about 20 minutes. Gradually stir in cream until smooth. Remove from heat; stir in vanilla. Serve warm with bread pudding. If desired, add a scoop of ice cream to each serving.

SPICY SEAFOOD STEW

This zippy stew is easy and quick to prepare. The hardest part is peeling and dicing the potatoes, and even that can be done the night before—just place the peeled potatoes in water and store them in the refrigerator to speed up assembly the next day.
—Bonnie Marlow, Ottoville, OH

PREP: 30 MIN. • **COOK:** 4¾ HOURS • **MAKES:** 9 SERVINGS

- 2   lbs. potatoes, peeled and diced
- 1   lb. carrots, sliced
- 1   jar (24 oz.) pasta sauce
- 2   jars (6 oz. each) sliced mushrooms, drained
- 1½ tsp. ground turmeric
- 1½ tsp. minced garlic
- 1   tsp. cayenne pepper
- ¼   tsp. salt
- 1½ cups water
- 1   lb. sea scallops
- 1   lb. uncooked shrimp (31-40 per lb.), peeled and deveined

In a 5-qt. slow cooker, combine the first eight ingredients. Cook, covered, on low until the potatoes are tender, 4½ -5 hours. Stir in water, scallops and shrimp. Cook, covered, until scallops are opaque and shrimp turn pink, 15-20 minutes longer.

SLOW COOKER BURGUNDY BEEF

When my adult children are coming over for dinner, this is their most-requested dish. It makes a convenient comfort meal during the busy holiday week!
—Urilla Cheverie, Andover, MA

PREP: 10 MIN. • **COOK:** 8¼ HOURS • **MAKES:** 10 SERVINGS

- 4   lbs. beef top sirloin steak, cut into 1-in. cubes
- 3   large onions, sliced
- 1   cup water
- 1   cup burgundy wine or beef broth
- 1   cup ketchup
- ¼   cup quick-cooking tapioca
- ¼   cup packed brown sugar
- ¼   cup Worcestershire sauce
- 4   tsp. paprika
- 1½ tsp. salt
- 1   tsp. minced garlic
- 1   tsp. ground mustard
- 2   Tbsp. cornstarch
- 3   Tbsp. cold water
     Hot cooked noodles

1. In a 5-qt. slow cooker, combine the first 12 ingredients. Cook, covered, on low until meat is tender, 8-9 hours.
2. Combine cornstarch and water until smooth; stir into pan juices. Cook, covered, on high until gravy is thickened, about 15 minutes. Serve with noodles.

PINEAPPLE-ORANGE SPICED TEA

The sweet aroma of this tea wafting from a slow cooker warms the coldest day. My daughter served it for a holiday open house, and coffee drinkers were instantly converted. I bring it to the office to spice up our break room beverage selections.
—Carole J. Drennan, Abilene, TX

PREP: 15 MIN. • **COOK:** 2 HOURS • **MAKES:** 12 SERVINGS

- 2 qt. boiling water
- 16 individual tea bags
- 2 cinnamon sticks (3 in.)
- 1 piece fresh gingerroot (½ in.), peeled and thinly sliced
- 4 whole cloves
- 1 cup sugar
- 1 can (12 oz.) frozen orange juice concentrate, thawed
- 1 can (12 oz.) frozen pineapple juice concentrate, thawed
- 1 cup pomegranate or cranberry juice
- ½ cup lemon juice
  Orange slices, optional

1. In a 5- or 6-qt. slow cooker, combine boiling water and tea bags. Cover and let stand for 5 minutes.
2. Meanwhile, place cinnamon sticks, ginger and cloves on a double thickness of cheesecloth. Gather the corners of the cloth to enclose the seasonings; tie securely with string. Discard the tea bags. Stir in the remaining ingredients; add the spice bag. Cook, covered, on low until heated through, 2-3 hours. Discard the spice bag. Stir before serving. If desired, serve with orange slices.

SLOW COOKER PRALINE SWEET POTATOES

I had a house full of relatives and was short on cooking space. I used the basic idea of the traditional sweet potato casserole and adapted it for the slow cooker. It's been a huge hit ever since!
—Joanna Stanforth, Mascoutah, IL

PREP: 15 MIN. • **COOK:** 4 HOURS • **MAKES:** 6 SERVINGS

- 3 cups mashed sweet potatoes
- 1 cup sugar
- 3 large eggs
- ½ cup 2% milk
- ¼ cup butter, melted
- 1 tsp. salt
- 1 tsp. vanilla extract

TOPPING
- ½ cup packed brown sugar
- ½ cup chopped pecans
- ¼ cup all-purpose flour
- 2 Tbsp. cold butter

In a greased 3-qt. slow cooker, combine the first seven ingredients. Cook, covered, on low for 3 hours. Combine brown sugar, pecans and flour; cut in butter until crumbly. Sprinkle over the sweet potatoes. Cook, covered, on low until a thermometer reads 160°, 1-2 hours longer.

SALTY-SWEET PEANUT TREAT

Who knew slow cooking could transform chocolate, peanuts and pretzels? When the clusters are done, we tuck them into mini muffin papers for a takeaway treat.
—Elizabeth Godecke, Chicago, IL

PREP: 10 MIN. • **COOK:** 1 HOUR + CHILLING
MAKES: ABOUT 6 DOZEN

- 24 oz. milk chocolate, coarsely chopped
- 2 cups salted peanuts
- ¼ cup packed brown sugar
- 1 tsp. vanilla extract
- 2 cups crushed pretzels

In a 3-qt. slow cooker, combine chocolate, peanuts and brown sugar. Cook, covered, on low, stirring halfway through cooking, until the chocolate is melted, about 1 hour. Stir in vanilla. Add pretzels; stir to combine. Drop by tablespoonfuls onto waxed paper-lined baking sheets. Refrigerate until set, 10-15 minutes. Store in an airtight container.

MELTING CHOCOLATE IN YOUR SLOW COOKER

To melt multiple kinds of chocolate, fill a slow cooker one-third full of hot water. Place chopped chocolate in jars, and set the jars in the water. Heat, uncovered, for about 30 minutes. Take care to keep water from getting inside the jars—moisture causes the sugar in chocolate to turn into syrup and the cocoa particles to clump, a process called seizing.

To melt a batch of one kind of chocolate, chop it up and place it in the slow cooker insert. Cover and cook on high for one hour. Reduce heat to low and continue cooking, covered, for an another hour or until it is completely melted, stirring every 15 minutes.

GINGERBREAD PUDDING CAKE

Sweet spices and molasses give my dessert a delightful old-fashioned flavor. It's pretty topped with a dollop of whipped cream.
—Barbara Cook, Yuma, AZ

PREP: 20 MIN.
COOK: 2 HOURS + STANDING
MAKES: 8 SERVINGS

½ cup molasses
1 cup water
¼ cup butter, softened
¼ cup sugar
1 large egg white
1 tsp. vanilla extract
1¼ cups all-purpose flour
¾ tsp. baking soda
¼ tsp. salt
½ tsp. ground cinnamon
½ tsp. ground ginger
¼ tsp. ground allspice
⅛ tsp. ground nutmeg
½ cup chopped pecans
6 Tbsp. brown sugar
¾ cup hot water
⅔ cup butter, melted
   Sweetened whipped cream,
   optional

1. Mix molasses and 1 cup water. Cream softened butter and sugar until light and fluffy; beat in egg white and vanilla. In another bowl, whisk together flour, baking soda, salt and spices; add to the creamed mixture alternately with the molasses mixture, beating well after each addition. Fold in pecans.
2. Pour into a greased 3-qt. slow cooker. Sprinkle with brown sugar. Mix hot water and melted butter; pour over the batter (do not stir).
3. Cook, covered, on high until a toothpick inserted in the center comes out clean, 2-2½ hours. Turn off slow cooker; let stand 15 minutes. If desired, serve with whipped cream.

SALMON SWEET POTATO SOUP

I created this recipe to have a healthier alternative to whitefish chowder, which is a favorite in the area where I grew up. Salmon and sweet potatoes boost the nutrition, and the slow cooker makes it convenient. It's especially comforting on a cold winter day!
—Matthew Hass, Franklin, WI

PREP: 20 MIN. • **COOK:** 5½ HOURS
MAKES: 8 SERVINGS (3 QT.)

1 Tbsp. olive oil
1 medium onion, chopped
1 medium carrot, chopped
1 celery rib, chopped
3 garlic cloves, minced
2 medium sweet potatoes, peeled and cut into ½-in. cubes
1½ cups frozen corn, thawed
6 cups reduced-sodium chicken broth
1 tsp. celery salt
1 tsp. dill weed
½ tsp. salt
¾ tsp. pepper
1½ lbs. salmon fillets, skin removed and cut into ¾-in. pieces
1 can (12 oz.) fat-free evaporated milk
2 Tbsp. minced fresh parsley

1. In a large skillet, heat oil over medium heat. Add onion, carrot and celery; cook and stir until tender, 4-5 minutes. Add garlic; cook 1 minute longer. Transfer to a 5-qt. slow cooker. Add the next seven ingredients. Cook, covered, on low until the sweet potatoes are tender, 5-6 hours.
2. Stir in salmon, milk and parsley. Cook, covered, until the fish just begins to flake easily with a fork, 30-40 minutes longer.

SLOW-COOKED TURKEY WITH HERBED STUFFING

I'm all for turkey dinner, especially around the holidays. A whole turkey won't fit in my slow cooker, so thank goodness for turkey breast. I cook it with my grandma's easy stuffing recipe for a happy meal that doesn't require any hard work.
—Camille Beckstrand, Layton, UT

PREP: 20 MIN. • **COOK:** 3 HOURS + STANDING • **MAKES:** 8 SERVINGS

2 boneless skinless turkey breast halves (1 lb. each) or 2 lbs. turkey breast tenderloins
1 jar (12 oz.) turkey gravy, divided
1 can (10½ oz.) reduced-fat reduced-sodium condensed cream of mushroom soup, undiluted
½ tsp. salt
½ tsp. poultry seasoning
¼ tsp. pepper
1 medium Granny Smith apple, finely chopped
2 celery ribs, thinly sliced
1 small onion, finely chopped
1 cup sliced fresh mushrooms, optional
6 cups seasoned stuffing cubes

1. Place turkey in a 5- or 6-qt. slow cooker. Whisk ¼ cup gravy, condensed soup and seasonings. Cover and refrigerate remaining gravy. Stir apple, celery, onion and, if desired, mushrooms into gravy mixture. Stir in stuffing cubes; spoon over turkey. Cook, covered, on low until a thermometer reads 170° and meat is tender, 3-4 hours.
2. Remove turkey from slow cooker; tent with foil. Let stand 10 minutes before slicing. Warm remaining gravy. Serve with turkey and stuffing.

SWEET & SOUR TURKEY MEATBALLS

Here's a great potluck or buffet recipe for Christmas parties that's seasonal, easy and delicious.
—Christine Wendland, Browns Mills, NJ

PREP: 30 MIN. • **COOK:** 2 HOURS • **MAKES:** ABOUT 5 DOZEN

4 thick-sliced peppered bacon strips
1 large egg, beaten
½ cup seasoned bread crumbs
3 Tbsp. minced fresh cilantro
1 tsp. salt
1 tsp. white pepper
2 lbs. ground turkey
1 jar (18 oz.) apricot preserves
1 can (14½ oz.) diced tomatoes, undrained
1 bottle (8 oz.) taco sauce
½ cup pomegranate juice

1. Preheat oven to 400°. Pulse bacon, covered, in a food processor until finely chopped. Combine egg, bread crumbs, cilantro, salt and pepper. Crumble turkey and bacon over the egg mixture; mix lightly but thoroughly. Shape into 1-in. balls.
2. Place meatballs in two ungreased 15x10x1-in. baking pans. Bake until no longer pink, 8-10 minutes.
3. In a 4-qt. slow cooker, combine preserves, tomatoes, taco sauce and juice. Stir in the meatballs. Cook, covered, on high until a thermometer inserted into several meatballs reads 165°, about 2-3 hours.

MAKE-AHEAD EGGNOG

Sipping homemade eggnog is a holiday tradition for many families. Our slow cooker version of the classic drink couldn't be easier to make.
—**Taste of Home** *Test Kitchen*

PREP: 10 MIN. • **COOK:** 2 HOURS • **MAKES:** 9 SERVINGS

6 cups whole milk
1 cup egg substitute
⅔ cup sugar
2 tsp. rum extract
1½ tsp. pumpkin pie spice
French vanilla whipped topping, optional

In a 3-qt. slow cooker, combine the first five ingredients. Cover and cook on low until heated through, 2-3 hours. Serve in mugs; dollop with whipped topping if desired.

Holiday Helper

To make your own whipped cream, refrigerate the bowl and beaters for about 30 minutes. Pour the cream into a deep, chilled bowl; whip on high until soft peaks form. For sweetened vanilla whipped cream, add 2 tablespoons confectioners' sugar and ½ tsp. pure vanilla extract to each cup of cream before whipping.

MUSHROOM & RICE PILAF

This easy rice pilaf is a lifesaver when you are hosting a holiday meal. Just place the ingredients in the slow cooker and forget about it until it's time to serve!
—*Kathleen Hedger, Godfrey, IL*

PREP: 15 MIN. • **COOK:** 3 HOURS • **MAKES:** 10 SERVINGS

½ cup butter, cubed
2 cups uncooked long grain rice
½ lb. sliced fresh mushrooms
8 green onions, chopped
2 tsp. dried oregano
2 cans (10½ oz. each) condensed beef broth, undiluted
1½ cups water

In a large saucepan, heat butter over medium heat. Add rice; cook and stir until lightly browned, 5-6 minutes. Transfer to a 3-qt. slow cooker. Add mushrooms, green onions and oregano. Stir in broth and water. Cook, covered, on low until the rice is tender and the liquid is absorbed, 3-4 hours.

MINI DESSERTS

*These single-serving sweets will satisfy everyone's craving
for a holiday dessert. Create a lovely plate for each guest,
or let them choose from an array of miniature treats.*

batter. Bake until a toothpick inserted in center comes out clean, about 20 minutes. Cool 10 minutes on a wire rack. Remove from pan; cool completely on wire rack.

3. For filling, beat cream cheese, butter and vanilla until blended. Gradually beat in confectioners' sugar until smooth.

4. To assemble, cut cake into ½-in. cubes. In juice glasses or small parfait glasses, alternate layers of cake and filling, ending with filling. If desired, sprinkle with additional cinnamon.

Holiday Helper

If you're serving all adults, try sprinkling the cake cubes with a little bit of brandy, schnapps or rum.

MINI BAKLAVA

Baklava holds amazing memories for me. My best friend made it for my bridal and baby showers—and then she taught me how to make it! These delicious little miniatures give you the taste of baklava in a bite-sized package.
—Margaret Guillory, Eunice, LA

PREP: 20 MIN. • **BAKE:** 10 MIN. + COOLING
MAKES: ABOUT 2½ DOZEN

½ cup butter
¼ cup sugar
1 tsp. ground cinnamon
1 cup finely chopped pecans
1 cup finely chopped walnuts
2 pkg. (1.90 oz. each) frozen miniature phyllo tart shells
Honey

1. Preheat the oven to 350°. In a small saucepan over medium heat, melt butter. Stir in sugar and cinnamon. Bring to a boil. Reduce heat; add pecans and walnuts, tossing to coat. Simmer, uncovered, until the nuts are lightly toasted, 5-10 minutes.

2. Place phyllo shells on a baking sheet lined with parchment paper. Spoon the nut mixture and butter sauce evenly into the shells. Bake until golden brown, 9-11 minutes. Cool completely on pan on a wire rack. Drizzle a drop of honey into each shell; let stand, covered, until serving. Serve with additional honey if desired.

MINI PUMPKIN SPICE TRIFLES

These miniature trifles are so much fun for holiday parties! The assembly takes a little longer than making one big trifle, but it's worth it to see everyone's reaction to getting their own!
—Rhiannon Brownell, Newport News, VA

PREP: 40 MIN. • **BAKE:** 20 MIN. + COOLING
MAKES: 8 SERVINGS

1 cup all-purpose flour
1 Tbsp. instant espresso powder
1 tsp. baking powder
1 tsp. ground cinnamon
½ tsp. baking soda
½ tsp. salt
½ tsp. ground nutmeg
½ tsp. ground allspice
1 cup pumpkin
¾ cup sugar
½ cup canola oil
2 large eggs

FILLING
6 oz. cream cheese, softened
¼ cup butter, softened
1 tsp. vanilla extract
2¾ cups confectioners' sugar
Additional ground cinnamon, optional

1. Preheat oven to 350°. Whisk together the first eight ingredients. In another bowl, beat pumpkin, sugar and oil until smooth; add eggs, one at a time, beating well after each addition. Gradually add the flour mixture; beat until well blended.

2. Line a 9-in. square baking pan with parchment paper; grease paper. Add

MINI SWEET POTATO PIES

My 2-year-old son helped me create this delicious recipe one day, and it was the first day he told me "I love you"! I will always remember making these with him.
—Emily Butler, South Williamsport, PA

PREP: 45 MINUTES
BAKE: 25 MIN. + COOLING
MAKES: 2 DOZEN

2 large sweet potatoes, peeled and cut into ¾-in. cubes
2 sheets refrigerated pie crust, room temperature
1 cup packed brown sugar, divided
¼ cup all-purpose flour
3 Tbsp. cold unsalted butter, cubed

1. Preheat oven to 400°. Place sweet potatoes in a greased 15x10x1-in. baking pan; bake until tender, 35-40 minutes.
2. Meanwhile, on a work surface, unroll one crust. Using a 2½-in. round cutter, cut out 12 circles. Press the circles into the bottoms and up the sides of 12 nonstick mini muffin cups. Repeat with the second crust. Chill until the filling is ready.
3. In a food processor, pulse flour, butter and ¼ cup brown sugar until crumbly; set aside for topping. Wipe out the food processor, then pulse the baked sweet potatoes and the remaining brown sugar until almost smooth. Fill the crust-lined cups three-fourths full with the sweet potato mixture. Sprinkle with topping.
4. Decrease oven setting to 325°. Bake until the crust is golden brown, 20-24 minutes. Cool for 5-10 minutes before removing from pan to a wire rack to cool completely.

MINIATURE ALMOND TARTS

My family requests these adorable little tarts each Christmas. I enjoy making them, as the almond paste in the filling reflects our Dutch heritage, and they're popular at special gatherings.
—Karen Van Den Berge, Holland, MI

PREP: 35 MIN. + CHILLING • **BAKE:** 25 MIN. + COOLING
MAKES: ABOUT 4 DOZEN

> 1 cup butter, softened
> 6 oz. cream cheese, softened
> 2 cups all-purpose flour
> FILLING
> 6 oz. almond paste, crumbled
> 2 large eggs, lightly beaten
> ½ cup sugar
> FROSTING
> 1½ cups confectioners' sugar
> 3 Tbsp. butter, softened
> 4 to 5 tsp. milk
>   Maraschino cherry halves (about 48)

1. In a large bowl, cream the butter and cream cheese until smooth. Gradually add flour until well blended. Refrigerate for 1 hour.
2. Shape into 1-in. balls. Place in ungreased miniature muffin cups; press into the bottom and up the sides to form a shell.
3. For filling, in a small bowl, beat the almond paste, eggs and sugar until blended. Fill each shell with about 1½ tsp. filling.
4. Bake at 325° for 25-30 minutes or until edges are golden brown. Cool for 10 minutes before removing to wire racks to cool completely.
5. For frosting, combine the confectioners' sugar, butter and enough milk to achieve desired consistency. Pipe or spread over tarts. Top each tart with a cherry half.

HOLIDAY MERINGUE MINIATURES

My kids love these melt-in-your-mouth meringues, and have such fun making them. The tiny treats were always on our Christmas cookie plate when I was a kid, and now the tradition continues.
—Susan Marshall, Colorado Springs, CO

PREP: 20 MIN. • **BAKE:** 1 HOUR + COOLING
MAKES: ABOUT 7 DOZEN

> 2 large egg whites, room temperature
> ½ tsp. white vinegar
>   Dash salt
> ½ tsp. almond extract
> ½ tsp. vanilla extract
> ½ cup granulated sugar
>   Red gel food coloring

1. Preheat oven to 225°. Beat egg whites with vinegar and salt on medium speed until foamy and doubled in volume. Beat in extracts. Gradually add sugar, 1 Tbsp. at a time, beating on high after each addition until the sugar is dissolved. Continue beating until stiff glossy peaks form (this may take 10 minutes).
2. Place a ½-in. round tip into a pastry bag. Paint five evenly spaced stripes of red food coloring inside the length of the pastry bag. Transfer meringue to pastry bag; pipe kiss-shaped dollops 1 in. apart onto parchment-lined baking sheets.
3. Bake for 1 hour until set and dry. Turn off the oven (do not open oven door); leave meringues in oven for 1 hour. Remove and cool completely on baking sheets. Remove meringues from the parchment paper; store in an airtight container at room temperature.

COFFEE LOVER'S MINI CHEESECAKES

My family knows I adore cheesecake. Anyone who wants one comes to me because they know I have many tried and tested recipes. But I was getting bored with the standard flavors. Then I had an idea—mocha cheesecake! After lots of experiments, I came up with this recipe. It's pretty good, if I do say so myself!
—Holly Sharp, Warren, ON

PREP: 30 MIN. • **BAKE:** 20 MIN. + CHILLING • **MAKES:** 2 DOZEN

 30 chocolate wafers, finely crushed
       (about 1⅔ cups crumbs)
 ¼   cup sugar
 2   Tbsp. butter, melted
 2   Tbsp. brewed espresso
FILLING
 8   oz. semisweet chocolate
 2   Tbsp. brewed espresso
 3   pkg. (8 oz. each) cream cheese, softened
 1   can (14 oz.) sweetened condensed milk
 4   large eggs, room temperature and lightly beaten
 2   cups frozen whipped topping, thawed
 24 chocolate-covered coffee beans
       Baking cocoa, optional

1. Preheat oven to 325°. Line 24 muffin cups with foil liners. Mix wafer crumbs and sugar; stir in butter and espresso. Press by tablespoonfuls into the bottoms of the liners.

2. For filling, melt chocolate in a microwave; stir in espresso until blended. In a large bowl, beat cream cheese until smooth; slowly stir in condensed milk until blended. Stir chocolate mixture into cream cheese mixture until combined. Add eggs; beat just until blended.

3. Fill each prepared cup with ¼ cup of the cheesecake batter. Bake until the centers are almost set, 17-20 minutes. Let cool in the pans for 10 minutes before removing to wire racks to cool completely. Refrigerate overnight, covering when completely cooled.

4. To serve, top with whipped topping and chocolate-covered coffee beans; if desired, dust with baking cocoa.

*"These are a
breeze to make
and a delight
to serve."*
—LORRAINE CALAND

MINI CHOCOLATE CAKES WITH CARAMELIZED BANANAS

This recipe represents one of my first times spreading my wings and try to go a bit fancy. It may look intimidating, but after you try it once, you'll have it down pat. These are a breeze to make and a delight to serve.
—Lorraine Caland, Shuniah, ON

PREP: 50 MIN. • **BAKE:** 15 MIN. + COOLING
MAKES: 8 RAMEKINS

- 5 oz. bittersweet chocolate, chopped
- ½ cup unsalted butter
- 4 large eggs
- ⅓ cup sugar
- 1 tsp. vanilla extract
- ⅛ tsp. salt
- ¼ cup all-purpose flour
  Baking cocoa

CARAMELIZED BANANAS
- 2 Tbsp. unsalted butter
- 2 medium bananas, cut into 1-in. slices
- 2 Tbsp. sugar

SAUCE
- 1 cup white wine or unsweetened apple juice
- ½ cup sugar
- 2 oz. bittersweet chocolate, chopped

1. Preheat oven to 400°. In a microwave, melt chocolate and butter; stir until smooth. Cool. Beat eggs, sugar, vanilla and salt on high speed until thick and pale, about 5 minutes. Sift in flour; mix just until combined. Fold in the chocolate mixture.

2. Spoon the batter into eight buttered 4-oz. ramekins dusted with cocoa. Place the ramekins on a baking sheet. Bake until a toothpick inserted in centers comes out clean, 12-15 minutes. Run a small knife around the sides of the ramekins. Invert onto cooling rack; let stand 5 minutes. Remove ramekins; place each cake on an individual plate.

3. Melt butter in a large skillet over medium heat. Toss banana slices with sugar until well coated; arrange in a single layer in skillet. Do not stir until bottoms are golden brown, 4-5 minutes. Turn; cook until second side is golden brown, 4-5 minutes longer. Remove from heat. Place bananas on plates with cakes.

4. For sauce, heat wine and sugar in a small saucepan over medium heat. Bring to a boil. Reduce heat; simmer until slightly thickened, about 10 minutes. Remove from heat; cool slightly. Whisk in chocolate. Pour over cakes.

Holiday Helper

You can make these in muffin cups if you don't have ramekins but you'll need to turn them over immediately after they come out of the oven so they don't stick.

CITRUS MINI CAKES

These moist, bite-size muffins are melt-in-your-mouth good. With their appealing look, they really dress up a party table. The recipe makes a big batch, so there's plenty to please a crowd.
—Linda Terrell, Palatka, FL

PREP: 15 MIN. • **BAKE:** 20 MIN. • **MAKES:** ABOUT 6 DOZEN

- 1 pkg. yellow cake mix (regular size)
- 1¼ cups water
- 3 large eggs
- ⅓ cup canola oil
- 3½ cups confectioners' sugar
- ½ cup orange juice
- ¼ cup lemon juice
  Toasted chopped almonds

1. In a large bowl, combine the cake mix, water, eggs and oil; beat on low speed for 30 seconds. Beat on medium for 2 minutes.

2. Fill well-greased miniature muffin cups two-thirds full. Bake at 350° for 10-12 minutes or until a toothpick inserted in the center comes out clean.

3. Meanwhile, in a large bowl, combine the confectioners' sugar and juices until smooth. Cool cakes for 2 minutes; remove from pans. Immediately dip cakes into glaze, coating well. Place top down on wire racks; sprinkle with almonds.

MINI FRUITCAKES

Fruitcake always looked so festive, but I didn't like the hard citron fruit, so I came up with my own recipe. I place these in Christmas-themed petit four cups and give them to friends with other cookies and candies. They keep well in the freezer in an airtight container. Just thaw them to room temperature and they taste fresh-baked and moist.
—Lisa McDermith, Highland, CA

PREP: 40 MIN. + COOLING • **BAKE:** 15 MIN.
MAKES: 2½ DOZEN

½ cup sherry
6 Tbsp. sugar
2 Tbsp. margarine

¾ cup all-purpose flour
½ tsp. baking powder
¼ tsp. baking soda
¼ tsp. ground cinnamon
1 large egg
¼ tsp. vanilla extract
½ cup finely chopped dried apricots
½ cup finely chopped dates
½ cup finely chopped green candied cherries
½ cup finely chopped red candied cherries
¾ cup finely chopped candied pineapple
¼ cup raisins
¼ cup golden raisins
½ cup finely chopped walnuts

1. Preheat oven to 350°. In a small saucepan, heat sherry, sugar and margarine until the sugar is dissolved. Cool. In a small bowl, whisk together flour, baking powder, baking soda and cinnamon. In another bowl, beat egg and vanilla; stir into the cooled sherry mixture until thoroughly combined. Add to the flour mixture; stir just until moistened.
2. In a large bowl, toss fruits and nuts to combine. Stir in the batter. Fill each of 30 greased mini muffin cups with 1 tablespoon of the batter. Bake until a toothpick inserted in centers comes out clean, 15-20 minutes. Cool in pan for 3-4 minutes before removing to a wire rack to cool completely.

MINI BLUEBERRY TARTS

These little tarts are a delightful treat at the holidays, especially for the busy cook. Using refrigerated pie crust means you won't spend tons of time on them. Watch your mini tarts around the 13-minute mark to make sure they don't brown too quickly.
—Allison Bell, Hillsdale, NJ

PREP: 25 MIN. • **BAKE:** 15 MIN. + COOLING
MAKES: 6 MINI TARTS

- 2 **cups fresh blueberries**
- ⅓ **cup sugar**
- 4 **tsp. cornstarch**
- 2 **sheets refrigerated pie crust**
- 1 **large egg yolk, lightly beaten**

1. Preheat oven to 425°. Crush half of the blueberries. Sift together sugar and cornstarch. Add whole and crushed blueberries; toss until the berries are well coated. Set aside.

2. On a lightly floured surface, unroll crusts. Cut out six 4½-in. circles; press circles into the bottoms and up sides of greased muffin cups. Evenly spoon in blueberry mixture. Cut out six 2-in. circles from remaining crust; place over filling. Brush with yolk.

3. Bake until the crust is golden and the filling bubbles, 13-17 minutes. Cool in pans 10 minutes; run a knife around the sides of the muffin cups and remove tarts to a serving plate.

Holiday Helper
If you like, sprinkle the tops of the tarts with coarse sugar just before baking; the sugar gives the little pies a beautiful, sparkling finish.

MINI APPLE CRISPS

My family and I pick apples at our local orchard every year, and this has become a favorite way to use the fruit. A mini crisp topped with ice cream makes a delicious after-school snack.
—Sabrina Olson, Otsego, MN

PREP: 20 MIN. • **BAKE:** 30 MIN.
MAKES: 6 SERVINGS

- ¼ cup butter
- 3 Tbsp. honey
- ½ tsp. vanilla extract
- ½ tsp. apple pie spice
- 1 cup crushed raw almonds
- 1 cup old-fashioned oats

FILLING
- 3 unpeeled medium apples, cut into ½-in. pieces
- 3 Tbsp. sugar
- 1 Tbsp. lemon juice
- 1 tsp. apple pie spice
  Vanilla ice cream, optional

1. Preheat oven to 350°. Grease six 6-oz. ramekins and set aside. Mix the first four ingredients. In a large bowl, combine almonds and oats; toss with the butter mixture until well coated. Press 2 Tbsp. into the bottoms of prepared ramekins.
2. For filling, combine apples, sugar, lemon juice and pie spice. Spoon filling evenly into the ramekins. Top with the remaining oat mixture. Bake until the topping is dark golden brown and fruit is tender, about 30 minutes. Serve warm; if desired, top with ice cream.

PUMPKIN PIE TARTLETS WITH MAPLE PECAN CRUST

After discovering I had multiple food sensitivities, I began developing holiday recipes that would be safe for me, but enjoyable for others, too. These tarts are delicious—with no gluten, eggs or dairy!
—Chantale Michaud, Guelph, ON

PREP: 45 MIN. + COOLING
BAKE: 35 MIN+ CHILLING
MAKES: 1½ DOZEN

- 2 cups old-fashioned oats
- 4 cups chopped pecans
- ½ cup maple syrup

- 2 tsp. ground cinnamon
- 1 tsp. sea salt
- 1 tsp. vanilla extract
- ¼ tsp. ground cloves

FILLING
- ½ cup maple syrup
- 3 Tbsp. cornstarch
- 2¼ cups canned pumpkin or homemade pumpkin puree
- ¼ cup cream of coconut, warmed
- 2 tsp. vanilla extract
- 2 tsp. ground cinnamon
- ½ tsp. sea salt
- ½ tsp. ground nutmeg
- ¼ tsp. ground ginger
- ¼ tsp. ground cloves

TOPPING
- ½ cup chopped pecans
- 2 tsp. maple syrup
  Dash sea salt

1. Preheat oven to 350°. Grease 18 muffin cups and set aside. Process oats in a food processor until a fine powder forms. Add the pecans; pulse until nuts are chopped. Add the next five ingredients; pulse until the mixture is moistened. Remove from food processor.
2. Fill prepared muffin cups with ⅓ cup of the oat mixture. Using a wet 1 Tbsp. measuring spoon, press the mixture into the bottom and up the sides of the muffin cups. Bake until lightly browned, about 10 minutes. Cool on a wire rack.
3. For filling, whisk together maple syrup and cornstarch. In a second bowl, mix the remaining filling ingredients, then add the maple syrup mixture. Spoon about 3 Tbsp. filling into each crust.
4. Combine topping ingredients; spoon about 1 teaspoon of topping onto each tartlet. Bake until dark golden and set, 35-40 minutes. Cool 10 minutes before removing tartlets to a wire rack; cool for 1 hour. If desired, refrigerate before serving.

apart on ungreased baking sheets. Bake until edges begin to brown, 8-10 minutes. Cool on pans 2 minutes. Remove to wire racks to cool completely.

3. Meanwhile, for filling, split vanilla bean lengthwise. Using a sharp knife, scrape seeds from center into top of a double boiler over simmering water; discard bean. Add egg whites, granulated sugar and vanilla extract. Whisking constantly, heat mixture until sugar is dissolved and a thermometer reads 160°, 8-10 minutes. Transfer to a stand mixer fitted with a whisk attachment.

4. Whisk the egg white mixture on high until it cools to room temperature, 8-10 minutes. Reduce speed to medium; gradually add butter, 1 Tbsp. at a time, beating well after each addition. Increase speed to high; beat until smooth.

5. To assemble, cut a small hole in the tip of a pastry bag or in one corner of a food-safe plastic bag. Transfer filling to bag. Pipe about 1 tsp. on bottoms of half of the cookies; cover with remaining cookies. Store in airtight containers.

MINI CHOCOLATE CHIP SANDWICH COOKIES

I created this recipe for the annual holiday cookie platters I make for family and friends, and it received rave reviews from both children and adults. If the buttercream doesn't come together after all of the butter has been incorporated, add some shortening one tablespoon at a time until the mixture starts to transform.
—Julie Thomas, Saukville, WI

PREP: 1 HOUR + CHILLING • **BAKE:** 10 MIN. + COOLING
MAKES: ABOUT 5 DOZEN

- 1 cup shortening
- 1 cup packed light brown sugar
- ½ cup granulated sugar
- 2 large eggs
- 1 tsp. vanilla extract
- 2¼ cups all-purpose flour
- 1 tsp. baking soda
- 1 tsp. salt
- 1 pkg. miniature semisweet chocolate chips (10 oz.)

FILLING
- 1 vanilla bean
- 3 large egg whites
- ½ cup granulated sugar
- ½ tsp. vanilla extract
- ¾ cup unsalted butter, room temperature

1. Preheat oven to 350°. Cream shortening and sugars until light and fluffy. Beat in eggs and vanilla. In another bowl, whisk flour, baking soda and salt; gradually beat into creamed mixture. Stir in chocolate chips. Chill dough for 1 hour.

2. Shape teaspoonfuls of dough into 1-in. balls. Place 1½ in.

A BAKER'S GIFT

If you have someone among your family and friends who loves to bake, you can create a beautiful baker's gift just for her—or him!

Think of it as a chance to check off items on a baker's wish list. Select a big mixing bowl, line it with pretty kitchen towels, then start filling it with little treasures. Choose from pot holders, baking mixes and cookbooks...cookie cutters in "extra" shapes that a baker might buy only for special occasions...whisks and spatulas to replace the tools that are used most often and might be getting a little worn...bottles of extracts and flavorings...jars of spices.

Arrange the contents inside, then wrap up the bowl in a holiday bow. Your loved one will be dipping into these treasures all year long!

mixture just until moistened. Fill prepared muffin cups about half full. Bake until the edges are golden brown and a toothpick inserted in the center of the cakes comes out clean, about 12 minutes. Run a small knife around the sides of the cups; cool on wire rack for 5 minutes before removing.

3. Serve warm with cranberry caramel sauce. If desired, serve with whipped cream or ice cream.

FINGER-LICKING GOOD MINI CREAM PUFFS

This recipe is quick and easy and the kids will love it! The delicate little cream puffs are somehow both fun and elegant, perfect for a family holiday celebration.
—Jennifer Erwin, Reynoldsburg, OH

PREP: 45 MIN. • **BAKE:** 30 MIN. + COOLING
MAKES: ABOUT 2½ DOZEN

- ½ cup water
- ¼ cup butter
- ½ cup all-purpose flour
- ¼ tsp. salt
- 2 large eggs

VANILLA FILLING
- 1 pkg. (3.4 oz.) instant vanilla pudding mix
- 1¾ cups 2% milk
- 1 cup frozen whipped topping, thawed
  Confectioners' sugar

1. Preheat oven to 400°. In a small saucepan, bring water and butter to a rolling boil over medium heat. Add flour and salt all at once; beat until blended. Cook, stirring vigorously, until a film forms at the bottom of the pan, about 4 minutes. Remove from heat; let stand 10 minutes.
2. Add eggs, one at a time, beating well after each addition until smooth. Continue beating until the mixture is smooth and shiny. Drop dough by 1-in. balls 1½ in. apart onto parchment-lined baking sheets. Bake until puffed, very firm and golden brown, 25-30 minutes. Cool on wire racks.
3. Meanwhile, whisk together pudding mix and milk for 2 minutes or until thickened; let stand 5 minutes. Fold in whipped topping. Cut puffs in half, fill with vanilla filling and replace the tops. Dust with confectioners' sugar; serve immediately.

MINI CARROT CAKES WITH CRANBERRY CARAMEL SAUCE

Two classic favorites, carrot cake and pineapple upside-down cake, inspired my recipe. Gorgeous and delicious cranberries replace the pineapple, and the mini cakes are cute and fun!
—Priscilla Yee, Concord, CA

PREP: 30 MIN. • **BAKE:** 12 MIN.
MAKES: 10 SERVINGS

- ¾ cup dried cranberries
- ⅓ cup packed brown sugar
- ¼ cup water
- 2 Tbsp. butter
- 2 Tbsp. honey
- ¼ tsp. vanilla extract

CAKES
- ⅔ cup all-purpose flour
- 1 tsp. pumpkin pie spice
- ½ tsp. baking powder
- ¼ tsp. baking soda
- ¼ tsp. salt
- 1 large egg
- ½ cup sugar
- ⅓ cup canola oil
- 1 tsp. vanilla extract
- 1 tsp. grated orange zest
- 1 cup shredded carrots
  Whipped cream or vanilla ice cream, optional

1. Preheat oven to 350°. Grease ten muffin cups; set aside. In a small saucepan, bring the first five ingredients to a boil over medium-low heat. Simmer until slightly thickened, about 2 minutes. Remove from heat; stir in vanilla extract. Keep warm.
2. Whisk together flour, pie spice, baking powder, baking soda and salt. In another bowl, mix egg, sugar, oil, vanilla and orange zest until blended; add carrots. Stir the flour mixture into the carrot

GRANDMA'S FAVORITE COOKIES

*Christmas cookies are always a highlight of the season,
and these recipes are the tried-and-true classics.
They're the cookies Grandma made, Mom made,
and your kids will make.*

SCOTTISH SHORTBREAD

My mother, who is of Scottish heritage, passed this recipe, as with most of my favorite recipes, on to me.
—Rose Mabee, Selkirk, MB

PREP: 15 MIN.
BAKE: 20 MIN./BATCH + COOLING
MAKES: ABOUT 4 DOZEN

  2 **cups butter, softened**
  1 **cup packed brown sugar**
  4 **to 4½ cups all-purpose flour**

1. Preheat oven to 325°. Cream butter and brown sugar until light and fluffy. Add 3¾ cups flour; mix well. Turn dough onto a floured surface; knead for 5 minutes, adding enough of the remaining flour to form a soft dough.
2. Roll dough to ½-in. thickness. Cut into 3x1-in. strips. Place strips 1 in. apart on ungreased baking sheets. Prick with fork. Bake until cookies are lightly browned, 20-25 minutes. Cool.

ALMOND SANDIES

Buttery, rich and delicious, these sandies are my husband's favorite cookie!
—Joyce Pierce, Caledonia, MI

PREP: 20 MIN.
BAKE: 25 MIN./BATCH + COOLING
MAKES: ABOUT 4 DOZEN

  1 **cup butter, softened**
  1 **cup sugar**
  1 **tsp. almond extract**
 1¾ **cups all-purpose flour**
  ½ **tsp. baking soda**
  ¼ **tsp. baking powder**
  ¼ **tsp. salt**
  ½ **cup slivered almonds**

1. Preheat oven to 300°. Cream butter and sugar until light and fluffy. Beat in extract. In another bowl, whisk together flour, baking soda, baking powder and salt; gradually add to the creamed mixture. Fold in almonds.
2. Drop by level tablespoonfuls onto ungreased baking sheets. Bake until the edges are lightly browned, 22-24 minutes. Cool for on baking sheets for 1-2 minutes before removing to wire racks.

GREAT-GRANDMA'S OATMEAL COOKIES

This recipe—a favorite of my husband's—goes back to my great-grandmother. At Christmastime, we use colored sugar for a festive touch.
—Mary Ann Konechne, Kimball, SD

PREP: 35 MIN.
BAKE: 15 MIN./BATCH + COOLING
MAKES: ABOUT 12 DOZEN

- 1½ cups shortening
- 2 cups sugar
- 4 large eggs, room temperature
- 4 tsp. water
- 4 cups all-purpose flour
- 2 tsp. baking soda
- 2 tsp. ground cinnamon
- ½ tsp. salt
- 4 cups quick-cooking oats
- 2 cups chopped raisins
- 1 cup chopped walnuts
  Additional granulated sugar or colored sugar

1. Preheat the oven to 350°. Cream the shortening and sugar until light and fluffy. Add eggs, one at a time, beating well after each addition. Beat in water. In a second bowl, whisk together the flour, baking soda, cinnamon and salt; add to the creamed mixture, and mix well. Stir in oats, raisins and walnuts.
2. On a surface sprinkled with additional granulated or colored sugar, roll dough to ¼-in. thickness. Cut with floured cookie cutters in desired shapes. Place cutouts 2 in. apart on greased baking sheets. Bake until set, 12-15 minutes. Remove to wire racks to cool.

BAKI'S OLD-WORLD COOKIES

My uncles have always called these "cupcake cookies" because of the unique and pretty way they're baked. My maternal grandmother mixed up many a batch.
—Marilyn Louise Riggenbach, Ravenna, OH

PREP: 25 MIN. + CHILLING • **BAKE:** 20 MIN.
MAKES: 2-3 DOZEN

- 1 cup butter, softened
- 1 cup sugar
- 2 large eggs
- 1 cup ground walnuts
- 1½ cups all-purpose flour
- 1½ tsp. ground cinnamon
- 1 tsp. ground cloves
- 2 tsp. vanilla extract
  Confectioners' sugar

1. Preheat oven to 350°. Cream butter and sugar until light and fluffy. Add eggs, one at a time, beating well after each addition. Add nuts. In another bowl, sift together flour, cinnamon and cloves; add with vanilla to creamed mixture. Refrigerate, covered, for 1 hour.
2. Fill 24 to 36 generously greased muffin cups one-third to half full. Press dough around sides, leaving a depression in the center. (If dough is too soft, add flour.)
3. Bake for 18 minutes, or until light brown. Cool for 2 minutes in tins; tap tins to remove the cookies to a wire rack. Dust with confectioners' sugar.

SACHER TORTE COOKIES

This cookie recipe will be a hit whether you are making it for your family or for a potluck. You can choose whichever fruit preserves you prefer.
—Audrey Thibodeau, Gilbert, AZ

PREP: 20 MIN. • **BAKE:** 15 MIN./BATCH + COOLING
MAKES: ABOUT 2½ DOZEN

- 1 cup butter, softened
- 1 pkg. (3.9 oz.) instant chocolate pudding mix
- 1 large egg
- 2 cups all-purpose flour
- ¼ cup sugar
- ½ cup raspberry, strawberry or apricot preserves

GLAZE
- ⅓ cup semisweet chocolate chips
- 2 tsp. shortening

1. Preheat oven to 325°. Cream butter and pudding mix until light and fluffy. Beat in egg. Add flour; gradually beat into the creamed mixture. Shape dough into 1¼-in. balls; roll in sugar. Place 2 in. apart on ungreased baking sheets. Using the end of a wooden spoon handle or your thumb, press a deep indentation in the center of each ball.
2. Bake until set, 15-18 minutes. Cool in pans for 2 minutes; remove from pans to wire racks. Fill each indentation with preserves; cool completely.
3. For the glaze, melt the chocolate chips and shortening in a microwave; stir until smooth. Cool slightly. Drizzle over cookies. Let cool completely.

GROSSMUTTER'S PEPPERNUTS

In the weeks before Christmas, my grandmother would bake peppernuts and store them until the big day. When we'd come home from school, the whole house would smell like anise and we knew the holiday season was about to begin.
—Marilyn Kutzli, Clinton, IA

PREP: 40 MIN. + CHILLING • **BAKE:** 10 MIN./BATCH + COOLING
MAKES: ABOUT 30 DOZEN

- 3 large eggs
- 2 cups sugar
- 2¾ cups all-purpose flour
- 1 tsp. anise extract or crushed aniseed

1. Beat eggs and sugar at medium speed for 15 minutes. Reduce speed; gradually add flour and anise. Beat until well combined. On a lightly floured surface, shape dough into ½-in.-thick ropes. Refrigerate, covered, for 1 hour.
2. Preheat oven to 350°. Cut ropes into ½-in. pieces; place on greased baking sheets. Bake until set, 6-8 minutes. Set baking sheets on wire racks and cool completely. Cookies will harden upon standing. Store in airtight containers.

HOLLY WREATHS

Cream cheese helps to keep these wreaths moist a long time, while adding a delicious, tangy flavor.
—Dee Lein, Longmont, CO

PREP: 20 MIN.
BAKE: 10 MIN./BATCH + COOLING
MAKES: ABOUT 3 DOZEN

- 1 cup butter, softened
- 3 oz. cream cheese, softened
- ½ cup sugar
- 1 tsp. vanilla extract
- 2 cups all-purpose flour
  Green candied cherries, thinly sliced
  Red Hots
  Decorating icing

1. Preheat oven to 375°. Cream butter and cream cheese. Add sugar; beat until light and fluffy. Stir in vanilla. Gradually beat in flour.

2. Using a cookie press fitted with a star piping tip, shape the dough into 2½-in. wreaths 1 in. apart on ungreased baking sheets. Bake until set (do not brown), 8-10 minutes. Cool on wire racks.

3. Decorate with green cherry pieces for leaves and Red Hots for berries. Use red decorating icing to form bows and adhere candy to wreaths.

Holiday Helper
Using a cookie press takes practice. If your dough is too soft to form crisp lines, chill it thoroughly and try again. Let your baking sheets cool completely before piping out more cookies—never use them hot from the oven.

"Everyone enjoys these, and they're perfect for Christmas!"
—CARLA HODENFIELD

CRANBERRY NUT SWIRLS

My sister-in-law came up with this recipe. We make these when we want to pull a fast one on the guys in our family—they claim they don't like cranberries in any shape or form, but everyone enjoys these, and they're perfect for Christmas!
—Carla Hodenfield, Ray, ND

PREP: 15 MIN. + CHILLING
BAKE: 15 MIN./BATCH + COOLING
MAKES: ABOUT 3½ DOZEN

½ cup butter, softened
¾ cup sugar
1 large egg
1 tsp. vanilla extract
1½ cups all-purpose flour
¼ tsp. baking powder
¼ tsp. salt
½ cup finely ground cranberries
½ cup finely chopped walnuts
1 Tbsp. grated orange zest
3 Tbsp. brown sugar
2 tsp. milk

1. Combine butter, sugar, egg and vanilla. Beat until light and fluffy, scraping the bowl occasionally. In another bowl, whisk together flour, baking powder and salt; add to the creamed mixture, beating well. Refrigerate at least 1 hour.
2. Combine cranberries, walnuts and orange zest; set aside. On a lightly floured surface, roll dough into a 10-in. square. Combine brown sugar and milk; brush over dough. Sprinkle with the cranberry mixture to within ½ in. of edges. Roll up tightly, jelly-roll style. Wrap in plastic; refrigerate until firm, several hours or overnight.
3. Preheat oven to 375°. Unwrap and cut the dough crosswise into ¼-in. slices. Place slices 2 in. apart on well-greased baking sheets. Bake until the edges are light brown, 14-15 minutes. Remove from pans to wire racks to cool.

MOM'S LEMON SUGAR COOKIES

These tender, soft sugar cookies have just a hint of lemon. If you like more lemon flavor, go ahead and kick it up a notch. It's also fantastic made with orange.
—Nancy Foust, Stoneboro, PA

PREP: 15 MIN. + CHILLING
BAKE: 10 MIN./BATCH + COOLING
MAKES: ABOUT 5 DOZEN

1 cup butter, softened
2 cups sugar
2 large eggs
2 tsp. grated lemon peel
2 tsp. lemon extract
4 cups all-purpose flour
1 tsp. baking soda
1 tsp. salt
1 cup buttermilk

1. Cream butter and sugar until light and fluffy. Add eggs, one at a time, beating well after each addition. Beat in lemon peel and extract. In another bowl, whisk together flour, baking soda and salt; add to the creamed mixture alternately with buttermilk, beating well after each addition. Cover and refrigerate for at least 2 hours.
2. Preheat oven to 375°. Drop dough by tablespoonfuls 2 in. apart onto ungreased baking sheets. Bake until lightly browned, 7-10 minutes. Remove to wire racks to cool completely.

HERMITS

Dress up a cookie plate with these old-fashioned spice bars full of raisins, molasses, cinnamon, ginger and nuts. These chewy cookies are said to be called hermits because they keep well—they're even better when hidden away like a hermit for several days!
—*Jeri Tirmenstein, Apache Junction, AZ*

PREP: 25 MIN. • **BAKE:** 10 MIN. + COOLING
MAKES: ABOUT 1 DOZEN

- ⅓ cup raisins
- 1 cup all-purpose flour
- ⅓ cup packed brown sugar
- ½ tsp. baking powder
- ½ tsp. ground ginger
- ½ tsp. ground cinnamon
- ¼ tsp. salt
- ¼ cup molasses
- 3 Tbsp. butter, melted
- 1 large egg white or 2 Tbsp. egg substitute
- 1 tsp. vanilla extract
- ⅓ cup chopped walnuts

1. Preheat oven to 375°. Cover raisins with boiling water. Let stand for 5 minutes; drain and set aside.
2. Whisk together next six ingredients. In another bowl, combine molasses, butter, egg white and vanilla; stir into the dry ingredients just until moistened. Fold in walnuts and raisins (the batter will be wet).
3. Divide the batter in half; spread each half into a 12x2-in. rectangle 2 in. apart on a parchment paper-lined baking sheet. (If necessary, wet your hands to keep the batter from sticking to them.) Bake until the edges are lightly browned and set, 10-15 minutes.
4. Transfer the rectangles to a cutting board; use a serrated knife to cut diagonally into 1½-in. bars. Remove bars to wire racks to cool. Store in an airtight container.

PEANUT BUTTER BLOSSOM COOKIES

This is an easy family favorite that makes my children smile.
—*Tammie Merrill, Wake Forest, NC*

PREP: 15 MIN.
BAKE: 10 MIN./BATCH + COOLING
MAKES: ABOUT 3 DOZEN

- ½ cup butter, softened
- ½ cup creamy peanut butter
- ½ cup sugar
- ½ cup packed brown sugar
- 1 large egg
- 1¼ cups all-purpose flour
- ¾ tsp. baking soda
- ½ tsp. baking powder
- ¼ tsp. salt
- 36 milk chocolate kisses

1. Preheat oven to 350°. Cream butter, peanut butter and sugars until light and fluffy. Beat in egg. In another bowl, sift together flour, baking soda, baking powder and salt; beat into the peanut butter mixture.
2. Drop dough by level tablespoonfuls 2 in. apart on ungreased baking sheets. Bake until light brown, 10-12 minutes. Remove from oven; immediately press a chocolate kiss into the top of each cookie. Cool on pans 2 minutes; remove from pans to wire racks to cool completely.

WHOLE WHEAT SNICKERDOODLES

These soft, chewy cookies make a super snack. Their light cinnamon taste is perfect with a cold glass of milk.
—Jana Horsfall, Garden City, KS

PREP: 15 MIN. • **BAKE:** 10 MIN/BATCH + COOLING
MAKES: ABOUT 2½ DOZEN

- 1 cup butter, softened
- 1½ cups sugar
- 1 large egg plus 1 large egg white, room temperature
- 1½ cups whole wheat flour
- 1¼ cups all-purpose flour
- 1 tsp. baking soda
- ¼ tsp. salt

TOPPING

- 2 Tbsp. sugar
- 2 tsp. ground cinnamon

1. Preheat oven to 400°. Cream butter and sugar until light and fluffy. Beat in egg and egg white. In another bowl, whisk together the flours, baking soda and salt; gradually beat into the creamed mixture.

2. In a small bowl, combine the topping ingredients. Shape dough into 1½-in. balls; roll in cinnamon sugar. Place balls 2 in. apart on ungreased baking sheets. Bake for 8-10 minutes. As they bake, the cookies will puff up, then flatten. Cool.

HARVEYS COCONUT MACAROONS

As the executive chef at Harveys, a resort hotel in Lake Tahoe, I modified this classic recipe, which originated a century ago at a renowned pastry shop in Vienna, Austria.
—Norbert Koblitz, Harveys, Lake Tahoe, NV

PREP: 15 MIN. • **BAKE:** 15 MIN./BATCH + COOLING
MAKES: ABOUT 4 DOZEN

- 1 cup sweetened shredded coconut
- 3½ cups almond paste
- 1 cup all-purpose flour
- ⅔ cup sugar
- 5 large eggs
- ½ cup chopped walnuts
  Red candied cherries, halved

1. Preheat oven to 350°. In a food processor or blender, process coconut until finely chopped; set aside. Beat almond paste until crumbled. Gradually add flour, sugar and coconut; mix well. Add eggs, one at a time, beating well after each addition; beat until smooth. Stir in nuts.

2. Cut a small hole in the tip of a pastry bag or in a corner of a food-safe plastic bag; insert a large star tip. Transfer dough to bag. Pipe 1-in.-diameter cookies 2 in. apart onto parchment paper-lined baking sheets. Top with cherries. Bake until golden brown, 15-20 minutes. Cool for 5 minutes before removing to wire racks.

2. Preheat oven to 400°. Unwrap dough and cut crosswise into ⅛-in. slices. Place 2 in. apart on ungreased baking sheets. Bake until edges are firm, 7-8 minutes. Remove from pans to wire racks to cool completely.

3. Combine all the frosting ingredients; beat until smooth. Spread over cookies; let dry completely. Store in airtight containers.

GRANDMA'S CHRISTMAS SPICE CUTOUTS

My great-grandmother made these, and the recipe was passed down in the family. When my mother started them—always the day after Thanksgiving—we knew Christmas wasn't far off. They are easy to decorate with family; my grandchildren always look forward to them.
—Elaine Phelps, Cornell, WI

PREP: 1 HOUR 20 MIN. + CHILLING
BAKE: 10 MIN./BATCH + COOLING
MAKES: ABOUT 7 DOZEN

2	cups molasses
2	cups dark corn syrup
½	cup shortening, melted
2	Tbsp. white vinegar
1	Tbsp. cold water
10	cups all-purpose flour
1	tsp. baking soda
1	tsp. powdered star anise
¼	tsp. ground cloves
⅛	tsp. ground cinnamon
⅛	tsp. ground nutmeg
	Dash salt

1. Combine the first five ingredients. Whisk together the remaining ingredients; add to the molasses mixture and mix well. Refrigerate, covered, for 3 hours or overnight.

2. Preheat oven to 375°. On a lightly floured surface, roll out the dough to ⅛-in. thickness. Cut into desired shapes with floured cookie cutters; place 1 in. apart on greased baking sheets. Bake until set, 10-12 minutes. Remove to wire racks to cool.

CHOCOLATE MINT CREAMS

This recipe came from an family friend and is always high on everyone's request list. I make at least six batches—some for Noel nibbling and some to give away as gifts.
—Beverly Fehner, Gladstone, MO

PREP: 20 MIN. + CHILLING
BAKE: 10 MIN./BATCH + COOLING
MAKES: ABOUT 6 DOZEN

1	cup butter, softened
1½	cups confectioners' sugar
2	oz. unsweetened chocolate, melted and cooled
1	large egg
1	tsp. vanilla extract
2½	cups all-purpose flour
1	tsp. baking soda
1	tsp. cream of tartar
¼	tsp. salt

FROSTING

¼	cup butter, softened
2	cups confectioners' sugar
2	Tbsp. milk
½	tsp. peppermint extract
	Green food coloring, optional

1. Cream butter and confectioners' sugar until light and fluffy. Add chocolate, egg and vanilla; mix well. In another bowl, whisk together flour, baking soda, cream of tartar and salt; gradually add to the creamed mixture, beating well. Divide dough in half; shape each piece into a 2-in.-diameter roll. Wrap in plastic; refrigerate until firm, about 1 hour.

PECAN SHORTBREAD TEA CAKES

*My Grandma Ellis made her shortbread cookies only at Christmas
because the ingredients were so indulgent. The results are, too!*
—Trisha Kruse, Eagle, ID

PREP: 45 MIN. • **BAKE:** 10 MIN./BATCH + COOLING
MAKES: ABOUT 6 DOZEN

- 2 cups butter, softened
- ½ cup sugar
- ½ cup packed brown sugar
- 2 tsp. vanilla extract
- 4 cups all-purpose flour
- ½ tsp. salt
- 72 pecan halves, toasted

CARAMEL GLAZE
- ½ cup packed brown sugar
- 3 Tbsp. 2% milk
- 2 Tbsp. butter
- 1½ cups confectioners' sugar
- 1 Tbsp. brandy

1. Preheat oven to 350°. Cream butter and sugars until light
and fluffy. Beat in vanilla. In another bowl, whisk together flour
and salt; gradually add to the creamed mixture and mix well.
Roll into 1-in. balls; place in greased miniature muffin cups.
Lightly press a pecan half into the center of each. Bake until
the edges are lightly browned, 10-12 minutes. Cool 10 minutes
before removing from pans to wire racks.

2. For caramel glaze, combine brown sugar, milk and butter in
a small saucepan over medium heat. Bring to a boil; cook and
stir for 1 minute. Remove from heat; cool 5 minutes. Gradually
beat in the confectioners' sugar and brandy. Drizzle glaze over
the cookies.

CREAM CHEESE SPRITZ

Before baking, I add bright sprinkles to these classics featuring a hint of orange and cinnamon. The recipe is from a booklet that came with a cookie press in the 1950s...and I still have the press!
—Sarah Bedia, Lake Jackson, TX

PREP: 15 MIN. • **BAKE:** 10 MIN./BATCH • **MAKES:** ABOUT 6 DOZEN

- 1   cup shortening
- 3   oz. cream cheese, softened
- 1   cup sugar
- 1   large egg yolk
- 1   tsp. vanilla extract
- 2½ cups all-purpose flour
- ½   tsp. salt
- ¼   tsp. ground cinnamon
- 1   tsp. grated orange zest
      Green food coloring, decorator candies and colored sugar, optional

1. Preheat oven to 350°. Cream shortening, cream cheese and sugar until light and fluffy. Beat in egg yolk and vanilla. In another bowl, whisk together flour, salt and cinnamon; gradually add to the creamed mixture and mix well. Stir in orange zest. If desired, add food coloring.
2. Using a cookie press fitted with the disk of your choice, press dough 1 in. apart onto ungreased baking sheets. Decorate with candies and colored sugar as desired. Bake until set (do not brown), 9-12 minutes. Remove from pans to wire racks to cool.

PEPPERMINT KISSES

These cookies really melt in your mouth. They're great when you don't want something rich and heavy.
—Lynn Bernstetter, Lake Elmo, MN

PREP: 20 MIN. • **BAKE:** 1½ HOURS + COOLING
MAKES: ABOUT 3 DOZEN

- 2   large egg whites
- ⅛   tsp. cream of tartar
- ⅛   tsp. salt
- ½   cup sugar
- 2   regular-size peppermint candy canes (one green, one red), crushed

1. Let egg whites stand at room temperature for 30 minutes.
2. Preheat oven to 225°. Add cream of tartar and salt to the egg whites; beat on medium speed until foamy. Gradually add sugar, 1 Tbsp. at a time, beating on high after each addition. Continue beating until stiff, glossy peaks form.
3. Cut a small hole in the tip of a pastry bag or in a corner of a food-safe plastic bag. Transfer the egg whites to the bag. Pipe 1½-in. cookies 2 in. apart onto parchment paper-lined baking sheets. Sprinkle half with crushed red candy canes, the other half with green.
4. Bake until firm but not brown, 1½-2 hours. Remove to wire racks to cool completely. Store in an airtight container.

GINGERSNAPS

My friends and neighbors look for these old-time cookies on the goodie trays that I give out every holiday. They're great for dunking in milk and they bring back the spicy flavor of Christmases past.
—Elizabeth Flatt, Kelso, WA

PREP: 20 MIN. + CHILLING
BAKE: 10 MIN./BATCH + COOLING
MAKES: ABOUT 2 DOZEN

- ⅓ cup shortening
- ½ cup sugar
- 1 large egg, room temperature
- 2 Tbsp. molasses
- 1 cup all-purpose flour
- 1 tsp. baking soda
- ½ tsp. ground cinnamon
- ½ tsp. ground cloves
- ½ tsp. ground ginger
- ⅛ tsp. salt
   Additional sugar

1. Cream shortening and sugar until light and fluffy. Beat in egg and molasses. In another bowl, whisk together next six ingredients; gradually beat into creamed mixture, mixing well. Refrigerate, covered, for at least 4 hours.
2. Preheat oven to 350°. Shape dough by tablespoonfuls into balls; roll in additional sugar. Place 2 in. apart on lightly greased baking sheets.
3. Bake until the edges are lightly browned and tops are set and starting to crack, 8-10 minutes. Cool for 2 minutes before removing to wire racks.

Holiday Helper

You can make this dough ahead of time and freeze it. Freeze balls of dough on waxed paper-lined baking sheets until firm. Then place the balls in resealable freezer bags for up to 3 months. To bake, place frozen balls 2 in. apart on lightly greased baking sheets. Bake until edges are lightly browned and tops are set and starting to crack.

CRINKLE-TOP CHOCOLATE COOKIES

When I baked these moist fudgy cookies for the first time, my three preschool children loved them! I like them because they're lower in fat and easy to mix and bake.
—Maria Groff, Ephrata, PA

PREP: 15 MIN. + CHILLING
BAKE: 10 MIN./BATCH + COOLING
MAKES: ABOUT 3½ DOZEN

- 2 cups (about 12 oz.) semisweet chocolate chips, divided
- 2 Tbsp. butter, softened
- 1 cup sugar
- 2 large egg whites
- 1½ tsp. vanilla extract
- 1½ cups all-purpose flour
- 1½ tsp. baking powder
- ¼ tsp. salt
- ¼ cup water
- ½ cup confectioners' sugar

1. In a microwave, melt 1 cup chocolate chips. Stir until smooth; set aside. Beat butter and sugar until crumbly, about 2 minutes. Add egg whites and vanilla; beat well. Stir in the melted chocolate.
2. In another bowl, whisk together flour, baking powder and salt; gradually add to the butter mixture alternately with water. Stir in the remaining chocolate chips. Refrigerate, covered, until easy to handle, about 2 hours.
3. Preheat oven to 350°. Shape dough into 1-in. balls. Roll in confectioners' sugar. Place 2 in. apart on baking sheets coated with cooking spray. Bake until set, 10-12 minutes. Remove to wire racks to cool.

6 TIPS FOR MAILING COOKIES

Good planning, good timing, good recipe selections and good packing methods are key when mailing cookies to family and friends.

1. Choose recipes that will ship well
Hard, crunchy cookies, slightly soft and chewy cookies, and dense cookies and brownies ship well. Extremely delicate cookies or those that require refrigeration don't. Avoid moist cookies topped with powdered sugar; the sugar will dissolve into a pasty mess by the time they arrive. Save these for a knockout in-person cookie plate.

2. Plan your time
Your goal is to ship as soon as possible. Spend the first few days making dough that can be refrigerated, followed by a marathon of oven time. If you make cookies in advance and freeze them, thaw them before shipping. Both warm and frozen cookies release moisture as they come to room temperature, which is bad in an enclosed space.

3. Keep them cool and dry
Remember: Air is the enemy of freshness! Keep your cookies in airtight food containers or resealable bags until you're ready to pack them. Your gift container should also be airtight. If you're using a baker's box, wrap the cookies in individual plastic bags or cellophane treat bags.

4. Pack in layers
Put a cushioning layer of crumpled plastic wrap on the bottom of the tin (if you want to use pretty tissue paper, add that first). Layer cookies in order of weight, with the heaviest on the bottom. Keep types of cookies together—crisp with crisp, soft with soft—and separate them with plastic. Otherwise, crisp cookies will absorb the moisture from your soft cookies, to the detriment of both. Individually wrap moist or strongly flavored treats. Use parchment paper for frosted cookies; with varying temperatures, frosting can soften and stick to plastic.

5. Pack snugly, but don't cram
Your cookies shouldn't bounce around, but should have a bit of "give" so they won't break with pressure. Use crumpled plastic wrap to fill empty spaces as you fill your tin. After you've closed the tin, gently shake it—if you hear bouncing, open it and add more cushioning. Choose a heavy-duty cardboard shipping box that's larger than your container by at least an inch on each side. Pack the extra space with bubble wrap, crumpled newspaper or packing peanuts.

6. Check your shipping methods
Whether you use USPS, FedEx or UPS, choose a method that will deliver within two or three days. There are special guidelines for care packages sent to military personnel overseas; these are on the USPS website, along with a pricing tool to estimate shipping costs.

LEMON SNOWDROPS
PICTURED ON PAGE 188

I save my snowdrop cookies for special occasions. The crunchy, buttery sandwich cookie has a puckery lemon filling.
—Bernice Martinoni, Petaluma, CA

PREP: 40 MIN. + CHILLING
BAKE: 10 MIN./BATCH + COOLING
MAKES: 2 DOZEN

- 1 cup butter, softened
- ½ cup confectioners' sugar
- ¼ tsp. salt
- 1 tsp. lemon extract
- 2 cups all-purpose flour
  Granulated sugar

FILLING
- 1 large egg, lightly beaten
- ⅔ cup sugar
- 2 tsp. grated lemon zest
- 3 Tbsp. lemon juice
- 4 tsp. butter
  Additional confectioners' sugar, optional

1. Preheat oven to 350°. Cream butter, confectioners' sugar and salt until light and fluffy. Beat in extract. Gradually beat in flour. Shape teaspoonfuls of dough into balls (if necessary, refrigerate dough, covered, until firm enough to shape). Place 1 in. apart on ungreased baking sheets; flatten slightly with bottom of a glass dipped in granulated sugar. Bake until light brown, 10-12 minutes. Remove cookies from pans to wire racks to cool completely.

2. For filling, whisk together egg, sugar, lemon zest and lemon juice in a small heavy saucepan over medium-low heat until blended. Add butter; cook over medium heat, whisking constantly, until thickened and a thermometer reads at least 170°, about 20 minutes. Remove from heat immediately (do not boil). Transfer to a small bowl; cool. Press plastic wrap onto the surface of the filling. Refrigerate until cold, about 1 hour.

3. To serve, spread lemon filling on half of cookies; cover with the remaining cookies. If desired, dust with confectioners' sugar. Store leftovers in refrigerator.

SPIRITED SWEETS

Each of these delicious, tempting treats is infused with wine, liquor or liqueur—giving a sophisticated, grown-up spin to your holiday desserts.

KAHLUA FUDGE

This tasty variation calls for only five ingredients, making it easy to serve up sweet and scrumptious holiday treats.
—Laura Hanks, Harleysville, PA

PREP: 20 MIN. • **COOK:** 5 MIN. + CHILLING
MAKES: ABOUT 2½ LBS.

- 1 tsp. plus 2 Tbsp. butter, divided
- 24 oz. white baking chocolate, coarsely chopped
- 1 cup sweetened condensed milk
- ½ cup chopped pecans, toasted
- ⅓ cup Kahlua (coffee liqueur)

1. Line a 9-in. square pan with foil; grease foil with 1 tsp. butter. In a heavy saucepan, cook and stir chocolate over low heat until melted. Add milk and the remaining butter; stir until blended. Remove from heat; stir in pecans and Kahlua.
2. Spread mixture into the prepared pan. Refrigerate, covered, 2 hours or until firm. Remove foil; cut fudge into 1-in. squares. Store between layers of waxed paper in an airtight container in the refrigerator.

CHAMBORD CREAM

I love serving this for holiday get-togethers; it's easy to make and is a great way to incorporate fruit into a buffet setting. During the Christmas season, I include starfruit to make it even more festive.
—Brittany Allyn, Mesa, AZ

TAKES: 10 MIN. + CHILLING
MAKES: 10 SERVINGS

- 3 oz. cream cheese, softened
- 3 Tbsp. plus 2 tsp. Chambord raspberry liqueur, divided
- 3 Tbsp. seedless raspberry jam
- 1 cup heavy whipping cream
  Assorted fresh fruit

Whisk together cream cheese, 3 Tbsp. Chambord and raspberry jam until very smooth. In another bowl, beat cream until soft peaks form. Gently fold whipped cream into the cream cheese mixture until combined. Spoon into small glasses; refrigerate. Just before serving, drizzle the remaining Chambord over the cream mixture. Serve with fresh fruit.

RUM VANILLA CRANBERRY SAUCE

Cranberry sauce is one of my favorite things. This jazzed-up version combines vanilla with rum to create a rich, flavorful sauce that's far from the usual!
—Ashley Lecker, Green Bay, WI

PREP: 5 MIN. • **COOK:** 35 MIN. + COOLING
MAKES: 2 CUPS

- 1 pkg. (12 oz.) fresh cranberries, rinsed
- 1 cup sugar
- 1 cup water
- 1 tsp. grated orange zest
- ½ cup orange juice
- ¼ cup rum
- 1½ tsp. vanilla extract

In a large saucepan, gently stir all the ingredients over medium heat. Bring to a boil. Reduce heat; simmer, uncovered, for 35 minutes. Remove from heat; cool.

the remaining layer; spread the top and sides of torte with the remaining glaze. If desired, garnish torte with toasted almonds. Refrigerate for several hours before slicing.

NOTE To toast nuts, bake in a shallow pan in a 350° oven for 5-10 minutes or cook in a skillet over low heat until lightly browned, stirring occasionally.

GIMLET BARS

I love a tangy gimlet when the weather turns steamy—but these bars are just the thing when the craving hits and summer seems too far away. Add more lime zest if you want these a bit tangier.
—Trisha Kruse, Eagle, ID

PREP: 20 MIN. + STANDING
BAKE: 35 MIN. + COOLING
MAKES: 4 DOZEN

> 2 cups all-purpose flour
> ½ cup confectioners' sugar
> ½ tsp. salt
> 1 cup butter

FILLING
> 4 large eggs
> 2 cups granulated sugar
> ⅓ cup all-purpose flour
> ¼ cup lime juice
> ¼ cup gin
> 1 Tbsp. grated lime zest
> ½ tsp. baking powder
> 1 drop green food coloring, optional

GLAZE
> 1½ cups confectioners' sugar
> 2 Tbsp. lime juice
> 2 Tbsp. gin
> 1 tsp. grated lime zest

1. Preheat oven to 350°. Grease a 15x10x1-in. baking pan; set aside. Whisk flour, confectioners' sugar and salt; cut in butter until crumbly. Press onto bottom of prepared pan. Bake until golden brown, about 10 minutes. Cool on a wire rack.
2. For the filling, whisk the first seven ingredients and, if desired, food coloring; spread filling over crust. Bake until set, about 25 minutes. Cool completely in pan on a wire rack.
3. For the glaze, whisk all the ingredients until smooth; spread evenly over the cooled bars. Let the glaze set before serving bars.

SACHER TORTE

You'll get chocolate, almonds, apricots— and Amaretto—in every bite of this classic, elegant dessert.
—Taste of Home *Test Kitchen*

PREP: 30 MIN. • **BAKE:** 25 MIN. + CHILLING
MAKES: 16 SERVINGS

> ½ cup chopped dried apricots
> ½ cup Amaretto
> 1 pkg. devil's food cake mix (regular size)
> 3 large eggs
> ¾ cup water
> ⅓ cup canola oil

FILLING
> ⅔ cup apricot preserves
> 1 Tbsp. Amaretto

GLAZE
> 1 cup heavy whipping cream
> ¼ cup light corn syrup
> 12 oz. semisweet chocolate, chopped
> 4 tsp. vanilla extract
> 1 cup toasted sliced almonds, optional

1. Preheat oven to 350°. Grease and flour two 9-in. round baking pans; set aside. Combine apricots and Amaretto; let stand 15 minutes. In another bowl, combine cake mix, eggs, water, oil and apricot mixture. Beat on low speed 30 seconds; beat on medium 2 minutes.
2. Pour batter into prepared pans. Bake until a toothpick inserted in the center comes out clean, 22-27 minutes. Cool in pans for 10 minutes before removing to a wire rack to cool completely.
3. For the filling, heat apricot preserves and Amaretto on low in a small saucepan, stirring occasionally, until the preserves are melted; set aside.
4. For the glaze, combine cream and corn syrup in a small saucepan. Bring just to a boil. Pour over chocolate; whisk until smooth. Stir in vanilla.
5. Using a long serrated knife, cut each cake horizontally in half. Place one layer on a serving plate; spread with half the filling. Top with another layer; spread with a third of the glaze. Cover with the third layer and the remaining filling. Top with

FROZEN MARGARITA MOUSSE

This creamy frozen mousse combines ready-to-drink margarita mix and whipped topping. It's easy to put together and the freezer does all the work. Garnish with additional crushed pretzels and kosher salt to enhance the sweet and salty flavor.
—*Debbie Glasscock, Conway, AR*

TAKES: 20 MIN. + FREEZING
MAKES: 6 SERVINGS

- 1 can (14 oz.) sweetened condensed milk
- ½ cup ready-to-drink margarita mix
- 1 Tbsp. sugar
- 1½ tsp. grated lime zest
- 1 Tbsp. lime juice
- 5 drops green food coloring, optional
- 1 carton (8 oz.) frozen whipped topping, thawed

PRETZEL TOPPING
- ⅓ cup finely crushed pretzels
- 4 tsp. butter, melted
- 1 Tbsp. sugar
  Lime slices

1. Combine the first five ingredients; mix well. If desired, add green food coloring; fold in thawed whipped topping.

2. For pretzel topping, combine pretzels, butter and sugar. Spoon the lime mixture into 6 glasses; top each with 1 Tbsp. of the pretzel topping. Freeze until firm, 4-6 hours. Serve frozen with lime slices.

Holiday Helper

This dessert can be easily adapted to different flavors of margarita mix. Simply choose your added fruit juice and zest to match (or complement) your chosen mix, and you have an entirely different flavor of mousse.

DARK CHOCOLATE BOURBON BALLS

This classic will take you back to Christmases past. The blended taste of bourbon and pecans is irresistible!
—*Taste of Home* Test Kitchen

TAKES: 30 MIN. + CHILLING • **MAKES:** ABOUT 4 DOZEN

- 1¼ cups finely chopped pecans, divided
- ¼ cup bourbon
- ½ cup butter, softened
- 3¾ cups confectioners' sugar
- 1 lb. dark chocolate candy coating, melted

1. Combine 1 cup pecans and bourbon; let stand, covered, for 8 hours or overnight.
2. Cream butter and confectioners' sugar, ¼ cup at a time, until crumbly; stir in pecan mixture. Refrigerate, covered, until firm enough to shape into 1-in. balls, about 45 minutes. Place on waxed paper-lined baking sheets. Refrigerate until firm, about 1 hour.
3. Dip in chocolate coating; allow excess to drip off. Sprinkle with remaining pecans. Let stand until set.

BERRIES IN CHAMPAGNE JELLY

My sister gave me this recipe a few years back when I wanted an elegant fruit dish to serve guests. A refreshing alternative to salad, it's sparkly and special enough to double as a light dessert.
—*Andrea Barnhoom, Scottsville, NY*

PREP: 40 MIN. • **COOK:** 10 MIN. + CHILLING • **MAKES:** 12 SERVINGS

- 4 envelopes unflavored gelatin
- 2 cups cold water
- 1½ cups sugar
- 4 cups champagne
- 2 cups sparkling grape juice
- 3 cups fresh raspberries
- 3 cups fresh blueberries
- 2 cups fresh blackberries

1. In a large saucepan, sprinkle gelatin over cold water; let stand for 2 minutes. Add sugar. Cook and stir over medium-low heat until gelatin and sugar are dissolved (do not boil). Remove from heat. Slowly stir in champagne and grape juice.
2. Transfer mixture to a 13x9-in. dish coated with cooking spray. Refrigerate, covered, for 8 hours or overnight. Using a potato masher, gently break up champagne jelly. Layer jelly and berries in 12 dessert dishes. Refrigerate, covered, for at least 2 hours before serving.

RAWHIDE'S WHISKEY CAKE

For several years, our neighbor gave us a moist, whiskey-flavored cake. I tweaked the recipe, and now my friends want this cake instead of platters of homemade cookies.
—Cindy Worth, Lapwai, ID

PREP: 15 MIN. + STANDING
BAKE: 1 HOUR + COOLING
MAKES: 16 SLICES

- 1 pkg. spice cake mix with pudding (regular size)
- 1 pkg. (3.4 oz.) instant vanilla pudding mix
- ¾ cup 2% milk
- ¾ cup whiskey
- ½ cup canola oil
- 4 large eggs
- 1⅓ cups coarsely chopped walnuts, divided

GLAZE
- 1 cup sugar
- ½ cup butter, cubed
- ½ cup whiskey
- 1 tsp. water

1. Preheat oven to 300°. Grease and flour a 10-in. tube pan.

2. Combine the first six ingredients; beat on low speed 30 seconds. Beat on medium speed 2 minutes; fold in 1 cup nuts. Pour batter into prepared pan; sprinkle with remaining nuts. Bake until a toothpick inserted in center comes out clean, about 60-65 minutes. Cool in pan.

3. For glaze, mix all ingredients in a small saucepan; bring to a boil over medium-high heat. Reduce heat; simmer for 10 minutes. Cool for 3 minutes. Pour one-third of glaze over top of cake, allowing some to flow over sides. Let stand 1 hour. Remove from pan to cool completely; cover.

4. The next day, reheat glaze; brush half over cake, cooling before covering. Repeat the following day, using remaining glaze.

3. Bake until the center is just set and the top appears dull, 60-70 minutes. Remove springform pan from water bath. Cool on a wire rack for 10 minutes. Loosen the sides from the pan with a knife; remove foil. Cool for 1 hour longer. Refrigerate overnight; cover when completely cooled.
4. Remove the rim from the pan. Top cheesecake with whipped topping and, if desired, cinnamon.

LIME & GIN COCONUT MACAROONS

I took these lime and coconut macaroons to our annual cookie exchange, where we name a cookie queen each year. These won me the crown!
—*Milissa Kirkpatrick, Angel Fire, NM*

PREP: 20 MIN.
BAKE: 15 MIN/BATCH + COOLING
MAKES: ABOUT 2½ DOZEN

- 4 large egg whites
- ⅔ cup sugar
- 3 Tbsp. gin
- 1½ tsp. grated lime zest
- ¼ tsp. salt
- ¼ tsp. almond extract
- 1 pkg. (14 oz.) sweetened shredded coconut
- ½ cup all-purpose flour
- 8 oz. white baking chocolate, melted

1. Preheat oven to 350°. Whisk the first six ingredients until blended. In another bowl, toss coconut with flour; stir in the egg white mixture.
2. Drop by tablespoonfuls 2 in. apart onto greased baking sheets. Bake until tops are light brown, 15-18 minutes. Remove from pans to wire racks to cool completely.
3. Dip the bottoms of the macaroons into melted chocolate, allowing excess to drip off. Place on waxed paper; let stand until set. Store in an airtight container.

RUMCHATA CHEESECAKE

When I tried RumChata at a friend's party, I knew it would make a great cheesecake. For a pretty presentation, drizzle it with caramel syrup or top with toasted coconut.
—*Christine Talley, Hillsboro, MO*

PREP: 35 MIN. + COOLING
BAKE: 1 HOUR + CHILLING
MAKES: 12 SERVINGS

- 1 pkg. (10 oz.) shortbread cookies, finely crushed
- 4 Tbsp. butter, melted
- 4 pkg. (8 oz. each) cream cheese, softened
- 1 cup sugar
- ¾ cup vanilla Greek yogurt
- ¾ cup RumChata liqueur
- 1 tsp. vanilla extract
- 4 large eggs, room temperature
- 1 carton (16 oz.) frozen whipped topping, thawed
    Ground cinnamon, optional

1. Preheat oven to 325°. Securely wrap bottom and sides of a greased 9-in. springform pan with a double thickness of heavy-duty foil. Combine cookie crumbs and butter. Press onto bottom of pan.
2. Beat cream cheese and sugar until smooth. Beat in yogurt, RumChata and vanilla. Add eggs; beat on low speed just until blended. Pour over crust. Place springform pan in a larger baking pan; add 1 in. of hot water to larger pan.

NO-MESS DIPPING

To keep your fingers clean while dipping confections in chocolate, all you need is a knife and fork. Drop each candy center in the melted chocolate, then scoop it out with a fork, holding it over the bowl to catch the drips. Use a knife to roll the coated candy off the fork and onto waxed paper to set.

When melting chocolate for dipping, be sure your equipment is bone-dry to prevent the chocolate from seizing (turning dry and lumpy). Melt slowly, and stir often, to prevent any one section from overheating. Finally, invest in the best chocolate you can afford, with a high cocoa-butter content. This is especially important for coating the outside of confections, and it will be the first thing to hit the taste buds.

CREME DE MENTHE TRUFFLES

I found the recipe for these sweets in a box of old recipe clippings and decided to try it. I'm so glad I did! The minty flavor is perfect for Christmas, and the filling just melts in your mouth.
—Joe Mattes, Amana, IA

PREP: 55 MIN. + CHILLING • **COOK:** 5 MIN.
MAKES: 4½ DOZEN

- 1　cup finely chopped pecans
- ½　cup butter, melted
- ¼　cup creme de menthe
- 4　cups confectioners' sugar
- 2　cups (12 oz.) semisweet chocolate chips
- 2　tsp. shortening

1. Combine pecans, butter and creme de menthe. Gradually beat in confectioners' sugar. Refrigerate, covered, until easy to handle, about 1 hour.
2. Lightly dust hands with confectioners' sugar; shape mixture into 1-in. balls. Place balls on waxed paper-lined baking sheets. Chill until firm, about 30 minutes.
3. In a microwave-safe bowl, melt chocolate chips and shortening; stir until smooth. Dip balls in the chocolate mixture; let excess drip off. Return to waxed paper; refrigerate until set. After serving, store leftovers in an airtight container in the refrigerator.

FUDGY LAYERED IRISH MOCHA BROWNIES

My husband and I are big fans of Irish cream liqueur, so I wanted to incorporate it into a brownie. I started with my mom's brownie recipe, then added frosting and ganache. This decadent recipe is the result.
—Sue Gronholz, Beaver Dam, WI

PREP: 35 MIN. • **BAKE:** 25 MIN. + CHILLING
MAKES: 16 SERVINGS

- ⅔ cup all-purpose flour
- ½ tsp. baking powder
- ¼ tsp. salt
- ⅓ cup butter
- 6 Tbsp. baking cocoa
- 2 Tbsp. canola oil
- ½ tsp. instant coffee granules
- 1 cup granulated sugar
- 2 large eggs, beaten
- 1 tsp. vanilla extract

FROSTING
- 2 cups confectioners' sugar
- ¼ cup butter, softened
- 3 Tbsp. Irish cream liqueur

GANACHE
- 1 cup semisweet chocolate chips
- 3 Tbsp. Irish cream liqueur
- 2 Tbsp. heavy whipping cream
- ½ tsp. instant coffee granules

1. Preheat oven to 350°. Sift together flour, baking powder and salt; set aside. In a small saucepan over low heat, melt butter. Remove from heat; stir in cocoa, oil and instant coffee granules. Cool slightly; stir in sugar and beaten eggs. Gradually add flour mixture and vanilla; mix well. Spread batter into greased 8-in. square pan; bake until center is set (do not overbake), about 25 minutes. Cool in pan on wire rack.

2. For frosting, whisk confectioners' sugar and butter (mixture will be lumpy). Gradually whisk in liqueur; beat until smooth. Spread over slightly warm brownies. Refrigerate until frosting is set, about 1 hour.

3. For ganache, microwave all ingredients on high for 1 minute; stir. Microwave for 30 seconds longer; stir until smooth. Cool slightly until ganache reaches a spreading consistency. Spread over frosting. Refrigerate until set, 45-60 minutes.

BOURBON PUMPKIN TART WITH WALNUT STREUSEL

My husband loves pumpkin pie, so I searched high and low for the perfect recipe. As soon as he tasted this tart, he told me to stop searching!
—Brenda Ryan, Marshall, MO

PREP: 45 MIN. + CHILLING • **BAKE:** 45 MIN.
MAKES: 14 SERVINGS

- 2 cups all-purpose flour
- ⅓ cup granulated sugar
- 1 tsp. grated orange zest
- ½ tsp. salt
- ⅔ cup cold butter, cubed
- 1 large egg, lightly beaten
- ¼ cup heavy whipping cream

FILLING
- 3 large eggs
- 1 can (15 oz.) solid-pack pumpkin
- ½ cup granulated sugar
- ½ cup heavy whipping cream
- ¼ cup packed brown sugar
- ¼ cup bourbon
- 2 Tbsp. all-purpose flour
- 1 tsp. ground cinnamon
- 1 tsp. ground ginger
- ¼ tsp. salt
- ¼ tsp. ground cloves

TOPPING
- ¾ cup all-purpose flour
- ⅓ cup granulated sugar
- ⅓ cup packed brown sugar
- ½ tsp. salt
- ½ tsp. ground cinnamon
- ½ cup cold butter, cubed
- ¾ cup coarsely chopped walnuts, toasted
- ¼ cup chopped crystallized ginger

1. Preheat oven to 350°. Combine flour, sugar, orange zest and salt. Cut in butter until crumbly. Add egg. Gradually add cream, tossing with a fork until a ball forms. Refrigerate, covered, until easy to handle, at least 30 minutes.

2. On a lightly floured surface, roll out dough into a 13-in. circle. Press onto bottom and up the sides of an ungreased 11-in. fluted tart pan with removable bottom.

3. Combine all filling ingredients; pour into the crust. For topping, whisk flour, sugar, brown sugar, salt and cinnamon. Cut in butter until crumbly. Stir in walnuts and ginger. Sprinkle over the filling.

4. Bake until a knife inserted in center comes out clean, 45-55 minutes. Cool on a wire rack. After serving, refrigerate any leftovers.

Holiday Helper
You can prepare your own pumpkin instead of using canned. Wash, peel and remove seeds from a pie pumpkin. Cut into chunks and steam until soft. Puree using a food mill or processor. Use cup-for-cup in place of canned pumpkin.

CRANBERRY-ORANGE TIRAMISU

This holiday version of tiramisu trades the Amaretto and coffee notes of the traditional dessert for the bright, seasonal flavors of cranberries and orange. The combination of orange liqueur and Marsala make this a delicious, potent meal-ender.
—Jerry Gulley, Pleasant Prairie, WI

PREP: 10 MIN. + COOLING
COOK: 25 MIN. + CHILLING
MAKES: 9 SERVINGS

    2   cups fresh cranberries
    1   cup sugar
    ½   cup orange juice
CUSTARD
    ⅓   cup Marsala wine
    3   Tbsp. sugar

    1   large egg yolk
    2   cartons (8 oz. each)
        mascarpone cheese
FRUIT DIP
    1¼ cups cranberry juice
    4   tsp. orange liqueur
    1¼ tsp. sugar
    1   pkg. (7 oz.) crisp ladyfinger cookies
    ½   tsp. baking cocoa

1. In a small saucepan, combine the cranberries, sugar and orange juice. Cook, uncovered, over medium heat until the berries pop and mixture is thickened, about 10 minutes. Cool completely.
2. For the custard, heat wine and sugar in a small heavy saucepan over medium heat until bubbles form around the sides of the pan. Whisk a small amount of the hot mixture into the egg yolk. Return all to the

pan, whisking constantly. Cook and stir over low heat until a thermometer reads at least 160° and the mixture coats the back of a spoon. Quickly transfer to a small bowl; place the bowl in a pan of ice water. Stir 1 minute. In a large bowl, beat cheese until smooth. Gradually beat in the custard; set aside.
3. For the fruit dip, combine cranberry juice, liqueur and sugar in a shallow bowl. Quickly dip ladyfingers into the mixture, allowing excess to drip off. Arrange in a single layer in an 8-in. square dish. Layer with 1 cup of the custard mixture and the cranberry mixture. Top with remaining ladyfingers and the remaining custard mixture. Refrigerate, covered, at least 4 hours or overnight.
4. Just before serving, dust with cocoa.

SPICED RUM & PEAR CAKE

The flavors in this cake make it stand out—with raisins, fresh sweet pear chunks, rich spices, crunchy walnuts and rum, it's a great addition to your holiday spread. You can swap apple juice for the rum, and it'll still be delicious!
—Julie Peterson, Crofton, MD

PREP: 25 MIN. • **BAKE:** 45 MIN+ COOLING
MAKES: 20 SERVINGS

- ½ cup spiced rum
- 2 cups granulated sugar
- 3 large eggs
- ¾ cup canola oil
- 2 tsp. vanilla extract
- 2½ cups all-purpose flour
- 2 tsp. baking powder
- 2 tsp. ground cinnamon
- 1 tsp. salt
- ½ tsp. ground allspice
- 4 large pears (about 2 lbs.), peeled and cut into ½-in. cubes
- 1 cup chopped walnuts
- 1 cup golden raisins

GLAZE
- 1 cup confectioners' sugar
- 2 Tbsp. rum

1. Preheat oven to 350°. Grease and flour a 13x9 in. baking pan; set aside. In a small heavy saucepan, heat rum over medium heat. Bring to a boil; cook until reduced by half, 8-10 minutes. Remove from heat; cool.
2. Beat sugar, eggs, oil, vanilla and the cooled rum until slightly thickened, about 5 minutes. Sift together the next five ingredients; gradually beat into the rum mixture. Stir in pears, walnuts and raisins. Transfer batter to prepared baking pan.
3. Bake until a toothpick inserted in center comes out clean, 45-50 minutes. Cool cake in pan on rack.
4. For glaze, mix confectioners' sugar and rum; spread over cake. Cut into squares.

Holiday Helper

Change up the flavor by switching out the rum. It's exceptional with dark rum or coconut rum. The cake would also be great with bourbon. And if you have black walnuts, try using them in this hearty dessert.

HONEY-BOURBON HOT CHOCOLATE

My husband and I like this grown-up version of hot chocolate on cold winter evenings. It's even better when made with honey-flavored bourbon, if you can find it in your local store.
—Andrea Harvath, Duncannon, PA

TAKES: 15 MIN. • **MAKES:** 4 SERVINGS

- 4 cups whole milk
- 4 oz. bittersweet chocolate, chopped
- 2 Tbsp. honey
- ¼ cup bourbon
- 2 tsp. vanilla extract
- Whipped cream and baking cocoa, optional

1. In a large saucepan, heat milk over medium heat until bubbles form around the sides of the pan. Remove from heat; whisk in chocolate and honey until the chocolate is completely melted. Return to heat; cook and stir until heated through.
2. Remove from heat; stir in bourbon and vanilla. If desired, top with whipped cream; sprinkle with cocoa.

GIFTS IN A JAR

*Gifts from the kitchen are gifts from the heart.
They're homemade and delicious—and can be enjoyed
year-round. Jars of jam, salsa or gift mixes are perfect
presents for co-workers, teachers and neighbors.*

BLUEBERRY MAPLE SUGAR PANCAKE MIX

We use maple sugar made at our farm, Bonhomie Acres, to make these pancakes, and serve them with 100 percent maple syrup, too. The delicious flavor demands nothing less!
—Katherine Brown, Fredericktown, OH

PREP: 15 MIN. • **COOK:** 5 MIN./BATCH
MAKES: 1 BATCH (ABOUT 2 CUPS MIX)

- 2 **cups all-purpose flour**
- 4 **tsp. baking powder**
- ½ **tsp. salt**
- ⅓ **cup maple sugar**
- ⅔ **cup dried blueberries**

ADDITIONAL INGREDIENTS

- 2 **large eggs**
- 1⅓ **cups 2% milk**
- ¼ **cup butter, melted**

1. Whisk together flour, baking powder and salt. Transfer to a 1-pt. glass jar. Top with maple sugar; cover. Place dried blueberries in a small plastic bag; attach to jar. Store in a cool dry place or in a freezer up to 3 months.

2. To prepare pancakes: Preheat lightly greased griddle over medium heat. In a small bowl, mix flour mixture and maple sugar. Whisk in eggs, milk and melted butter. Stir in blueberries.

3. Pour batter by scant ¼ cupfuls onto griddle; cook until bubbles on top begin to pop and bottoms are golden brown. Turn; cook until second side is golden brown.

Holiday Helper

When you give a mix like this as a gift, be sure to write up the instructions for making the pancakes (or cookies, or brownies...) on a pretty label and attach it to the jar with ribbon or decorative cord.

GRANOLA STREUSEL CRANBERRY MUFFIN MIX

These muffins are great for breakfast. Once the family gets a taste, these delicious treats will disappear quickly!
—Karen Moore, Jacksonville, FL

TAKES: 30 MIN. • **MAKES:** 1 DOZEN

- 2 cups all-purpose flour
- ½ cup nonfat dry milk powder
- ½ cup sugar
- 3 tsp. baking powder
- 1 tsp. pumpkin pie spice
- ½ tsp. salt
- ¾ cup dried cranberries
- 2 crunchy oat and honey granola bars (0.74 oz. each), finely crushed
- 2 Tbsp. sugar

ADDITIONAL INGREDIENTS

- 1 large egg, lightly beaten
- ¾ cup water or 2% milk
- ⅓ cup canola oil
- 2 Tbsp. butter, melted

1. Whisk first six ingredients. Place in a 1-qt. jar; top with cranberries. In a small plastic bag, combine the crushed granola bars and sugar. Add bag to jar; cover. Store in a cool dry place up to 3 months.
2. To prepare muffins: Preheat oven to 375°. Place muffin mix in a large bowl. In a small bowl, whisk egg, water and canola oil until blended. Add to the muffin mix; stir just until moistened. Fill paper or foil-lined muffin cups three-fourths full. Combine the streusel mix from the plastic bag with melted butter. Sprinkle evenly over the muffin cups.
3. Bake until a toothpick inserted in the center comes out clean, 15-18 minutes. Cool for 5 minutes before removing from pan to a wire rack. Serve warm.

ANNIE'S ORIGINAL SALSA

I spent five years working on this recipe, testing and adjusting the acidity level to get approval from the state extension service that this was safe to can with a boiling water bath. When my oldest daughter got married, we gifted wedding guests with 300 small jars of salsa.
—Angela Barnes, Big Rapids, MI

PREP: 45 MIN. • **PROCESS:** 15 MIN.
MAKES: 7 PINTS

- 2 cups tomato sauce
- 2 cups tomato paste
- 2 cups chopped onions
- 1 cup chopped green pepper
- 3 to 5 chopped jalapeno peppers, seeded
- ½ cup chopped fresh cilantro
- 6 garlic cloves, minced
- ⅔ cup white vinegar
- ⅓ cup sugar
- 2 Tbsp. canning salt
- 2 tsp. ground cumin
- 2 tsp. pepper
- 8 cups chopped peeled tomatoes, drained (about 5 lbs. medium tomatoes)

1. In a stockpot, combine the first 12 ingredients. Stir in the tomatoes. Bring to a boil over medium-high heat. Reduce heat; simmer, uncovered, until the vegetables are tender, about 20 min.
2. Ladle the hot mixture into hot 1-pint jars, leaving ½-in. headspace. Remove air bubbles and adjust headspace, if necessary, by adding more of the hot mixture. Wipe rims. Center lids on jars; screw on bands until fingertip tight.
3. Place jars into canner with simmering water, ensuring that they are completely covered with water. Bring to a boil; process for 15 minutes. Remove jars and cool.
NOTE The processing time listed is for altitudes of 1,000 feet or less. For altitudes up to 3,000 feet, add 5 minutes; 6,000 feet, add 10 minutes; 8,000 feet, add 15 minutes; 10,000 feet, add 20 minutes.

MAKING VANILLA EXTRACT

Vanilla is a must-have in every kitchen, and with vanilla prices at an all-time high, the gift of homemade extract—fragrant and delicious—is sure to be warmly received.

Use a sharp knife to slice down the middle of each of 6 vanilla beans, revealing the seeds. Do not remove the seeds.

Place the beans (with the seeds) in a tall jar with an airtight seal. Pour in 2 cups of vodka until the beans are covered by at least 1/2 in.

Seal the jar tightly. Let the beans soak for 6 weeks. Gently shake the jar once a week. After 6 weeks, open the jar. The extract is ready if it's deeply fragrant. Remove the beans and reseal the jar.

MOMMA WATTS' CRAZY HERBY SALT BLEND

The recipe for this delicious salt blend came from my best friend Annabelle's mom, Mary Watts—Momma Watts to me and my friends! Last year I made it for my friends; it's the best gift to make at home.
—Ava Romero, South San Francisco, CA

TAKES: 10 MIN. • **MAKES:** ABOUT 2 CUPS

- 2 Tbsp. dried rosemary, crushed
- 1 to 2 Tbsp. fennel seed
- 2 cups kosher salt
- ½ tsp. garlic powder

In a spice grinder or with a mortar and pestle, grind rosemary and fennel until powdery. Stir the rosemary mixture into salt; add garlic powder. Transfer mix to clean 3- or 4-oz. jars. Store in a cool, dry place up to 6 months.

Holiday Helper

You can substitute two or three star anise for the fennel seeds in this blend. Choose one or the other; using both will overpower the flavors.

3. Drop by tablespoonfuls 1½ in. apart on parchment-lined baking sheets. Bake until lightly browned, 10-12 minutes. Remove from pans to wire racks to cool completely. Store in an airtight container.

EASY MEXICAN BROWNIE MIX

I was hosting a fun Mexican-themed cocktail party and needed a quick dessert. Dressing up an ordinary box brownie mix made life easy and delicious!
—*Susan Stetzel, Gainesville, NY*

TAKES: 30 MIN. • **MAKES:** 1 BATCH (ABOUT 4 CUPS MIX)

- 1 pkg. fudge brownie mix (13x9-in. pan size)
- 2 tsp. ground cinnamon
- 1 tsp. ground ancho chili pepper
- ¾ cup dark chocolate chips

ADDITIONAL INGREDIENTS
- 2 large eggs
- ½ cup canola oil
- ¼ cup water

1. Whisk together brownie mix and spices. Transfer mixture to a 1-qt. glass jar. Top with chocolate chips. Cover and store in a cool dry place up to 3 months.
2. To prepare brownies: Preheat oven to 350°. Whisk eggs, oil and water until blended. Gradually add chocolate the chips and brownie mix, mixing well. Spread batter into a greased 13x9-in. baking pan.
3. Bake until a toothpick inserted in center comes out clean (do not overbake), 20-25 minutes. Cool completely in the pan on a wire rack.

SALTED CASHEW OATMEAL COOKIE MIX

My son absolutely loves cashews, so I loaded my oatmeal cookies with them at Christmas—he loved them! The mix makes a great gift for friends, co-workers and teachers; all they have to do is add butter, vanilla and eggs.
—*Richard Hatch, Glen Burnie, MD*

PREP: 20 MIN. • **BAKE:** 10 MIN./BATCH + COOLING
MAKES: 1 BATCH (ABOUT 4 CUPS MIX)

- 1 cup all-purpose flour
- ¾ tsp. baking soda
- ¾ tsp. ground cinnamon
- ½ cup packed light brown sugar
- ½ cup sugar
- 1⅓ cups old-fashioned oats
- 1 cup salted whole cashews

ADDITIONAL INGREDIENTS
- ⅔ cup butter, softened
- ¾ tsp. vanilla extract
- 1 large egg plus 1 large egg yolk

1. Whisk flour, baking soda and cinnamon. In a 1-qt. glass jar, layer flour mixture, sugars, oats and cashews in order listed. Cover and store in a cool dry place up to 3 months.
2. To prepare cookies: Preheat oven to 350°. Beat butter and vanilla extract until light and fluffy. Add egg and yolk and beat until well blended. Add cookie mixture; mix well.

GOOD MORNINGS GRANOLA

I've made this granola since my kids were little. Now they take it with them to college and share it with friends. My daughter (who is majoring in nutrition) says it's good on a whole wheat peanut butter sandwich because it adds a healthy crunch to a quick lunch.
—Janet Ellsworth, Lexington, OH

PREP: 15 MIN. • **BAKE:** 30 MIN.
MAKES: 9 CUPS GRANOLA (18 SERVINGS)

4½ cups old-fashioned oats
1   cup coarsely chopped
    pecans or walnuts
½   cup chopped or slivered almonds
½   cup chopped cashews
⅓   cup unsalted sunflower kernels
⅓   cup pumpkin seeds
⅛   cup to ¼ cup sesame,
    chia or flax seeds
⅓   cup molasses
⅓   cup maple syrup
⅓   cup honey
⅓   cup canola oil
2   Tbsp. orange juice
2   tsp. ground cinnamon

1. Preheat oven to 325°. In a large bowl, combine oats, nuts and seeds. In a small saucepan, whisk remaining ingredients; heat through over medium heat (do not boil). Pour over oat mixture; toss to coat.
2. Spread evenly in two 15x10x1-in. baking pans. Bake, stirring and rotating pans halfway through, until dark golden brown, 30-35 minutes. Cool completely on wire racks. Store in glass jars or other airtight containers for up to 3 months.

 Holiday Helper
Put your own stamp on this granola by swapping in any combination of unsalted nuts and seeds you like. Just be sure to limit the total amount of nuts to 2 cups and total amount of seeds to 1 cup. You can even change up the oil—try blending the canola with olive and soybean oil. For extra crunch, toast the oats, nuts and seeds at 325° for 7-8 minutes before combining with liquids, then bake as directed.

APRICOT AMARETTO JAM

This thick, chunky apricot jam was my grandma's recipe; it's lovely to make something for my family and friends that she made for hers!
—Linda Weger, Robinson, IL

PREP: 30 MIN. • **PROCESS:** 10 MIN.
MAKES: 8 HALF-PINTS

4¼ cups crushed peeled
    apricots, (about 2½ lbs.)
¼   cup lemon juice
6¼ cups sugar, divided
1   pkg. (1¾ oz.) powdered fruit pectin
½   tsp. unsalted butter, optional
⅓   cup amaretto

1. In a Dutch oven, combine apricots and lemon juice. In a small bowl, combine ¼ cup sugar and pectin; stir into the apricot mixture. If desired, add butter. Bring to a full rolling boil over medium-high heat, stirring constantly. Gradually stir in the remaining sugar. Return to a full rolling boil, stirring constantly, for 1 minute.
2. Remove from heat; stir in amaretto. Cool jam in Dutch oven for 5 minutes, stirring occasionally. Ladle hot mixture into eight hot sterilized half-pint jars, leaving ¼-in. headspace. Wipe rims. Center lids on jars; screw on bands until fingertip tight.
3. Place jars into canner with simmering water, ensuring that they are completely covered. Bring to a boil; process for 10 minutes. Remove jars and cool.
NOTE The processing time listed is for altitudes of 1,000 feet or less. Add 1 minute to the processing time for each 1,000 feet of additional altitude.

PAM'S PINEAPPLE CRANBERRY SALSA

Apples and cranberries give this salsa a holiday flavor, while garlic and jalapenos give it just the kick salsa needs. You can serve it up as a dip with chips, like a regular salsa, or as a complement to meat dishes. Sometimes I substitute half the sugar with Splenda to lessen the calories. Works and tastes great!
—Pam Leni, Rockford, IL

PREP: 45 MIN. • **PROCESS:** 20 MIN.
MAKES: 6 PINTS

- 2 pkg. (12 oz. each) fresh cranberries
- 2 medium Granny Smith apples, peeled and cut into 1-in. chunks
- 1 large onion, cut into 1-in. chunks
- 1 large green pepper, cut into 1-in. chunks
- 4 garlic cloves
- 2 pickled seeded jalapeno peppers
- 1 can (20 oz.) crushed pineapple
- 1 cup sugar
- 1 cup packed brown sugar
- 2 tsp. salt
- ½ tsp. ground cinnamon
- ¼ tsp. ground cumin
- 1½ cups orange juice
- 2 Tbsp. white vinegar
- 2 tsp. lime juice

1. Working in batches, pulse the first six ingredients in a food processor until finely chopped. Transfer to a stockpot. Stir in the remaining ingredients. Bring to a boil over high heat. Reduce heat; simmer, uncovered, until tender, about 15 minutes.

2. Ladle the hot mixture into six hot 1-pint jars, leaving ¾-in. headspace. Remove any air bubbles and adjust headspace, if necessary, by adding more hot mixture. Wipe rims. Center lids on jars; screw on bands until fingertip tight.

3. Place jars into canner with simmering water, ensuring that they are completely covered. Bring to a boil; process for 20 minutes. Remove jars and cool.

NOTE The processing time listed is for altitudes of 1,000 feet or less. For altitudes up to 3,000 feet, add 5 minutes; 6,000 feet, add 10 minutes; 8,000 feet, add 15 minutes; 10,000 feet, add 20 minutes.

"Apples and cranberries give this salsa a holiday flavor."
—PAM LENI

HABANERO STRAWBERRY JAM

This spicy-sweet jam is delicious layered over a bar of cream cheese and served with crackers, or slathered on a toasted English muffin.
—Sarah Gilbert, Aloha, OR

PREP: 40 MIN. • **PROCESS:** 10 MIN. • **MAKES:** 9 HALF-PINTS

- 4½ cups crushed strawberries
- ½ cup minced seeded habanero peppers
- ¼ cup lemon juice
- 1 pkg. (1¾ oz.) powdered fruit pectin
- 7 cups sugar

1. In a Dutch oven, combine strawberries, peppers and lemon juice. Stir in pectin. Bring to a full rolling boil over high heat, stirring constantly. Stir in sugar; return to a full rolling boil. Boil and stir 1 minute.
2. Remove from heat; skim off foam. Ladle hot mixture into nine hot half-pint jars, leaving ¼-in. headspace. Wipe rims. Center lids on jars; screw on bands until fingertip tight.
3. Place jars into canner with simmering water, ensuring they are completely covered. Bring to a boil; process for 10 minutes. Remove jars and cool.
NOTE The processing time listed is for altitudes up to 1,000 feet. Add 1 minute to the processing time for each additional 1,000 feet of altitude.

ALL-PURPOSE MEAT SEASONING

My wonderful mother-in-law, Margarette, gave me this recipe. I like to sprinkle it over boneless pork tenderloin before baking. You can try sprinkle more over meat after cooking, too.
—Rebekah Widrick, Beaver Falls, NY

TAKES: 10 MIN. • **MAKES:** 1½ CUPS

- ¾ cup packed brown sugar
- 3 Tbsp. kosher salt
- 3 Tbsp. paprika
- 3 Tbsp. chili powder
- 2 Tbsp. garlic powder
- 2 Tbsp. onion powder
- 1 Tbsp. ground cumin
- 1 Tbsp. dried oregano

Combine all ingredients. Transfer to an airtight container. Store in a cool dry place up to 1 year.
NOTE The seasoning caramelizes quickly when the meat is seared in a skillet.

BBQ SPICED KETCHUP

I once bought my ketchup-loving husband a bottle of flavored ketchup from a fancy kitchen store; he loved his gift, but I didn't love the price! So I experimented and came up with my own spiced ketchup, and now my husband and I are both happy! I kept two half-pint jars in my refrigerator without processing because I knew we would go through them fast—and we did!
—*Nancy Murphy, Mount Dora, FL*

PREP: 35 MIN. • **PROCESS:** 20 MIN. • **MAKES:** 5 HALF-PINTS

- 4 cups ketchup
- 1 cup cider vinegar
- ¼ cup packed dark brown sugar
- ¼ cup molasses
- 2 Tbsp. honey
- 1 Tbsp. Worcestershire sauce
- 2 tsp. kosher salt
- 2 tsp. ground mustard
- ½ tsp. pepper
- ½ tsp. celery seed
- ½ tsp. garlic powder
- ½ tsp. paprika
- ½ tsp. chili powder

1. In a Dutch oven, combine all ingredients. Bring to a boil over medium-high heat. Reduce heat; simmer, uncovered, until mixture is thickened, 25-30 min.

2. Ladle hot mixture into five hot ½-pint jars, leaving ½-in. headspace. Remove air bubbles and adjust headspace, if necessary, by adding hot mixture. Wipe rims. Center lids on jars; screw on bands until fingertip tight.

3. Place jars into canner with simmering water, ensuring that they are completely covered with water. Bring to a boil; process for 20 minutes. Remove jars and cool.

NOTE The processing time listed is for altitudes up to 1,000 feet. For altitudes up to 3,000 feet, add 5 minutes; 6,000 feet, add 10 minutes; 8,000 feet, add 15 minutes; 10,000 feet, add 20 minutes.

A CUP OF COFFEE CAKE

This mix is easy, delicious—and full of the flavors teachers need to get through their day! Instant coffee works fine as a substitute for the brewed, if you like.
—Deborah Dubord, Fayette, ME

PREP: 10 MIN. • **BAKE:** 25 MIN.
MAKES: 1 BATCH (ABOUT 3½ CUPS MIX)

    1½ cups all-purpose flour
     ½ tsp. salt
     ½ tsp. baking soda
     1 cup packed brown sugar
     ½ cup chopped walnuts
     ½ cup semisweet chocolate chips
ADDITIONAL INGREDIENTS
     1 large egg
     ½ cup brewed coffee,
        room temperature
     ½ cup canola oil

1. Whisk together flour, salt and baking soda. Transfer to a 1-qt. glass jar. Layer with brown sugar. Place walnuts and chocolate chips in a small plastic bag and layer on top of brown sugar. Cover and store in a cool, dry place up to 3 months.
2. To prepare coffee cake: Preheat oven to 350°. Whisk egg, coffee and canola oil. Add brown sugar and flour mixture; mix until combined. Pour batter into a greased 8-in. square baking pan. Sprinkle with chocolate chips and nuts. Bake until a toothpick inserted in center comes out clean, 25-30 minutes. Cool on a wire rack.

 Holiday Helper
This coffee cake mix makes a great present on its own, but it can also be part of a larger gift basket. If you want to dress it up a bit more, add a lovely (or humorous!) coffee mug, a bag of coffee beans or a gift card to a local coffee shop.

PLUM CONSERVE

My mouthwatering conserve is a versatile gift. It makes a lovely garnish for rolls during holiday feasts, is delicious paired with cheese as an appetizer, and makes a great dessert topping for ice cream or pound cake.
—Ginny Beadle, Spokane, WA

PREP: 40 MIN. • **PROCESS:** 10 MIN.
MAKES: 7 HALF-PINTS

    2 lbs. medium Italian plums,
        pitted and quartered
    1½ cups dried cranberries
     ½ cup quartered and thinly
        sliced mandarin oranges
     ½ cup orange juice
     3 cups sugar, divided
     1 pkg. (1¾ oz.) powdered
        fruit pectin
     1 cup coarsely chopped walnuts

1. In a Dutch oven, combine plums, cranberries, oranges, orange juice and 2½ cups of sugar. Mix the remaining sugar with the pectin; set aside. Bring the fruit mixture to a full rolling boil over high heat, stirring constantly, until slightly thickened and plums soften, about 15 minutes. Stir in pectin mixture and walnuts; return to a full rolling boil. Boil and stir 1 minute.
2. Remove from heat. Ladle hot mixture into seven hot half-pint jars, leaving ¼-in. headspace. Remove air bubbles and adjust headspace, if necessary, by adding more hot mixture. Wipe rims. Center lids on jars; screw on bands until fingertip tight.
3. Place jars into canner with simmering water, ensuring that they are completely covered. Bring to a boil; process for 10 minutes. Remove jars and cool.
NOTE The processing time listed is for altitudes up to 1,000 feet. Add 1 minute to the processing time for each additional 1,000 feet of altitude.

General Recipe Index

This index lists every recipe in the book by food category, major ingredient and/or cooking method, so you can easily locate recipes to suit your needs.

P. 13

P. 28

P. 77

P. 98

P. 172

Alphabetical Recipe Index

This index lists every recipe in the book in alphabetical order. Just search for the titles when you want to find your favorites.

P. 178

P. 123

P. 214

P. 224